The Soviet Union: Looking to the 1980s

Papers of the Symposium: "The Futures of the Soviet Union,"
Sponsored by the Earhart Foundation
September 13 - 15, 1978
Hoover Institution, Stanford University
Stanford, California

Edited by Robert Wesson

The Soviet Union: Looking to the 1980s

HOOVER INSTITUTION PRESS
Stanford University, Stanford, California

KRAUS INTERNATIONAL PUBLICATIONS
Millwood, New York

A U.S. Division of Kraus-Thomson Organization Ltd.

©Copyright 1980 Board of Trustees of the Leland
Stanford Junior University.

All rights reserved.
No part of this work covered by the
copyright hereon may be reproduced or used
in any form or by any means—graphic, electronic,
or mechanical, including photocopying, recording or taping,
information storage and
retrieval systems—without written permission
of the publisher.

First Printing

Printed in the United States of America

Library of Congress Cataloging in Publication Data

The Soviet Union, looking to the 1980s.

    Includes index.
    1. Russia—Congresses. I. Wesson, Robert G.
II. Earhart Foundation.
DK2.5.S64   947.085   79-24546
ISBN 0-527-95452-7

Contents

vii	Preface *Robert Wesson*
3	Introduction *Donald W. Treadgold*
15	Soviet Foreign Policy: Looking Back to the Future *Leopold Labedz*
31	Sino-Soviet Relations *Klaus Mehnert*
45	Soviet-East European Relations *Jan F. Triska*
65	Military Stance and Outlook *Col. William F. Scott and Harriet Fast Scott*
89	Economic Prospects *Joseph S. Berliner*
111	Prospects for the Consumer *Gertrude E. Schroeder*

129	The Nationalities Question *Teresa Rakowska-Harmstone*
155	Political Dissent *Frederick C. Barghoorn*
177	The Problem of Succession *Myron Rush*
191	Images of the Future and Lessons of the Past *George W. Breslauer*
205	The Soviet Image of the Future *Donald R. Kelley*
225	The Soviet Order *Robert Conquest*
247	The Soviet Union—Approaching 1984 *Andrei Amalrik*
263	Conclusion *Robert Wesson*
279	Contributors
283	Index

Preface

Lenin was overcome by joy at the beginning of 1918 when he saw by the calendar that his radical state had outlasted the seventy-two days of the Paris Commune. Now it has passed its sixtieth birthday, having survived a near infinity of troubles and even more prophecies of its demise. It is solid indeed, and its achievements have been impressive, as several contributors to this volume underline.

Yet the Soviet Union may well be approaching major change. The fact that it has been outwardly stable and fixed during more than fifteen years of the stewardship of Leonid Brezhnev rather increases than decreases the likelihood of deeper change if the congealed system is overstrained. While the Soviet state and society appear outwardly unperturbed, their inner evolution has continued, and subsurface tensions have seemingly accumulated. Problems of various kinds, as discussed by contributors to this volume, pile up and must sooner or later require action. At the same time there looms a succession crisis, and in the Soviet past, succession crises have always brought new political directions and major changes of style and temper.

It was hence appropriate for a group of specialists in various aspects of Soviet affairs to meet at the Hoover Institution, Stanford

University, under the sponsorship of the Earhart Foundation, from September 13 to 15, 1978, to discuss "The Futures of the Soviet Union"—the plural implying not crass speculation but the desire to examine alternatives. The papers presented at the symposium form the body of this book. The only exception is that of Klaus Mehnert, whose travel to China prevented his personal participation. In most cases, papers were substantially revised after the spirited discussions. My own editing has been minimal, consisting mostly of minor abridgements. The style as well as substance of each chapter is entirely that of its author. The contribution of Andrei Amalrik, however, is in my translation.

The contributors have examined the principal aspects of Soviet affairs. In his introductory statement, Donald Treadgold points out some of the constants of Soviet behavior and pressures for change. Leopold Labedz looks at the main issues of Soviet foreign policy, particularly the continuing ideological drive. Concentrating on Eastern Europe, Jan Triska sees prospects for a burdensome relationship; and Klaus Mehnert examines a problem that will apparently continue to loom large, the antagonism with China. Soviet foreign policy rests heavily on military power, which Col. William Scott and Harriet Scott find formidable. But in the longer run, Soviet military capacity is limited by the strength of the economy, the prospects of which Joseph Berliner finds doubtful. The question of whether the Soviet economy can continue to go forward is central to any estimate of Soviet prospects, and Gertrude Schroeder has supplemented Berliner's observations by considering the economy from the point of view of the somewhat neglected Soviet consumer.

Roughly parallel with the problem of economic management is the problem of keeping harmony between dominant Russian and subordinate minorities. Like the economic problem, the nationalities problem is becoming continually more acute, as Teresa Rakowska-Harmstone makes clear. Dissent is also rising among the Russian intelligentsia, and Frederick Barghoorn sees in it tendencies to democratization.

The door to change will most likely be opened by a succession crisis, the prospects for which Myron Rush examines. George Breslauer, considering several possible scenarios, is more inclined than most of the contributors to regard something like the present condition as viable. Soviet institutions were invited to send a scholar or a paper to present a Soviet viewpoint of future prospects, but they were unable to do so. However, Donald Kelley describes the Soviet vision of the future as it has developed in the Brezhnev era. Robert Conquest discusses the nature of Soviet society as it has come down from the Russian past. Finally, Andrei Amalrik presents a scheme for the analysis of the Soviet system into which nearly all of the preceding could be fitted. In the conclusion I have tried to do little more than bring together some highlights of the various papers.

ROBERT WESSON

Santa Barbara,
November 17, 1978

The Soviet Union: Looking to the 1980s

Donald W. Treadgold

Introduction

Despite the determinism which characterizes Marxism as a theory of history, the Russian Bolsheviks under Lenin's leadership from the time they were organized as a faction (1930) within the Russian Social Democratic Labor Party stressed the need to take the initiative, decide on strategy and tactics and then act thereupon and, if need be, seize history by the throat to bring about the results they desired. Yet events have often turned out quite differently from the promise of the blueprint. Trotsky is supposed to have said of Ramon Mercader that he was "rather light-minded. . . . Nevertheless, he can be won closer. In order to build the party we must have confidence that people can be changed."[1] Mercader in due course assassinated Trotsky.

This story illustrates the dilemma of the Bolsheviks in 1917. They adhered to a fundamentally determinist creed—whatever limited concessions Marx and Engels were at times prepared to make to voluntarism—which led them confidently to regard objective conditions as propitious for their appointed task of carrying the proletarian revolution through successfully in Russia and the world. However,

1. Quoted in Isaac Don Levine, *The Mind of an Assassin* (New York, 1959), p. 104.

both national and international developments turned out unaccountably contrary to expectations. In 1919, in 1921, in the early 1930s, and in 1941, the Soviet state seemed to teeter on the edge of complete failure. The crises were somehow surmounted, and yet in 1978 all was far from well.

A key persistent tension in Soviet affairs is that of ideology and power. In the arresting formulation of Leopold Labedz, the chiliasm and the soteriology are permanent while the rest of the ideology is subject to alteration. If the doctrines of the final outcome and of human salvation may be taken to represent the core of Marxism-Leninism as it is taught today in the USSR, stress may be placed either on the unchanging core or the changing peripheries of the teaching—or, to put it another way, either on the long-term plans and expectations of the Soviet leaders or their short-term strategy and tactics.

The Bolshevik party came to power almost overnight in a vast country, the largest on earth, without previously having administered a square mile of territory, and the leaders catapulted into high administrative positions in the new state had never before been appointed or elected to any governmental office. (The closest thing to governmental experience might be found in the few Bolshevik Duma deputies—the leader of whom, Roman Malinovsky, had turned out to be a police spy.) Of course, several of them did have the experience of responsibility, which they took very seriously, in the central organization of the party, its ideological organs, and its local units; but governing the country was quite different. It is no wonder that their success in mastering that challenge did much to validate their belief in the truth of their doctrines.

The Bolsheviks temporarily lost control of much of the country during the civil war. Trotsky, fresh from his failure as foreign commissar, assumed the post for defense and, without even Hitler's experience as corporal, proceeded to organize an ultimately victorious Red Army. Lenin presided over the government and led it to triumph over its varied internal and external enemies; in the process he pursued such disastrous domestic policies as to face deep internal crisis at the moment of military success in 1920-21. In fact Lenin, facing that crisis, had moments of terrible suspicion that the whole revolution had gone wrong, a suspicion which he did his best to overcome. The hope that the revolution would spread westward recurred in 1918, 1919, and 1920, and was evidently not shelved even provisionally until the failure of the German adventure of 1923; but increasingly the Communists (so renamed in 1918) found themselves compelled to act without reference to what might happen in the West.

The Comintern, founded in 1919, consisted mainly of tiny,

powerless splinters of the Social Democratic parties of the Second International. Bertram D. Wolfe has convincingly suggested that the endless and often ridiculous intra-party struggles in many foreign Communist parties were ordered, provoked, or welcomed by Lenin, who had in mind the Russian experience.[2] Lenin had excommunicated, denounced, exposed, branded, and otherwise roughly treated many if not most of his fellow Social Democrats and indeed fellow Bolsheviks. Out of this shambles came, as he saw it, one nugget of pure ideological gold, the nucleus that fell in line with his injunctions in the April Theses of 1917, which nonplussed even his closest associates at the time, and marched to the triumph of October and conquest of power throughout the former Russian Empire. Those who would draw a sharp line between ideology and power should contemplate Lenin's management of the Communist International in, say, 1921. He believed that the achievement of correct ideology pointed not away from power, but toward it. There were to be many instances in which Lenin's successors made similar determinations. That they may have done so wrongly is irrelevant to their motives. As the 1920s wore on, the control of the Comintern fell with increasing obviousness into the hands of the Russian party, which was undergoing a process of centralization and was being taken over by Stalin.

It was only in the period of the First Five Year Plan that Stalin and his henchmen, having successfully assumed the mantle of Lenin, proceeded to undertake the "second revolution" (Isaac Deutscher's phrase). The task of completing the nationalization of industry, trade, and finance was extended to include large-scale construction of new industry and, most fateful of all Soviet economic decisions, collectivization of agriculture. The welfare of the consumer was a permanent casualty of the policies then adopted. For decades thereafter the ratio of consumer goods to total production declined, and only the absolute rise in their value of the 1970s has somewhat improved the lot of the ordinary urban shopper; as Gertrude Schroeder points out, the ratio of consumption to gross national product is currently not increasing. Surplus labor (at least from the planners' standpoint) was removed from the farm to the factory; and industrial output soared, not without large-scale waste, inefficiency, and suffering.

In the agrarian sector the story was still more grim. Millions of villagers died or were sent to concentration camp or exile; the resistance of virtually the whole peasantry to collectivization decimated livestock holdings, while the "grain factories" lacked the farm machinery that was supposed to compensate for animal losses.

2. In his memoirs, shortly to be published, which I have been privileged to read in manuscript.

6 Treadgold

However, the peasants won a concession important to the whole population—the retention or restoration of the private garden plot, which the collective farmer might till for himself, selling its produce in the free market. As a result, to this day the tiny fraction (under 3 percent) of tilled area consisting of private plots provides a substantial part of the food consumed in the USSR—from 25 percent to 75 percent depending on the item or items specified or stressed, most significantly in the categories of meat, dairy products, and vegetables. The Soviet leaders inflicted agricultural disaster on themselves, though the social and political calculations are more difficult to make and perhaps the long-range effects of forcing the peasantry into overall economic planning and altering their traditional outlook justified collectivization from the standpoint of Stalin and his successors. One must assume that the Soviet leaders are well informed about the actual state of Soviet agriculture past and present, though rarely has there been such public frankness as Krushchev's 1953 admission that total livestock holdings remained in part below the level of 1916. They have clearly considered abolition of the private plots, as clearly have decided on their retention for the time being, and have never hinted that the possibility of abandoning collectivization has crossed their mind.

Stalin's successors doubtless believed that he made many mistakes in the course of his heavy-handed takeover of the party machinery in the 1920s, in the economic transformation over which he presided in the early 1930s, and finally in the great purges he carried out in the late 1930s. However, the closest to frank discussion of these problems that they have come, in Khrushchev's statements of 1956-61, never called into question the objectives Stalin pursued. The indictment of Stalin's crimes to be found in Khrushchev's "secret speech" at the 20th Congress of the CPSU in 1956 centered on the fact that Stalin had liquidated people loyal to himself, not his destruction of the military, trade union, and above all party leadership per se. There can be no doubt that official Soviet historiography in 1978 is embarrassed by the fact that all of the highest leaders from 1917 to 1964 except for Lenin himself, are said to have been either betrayers of the Revolution (Lenin's entire Politburo except for Lenin and Stalin) or gravely deficient in some other aspect (Stalin and Khrushchev). The degree of deficiency or crime attributed to the 1917-64 leadership has had its ups and downs in this or that particular. Given the shortcomings admitted, however, it is awkward for Soviet historians to argue that the record has been positive overall.

The crisis of 1941 was surely provoked in part by Stalin's previous actions. The disappearance of the best generals in the purges, the dissatisfaction of the Russian and Ukrainian peasantry with both the system of collective farms and the closure of Orthodox churches in the villages, the atmosphere of universal fear generated by the purge period (1936-38 especially), and Stalin's own miscalculations of what was to be expected from his pact with Hitler—all contributed to a catastrophic military defeat. Stalin's personal panic and virtual incapacitation in the summer and fall of 1941 are well documented. The comeback that the Soviet regime made was a remarkable feat as little noticed in Western writing on the period as was the depth of the catastrophe that preceded it. Three factors may be counted as crucial: Hitler's suicidal refusal to recognize or try to use the Soviet population's antipathy to Communism; U.S. and other Allied military and economic aid, coupled with the solidarity publicly proclaimed with the Soviet regime; and Stalin's own adroitness in making concessions, real or pretended, to Russian national feeling and religious belief, notably in the abolition of the Comintern and the permission to the Orthodox church to elect a new patriarch.

Stalin's wartime participation in the alliance with America and Britain came as a new departure and a surprise to many, in the USSR and in Allied countries. However, the alliance could be portrayed as growing naturally out of aspects of earlier Soviet diplomacy—if one skipped over the period of the Nazi-Soviet Pact (1939-41). During the 1920s and 1930s normal diplomatic relations were established with a range of countries in Europe and Asia, climaxed by U.S. recognition in 1933. To be sure, a number of sharply differing policies were adopted consecutively by Moscow in regard to foreign Communist parties. After 1924 a united front policy, chiefly significant in Britain and China, sought to advance Communist fortunes by finding a temporary and conditional bourgeois partner in the countries concerned. Nowhere was the policy successful, and in China the consequence seemed for several years to have been the virtual destruction of Communism. After 1928 occurred a reversal which led to denunciation of bourgeois reformists as social fascists. The chief result seemed to be Hitler's accession to power. While many people in the West lamented that event, a bad conscience about the damage the Versailles Treaty had inflicted on Germany prevented them from laying much blame on Stalin's shoulders. By 1936 the Comintern reversed itself again and called for a popular front against Fascism (meaning chiefly Nazism) and Japanese militarism, evoking much sympathy in the West. Meanwhile, the defense of the Republic in the Civil War in Spain seemed to rally liberals and Communists together in a common cause. (The part that the USSR and the NKVD played in undermining the Spanish Republic before Franco finally crushed it did not become well known till later.) At the same time, the Communists seemed to be the Chinese faction most interested in resisting Japan, and many Westerners also pinned their hopes on Mao Tse-tung as the best hope for real reform in China. If Stalin had left

8 Treadgold

Britain and France in the lurch in August 1939, it was also true that the two Western powers had not shown much sense of urgency in the negotiations with the USSR that were abruptly terminated by announcement of Stalin's pact with Hitler.

Thus the "Grand Alliance" (Winston Churchill's term) of World War II—though the USSR never acknowledged that it was fighting any war other than the Great Fatherland War—was for the duration of the fighting a great success in Western public opinion. If some Soviet citizens wondered why Roosevelt and Churchill hastened to embrace Stalin, many of them also regarded the Allied connection as a guarantee of domestic reform at the end of the war. As victory came near, however, signs were plentiful that Stalin was not interested in making the world safe for democracy in Wilsonian style and that he was not enthusiastic about closer postwar ties with the West. Among those portents were Soviet quiescence and refusal to facilitate Western assistance at the time of the Warsaw rising, and the subsequent roughness with which the Soviet army installed Communist-front regimes in Eastern Europe. Roosevelt's last months were clouded by exchanges with the Soviets reflecting his dismay and disappointment at Stalin's conduct. Truman as president oversaw an end to hostilities in Europe and then Asia, and by that time the situation had changed enough to rule out any Soviet part in the Asian settlement comparable to that which had enabled Russians to move as far west as Thuringia in Germany.

Stalin cautioned his chief lieutenants on both continents, Tito and Mao, to show restraint and a healthy respect for the new U.S. nuclear weapons; but Soviet-style Communism emerged triumphant throughout Eastern Europe and portions of Eastern Asia. Leaving U.S. public opinion to seek scapegoats and trade indictments for what had happened, Stalin turned his attention to the problem of restoring the Soviet regime to the areas from which it had been driven for substantial periods (and establishing it in newly annexed territories) as well as to the millions of people who had come under Soviet control in Europe. A campaign for ideological purity launched by Andrei Zhdanov meant cutting the tenuous new ties with the West and ending hopes that they would continue or be expanded. After Zhdanov's mysterious death, the campaign was continued in a slightly different form under Stalin's aegis. Economic reconstruction was pursued along with renewed cultural repression, but the scarcely calculable losses in property and human beings meant that the recovery had to start from a level of misery and deprivation unequaled in Europe. Moreover, economic revival had to proceed slowly, lacking the capitalist dynamic that the Germans and Japanese soon learned to master, with Western help of a kind that the Soviets refused for themselves and denied to all Eastern Europe by rejecting the Marshall Plan.

Introduction 9

In the bleak years just after the end of the war and before Stalin's death, the Soviet people suffered in many ways. The concentration camps were filled with traitors real or imagined, scarcely veiled anti-Semitism wrecked Soviet Jewish culture, and indications are that the trumped-up "doctors' plot" which Stalin purported to discover in his last weeks was to be the prelude to renewed purges of more of the population than the Jews.

The quandary of the post-Stalin regime was soon evident, and its twin dangers continue in 1978. On the one hand there could not be a total repudiation of Stalin without undermining the legitimacy of his successors (unless they were willing to proclaim themselves something other than Communists). On the other hand they regarded the severity of his rule, at least in the last years, as counterproductive, constituting an impediment to their economic, military, and cultural objectives. Moreover, the statements they made immediately following Stalin's death hinted that they feared popular disorder if there were not some lessening of repression. There could not be too little de-Stalinization, but there must not be too much; for the ensuing quarter-century the leaders' estimate of what was the right amount varied, but the problem continued before, during, and after the more or less overt pursuit of de-Stalinization by Khrushchev. Malenkov identified himself by placating the population with a greater supply of consumer goods; Beria—in an unexpected stance for the chief of the secret police—evidently was willing to consider some legal and even constitutional change. The hesitance of the regime to continue Stalin's methods was obvious. The response was disorder, in both the USSR and Eastern Europe, notably the Berlin rising. Beria was sacrificed.

Khrushchev, the party secretary, sparred with Malenkov, the chief of the administration, charging him with right deviationism and thereby toppling him. But Khrushchev soon found himself following some of Malenkov's policies and began to tinker with the economic system in a puzzling manner, while he allowed the newly vocal intellectuals to stir up the mud of the Stalin epoch and call for greater cultural freedom (though at the same time he viciously attacked religion, especially Orthodox Christianity). He tried to deal with Mao's China, which was unhappy at facing its Stalinist tasks in the second revolution just at the moment when Moscow was undermining the stature of the chief prophet of that transformation, and ended by bringing Moscow-Peking relations to open hostility. He also made overtures to the West, interspersed with bluster that many feared was more than that. The most serious crisis of U.S.-Soviet relations since 1921, the Cuban face-off of 1962, was followed by a resumption of his quest for a more regular relationship with the capitalist powers.

Khrushchev was abruptly removed from office in October 1964. His successor, Brezhnev, tried to paper over the split with Peking and still leave the door open for more normal relations with the West. The invasion of Czechoslovakia in 1968, like the suppression of the Hungarian uprising in 1956, interrupted the process. The gradually intensifying war in Vietnam produced a welcome degree of U.S. domestic turmoil, but also constituted a significant drain on Soviet resources. Thus Brezhnev was ready to respond to the Nixon-Kissinger initiative of 1972 which produced an agreement for nominal peace in Vietnam, and which also bade fair to open the way to importation of Western technology which Brezhnev thought might ease the Soviet way out of its increasingly intractable economic predicament. Kissinger began his fateful travels with the trip to China, to be sure, and the establishment of a Peking-Washington link was a bitter pill to swallow; but Brezhnev saw no alternative.

Détente, however, did not realize the hopes the Soviets evidently placed in it; and difficulties multiplied. The trade agreement foundered on the Jackson-Vanik Amendment; the talks to limit nuclear weapons were slow and painful; in different ways relations were cooled by Soviet setbacks in the Middle East and gains in Africa—coming after the take-over of South Vietnam by the Moscow-oriented Hanoi regime. Moscow watched incredulously as its new friend, Nixon, was driven from the presidency, and lamented the failure of his successor, Ford, to win election in his own right. The Carter presidency's handling of the human rights issue brought a new frigidity to Washington-Moscow relations. In some ways the issue was itself created by the crackdown on dissidence inaugurated by the Soviet regime with the trial of Siniavsky and Daniel in 1966, trials of those who protested that trial, and so forth. However, the SALT talks continued and commercial and cultural connections were maintained and modestly expanded.

To a large extent the crisis of 1941, itself the product of Stalin's misdeeds and miscalculations, has hung over the past thirty-seven years. How thoroughly alienated the Soviet population had become at that point was amply attested by evidence that became available during and after World War II, including the Smolensk party archives and the massive documentation of the Harvard Russian Research Center's refugee interview project. The resistance of many Soviet citizens to forced repatriation at Allied hands shocked many Westerners at the time, even if their puzzlement did not lead to abandonment of that ugly enterprise. But popular dissatisfaction did not produce any kind of liberalization. The shape of the Soviet regime, politically and economically (though in the cultural field there has been more change), remains in its main lines what it was when Hitler attacked the USSR. The trivial changes introduced by the new Soviet Constitution of 1977 are the best evidence of that fact. Over the postwar decades, the Soviet population came to accept the reality that the regime retained power and was unlikely to alter its chief features.

What of the future? One of the least likely outcomes is a mass uprising that will topple the regime. There is no evidence that the Soviet leaders have anything short of full control of the army and police, and no evidence that a falling out impends among the leaders themselves; probably only thus could the regime be seriously threatened. Indeed, whatever disagreements may exist among the members of the Politburo, we know less about them than we did in the 1950s. If impatient youths wait in the wings for the old men who rule to die or retire, they are keeping very quiet.

The immediate economic problems, discussed in the papers that follow, are substantial but not dramatic, and no immediate emergency is foreseeable. The military strength of the USSR, immensely increased over the past decade or so, can be employed at home as well as abroad; and if the lie that Czechoslovakia was in danger of imminent invasion from the West in 1968 could be successfully fed the Soviet troops, almost any invented story is probably enough to put the army into action against domestic rioters.

The main dangers of the current situation may be neither economic nor political, neither tangible nor immediate, but they doubtless worry the Soviet leadership. They relate to ethnic and cultural problems, some of which are ultimately religious.

The ethnic problems have both changed and matured in the twentieth century. The Ukrainians have greatly sharpened their sense of identity, of their past, of their differentness from Great Russians. As the Baltic peoples, especially the Latvians, face possible submergence of their language and culture by immigrating Russians, they become restive and a few may become desperate. The Georgians and Armenians, habituated to greater latitude of treatment and often contemptuous of the big brother to the north, recently dared to voice their ethnic pride in discussion of the constitutional provisions regarding language. The Turkic peoples of European and Asiatic Russia may be potentially the most troublesome of all; their numbers have grown as Russian birth rates have fallen (though their growth may now be slowing), and their exposure to the modern world through Soviet education, with all its defects, may have stimulated dangerous thoughts. In all these and other cases, minorities in the USSR share some of the aspirations of nationalism and national feeling that have been sweeping the globe; and there is no way to insulate them from such impulses. The partly veiled, partly explicit (in *samizdat*) revival of Russian national feeling is less immediately threatening to the Soviet system than minority nationalism, but in the long run even more dangerous. Not even the Ukrainians (the largest non-Russian group) are going to overthrow the Moscow government, but one day

Russians conceivably might. There is doubtless some more or less surreptitious patronage and encouragement of Russian national consciousness, perhaps as a safety-valve but perhaps also as a trend for which there is real sympathy, on the part of highly placed Soviet officials. There is clearly, also, uneasiness in the Politburo about the ideological heresy latent and overt in Russian nationalism.

The cultural problems are partly related to Russian ethnicity. The attitude of Soviet youth toward Marxism-Leninism is a matter of grave concern. To be sure, there are a few dissidents who draw up political programs, but as far as the outsider can tell these are possibly interesting portents of the future rather than perils of the present for the Soviet system. Much more significant is the growing trend of abstention from politics of any kind, of avoidance of political entanglements, which may mean also sacrifice of any possibility for promotion, advancement, or influence. The drop-out phenomenon which has recently become common in the West may be found occasionally in the USSR, but the Soviet analogue does not seem very close; it is more a wish to "cultivate one's own garden" in the style of Candide, to accept an inferior post provided that one can do something rewarding without risking charges of parasitism. It may be connected with Solzhenitsyn's injunction to intellectuals, "do not tell lies;" whether or not the young people concerned have ever heard of him, many are voicing imperatives of honesty and integrity simply in relation to their own lives.

The Soviet leaders plainly are troubled about the fact that sixty years of indoctrination has produced youth not more enthusiastic about the Soviet system and its achievements but substantially less so than was the case, at least on the surface, two decades ago. The contrast between the fantasies of Soviet propaganda and easily perceptible realities has long been present; the willingness to internalize a kind of schizophrenia able to accommodate both is certainly in decline. A contrary point needs mention. In the eyes of some Soviet youth, the continuing expansion of Communism in the world and the influence of Marxism-Leninism in areas and countries where the governments are not officially Communist may serve as some kind of justification for the Soviet system, however much they may dislike aspects of it in the USSR; yet others may see in these developments only a new kind of imperialism which repels and horrifies them.

The flight from Marxism-Leninism, dislike for required school and university courses in the subject, and boredom with ideologically phrased statements in which the line is laid down in this or that area of learning are evident. Escape (even if not complete) is possible, indeed, within the system—notably in the natural sciences, certain branches of technology, and the more esoteric or remote fields of scholarship. Some of those havens for the apolitical youth may be prestigious, and if the special field in question is of the very highest value to the regime, its practitioners may be able to get away with words and deeds that would be most unwise for the ordinary citizen.

The well-educated and deeply thoughtful Soviet person may, either professionally or avocationally, be drawn to the arts, philosophy, and religion. If Marxism is ultimately a phenomenon of the religious consciousness of man, or a substitute for religion, then the passage may be easy from Marxism to religion and, for the Russian, to Christianity. A private letter just received from Leningrad states, "The intelligent Christians in Leningrad and Moscow are all new Christians"—that is, are recent converts. Soviet atheist posters are now referring mockingly to the 'new fashion' of religious belief; how far we have come from the days when ancient believing grandmothers were expected to die shortly and leave the USSR an atheist paradise. For many Russians, Orthodox Christianity is closely linked with their national past, though for some it is attractive precisely because it disavows any discrimination or preference for any nationality. The return to Judaism of Jews secularized for two or three generations is more directly traceable to events outside the USSR, and yet may not be wholly explained thereby. Of Islam and Buddhism we know less, but Central Asia stirs with all sorts of ideas unwelcome to the leadership in Moscow. *Samizdat* today, proliferating in quantity and varying in quality, provides samples of all the varieties of non-Communist thought just mentioned and more.

The Soviet leaders in 1978 have achieved much. If the world revolution that Lenin expected was delayed, and the "itinerary of revolution" (Zinoviev) proved to be in the direction of the east and south rather than the west, the spread of Communism was resumed after World War II and is clearly continuing. Soviet military and specifically nuclear power have come roughly to parity with—some believe even superiority over—that of the U.S., and no international issue can be addressed without consideration of the Soviet Union, its position, capabilities, and intentions.

Domestically, industry has expanded vastly and agriculture has been collectivized. The party and its creature, the state, have come to manage all aspects of economic, political, and cultural life and continue to do so, albeit with a less heavy hand than under Stalin. The Brezhnev regime has proclaimed the achievement of "developed socialism," since the transition to full communism prophesied by Khrushchev seems to have been postponed. The diminution or even exhaustion of revolutionary fervor annoys or may possibly frighten Soviet leaders, yet the Third World elites they wish to influence know that Moscow has the missiles and the money, not Peking. Many of the youth who are expected to be tomorrow's leaders show a troublesome hesitation to prepare for that role, and ethnic and cultural trends which do not harmonize with the official ideology proliferate despite success in stamping out this or that manifestation—as in the tale of the sorcerer's apprentice. Whether this portends a crisis in the USSR that is bound to deepen and become disabling, or whether current problems are only natural and unavoidable concomitants of steadily increasing Soviet success, is a question that Brezhnev and his successors must consider. There is little evidence that they think history is about to liquidate their great venture, and much to suggest that they retain their vision of a bright Communist future not much different from Lenin's.

It is said that when Scipio Africanus and Polybius stood watching Carthage burn, the great Roman general wept. Polybius asked why, and Scipio replied, "When looking down on Carthage, I think of the day when the same will happen to Rome." Rome did fall, and yet it emerged again as something different but still great, while Carthage belongs only to the past. It is tempting, in viewing the relationship between the USSR and the West, to compare one to Carthage and the other to Rome. However, one benefit of history, as a wise man has said, is that it enables one to avoid being victimized by false historical analogies. Russia and America may each have a future that holds destruction, even greater power, or merely continuation of existing conditions for a long period without apocalyptic change one way or the other. Whichever fate lies ahead for the USSR, its past certainly contains clues for its future, but interpreting the clues requires careful attention to the evidence and the avoidance of wishful thinking.

Leopold Labedz

Soviet Foreign Policy: Looking Back to the Future

History is open and not foreordained. Even if the determinants of Soviet policy dynamics were laid bare, it would be impossible to know what the prospects of history might be without knowing what kinds of responses it might encounter. Therefore, specific forecasts are impossible in principle because Soviet adversaries may cooperate or quarrel, exert pressures or submit to them, resist or capitulate. The Soviet Union may have limited options, but even within limited options, there is always room for fundamentally divergent choices, an exercise of political will which escapes prediction.

If scientific foretelling of Soviet policies is not possible, either as Marxist historical prophecy or as behavioural extrapolation from the present, there remains what Favier called in the 18th century *la conjecture raisonnée*, before the Hegelian nonsense was introduced into the idea of history. That, of course, requires judgment rather than methodology which aims at scientific exactitude. Besides, the Western record of foreign policy anticipation based on this kind of scientific attitude shows that academic Sovietology reflects the general political climate of the day, and that Soviet policies are interpreted more as a function of current political hopes than of the Soviet historical background. In looking at the future of Soviet foreign policy it may be, therefore, pertinent to look first backwards, to recall the errors of judgment which so often in the past distorted Western perspective on Soviet developments.

There seems to be a kind of *éternel rétour* in Western expectations of Soviet policy developments. This applies to progressives and reactionaries, Marxists and behaviorists, experts and non-experts. One remembers how their expectations were regularly falsified. They looked for the Soviet Union to take an "anti-fascist" stand against Nazi Germany; they got the Hitler-Stalin Pact instead. They expected that the Yalta Agreement would usher in the postwar era of cooperation with "Uncle Joe;" they saw the Prague coup, the Berlin blockade, and the Korean war. They expected détente to "end the era of confrontation," and got Angola, the Horn of Africa, Afghanistan, and Yemen. They always evaded the old truth that only power checks power, that expansion cannot be stopped without resistance.

The first question to ask about the future of Soviet policy concerns the tendencies in the world balance of power or, in Soviet parlance, "the correlation of forces." There is no denying the Soviet rise in the international power balance. Since World War II the Soviet Union has first established its domination in Eastern Europe and then expanded its influence to a number of states—from Cuba to Angola, from Yemen to Ethiopia, from Vietnam to Afghanistan. It has achieved apparent military parity with the U. S. and has continued its efforts towards military preponderance in Europe. It has undermined American strategic predominance in the world, and has progressed some way towards the goal of Finlandizing the foreign policies of West European states. Who would have presumed when NATO was established that thirty years later the Soviet Union would be telling the Western powers whether or not to give weapons to their allies or friendly states, issuing warnings against rapprochement with China, and aligning some of the non-aligned on its side? When the Soviet Union was establishing its control over Eastern Europe, Western unease was assuaged with an argument about the Soviet need for security. Those using this argument never imagined that thirty-five years later the Soviet Union would try to establish bases on five continents, that fifteen years after the 1962 missile crisis and Soviet withdrawal from Cuba, Cuban troops would be in evidence throughout Africa.

Soviet ascendancy has not of course proceeded without strains and stresses. There have been "disturbances" in Eastern Europe and occasional losses of acquired positions, as in Egypt or Somalia. Were these occurrences the growing pains of an expanding empire which continues its advance in spite of occasional setbacks, or are there some indications that the Soviet Union may not be the wave of the future it imagined itself to be?

Soviet Foreign Policy: Looking Back to the Future

It is a truism that the Soviet Union has emerged as a combination of a universal Communist "church" and a state within the international system of states. The duality of its policies was rooted in its origin as a party-state. On one level it was part and parcel of the international movement; on another, it continued the tradition of the tsarist empire. Its expansionist aims were enhanced by the replacement of the Russian Byzantine legacy—the dream of a Third Rome—with the universalist challenge of the Third International. The Soviet Union was established as a state open to new members, until "the International becomes the human kind."

Sixty years later the universalist claims of the Soviet Union look feeble. The Third International has been defunct for thirty-five years, the Cominform for twenty-two years, and the ad hoc meetings of the Communist parties only provide an occasion for manifestations of polycentrism. The proliferation of Communist disputes (Sino-Soviet, Sino-Albanian, Soviet-Albanian, Sino-Vietnamese, Sino-Cuban, Vietnamese-Cambodian, Soviet-Cambodian, and so on) and the relations between Communist states offer a commentary on proletarian solidarity. It is symbolized by the "fraternal" Soviet aid to Hungary in 1956, to Czechoslovakia in 1968.

The political ambivalence of Soviet policies is rooted in the fact that ideology cannot be jettisoned—and this ambivalence is becoming increasingly transparent. There are diminishing political returns from Soviet ideological ventures. The point has been reached at which imperial expansion props up doctrinal authority, instead of the doctrinal mission promoting imperial expansion.

One could observe similar processes in the Roman Empire after Constantine and Theodosius, but a totalitarian state like the Soviet Union, with its Party controls and ideology of a secular utopia, offers no real parallel with ancient Rome. The role and consequences of Christianity as the Roman state religion (even in the hostile interpretation of Gibbon) are not comparable with the role and manipulative potential of Communist ideology in the Soviet Union. But, in any case, the relation between the universalistic claims of a state and its imperial expansion is relevant to the understanding of its long-term prospects.

The external loss of the universalistic momentum is accompanied by the internal loss of the utopian perspective. This process is also protracted. How long can one stay on the road to utopia? We simply do not know, but it is difficult to imagine any temporary solutions to Soviet dilemmas (which arise from the impossibility of discarding ideological legitimation) other than those of (internally) postponing utopia, and (externally) promoting further expansion. The strategy and tactics of such an escape forward depend on future circumstances which cannot be divined in detail. One can guess that, short of an unpredictable internal upheaval due to some disaster, such as several consecutive catastrophic harvest failures coinciding with a succession struggle and the loss of authority at the top, there will be a continuation of the effort to shift still further the balance of power in the Soviet favor.

Europe remains the supreme prize because only by gaining control or, at least, strong influence in Europe, can the Soviet Union fundamentally improve its global strategic position. A frontal assault, in spite of weakening NATO's central sector and its northern and southern flanks, would still involve unacceptably high risks, so the old step-by-step salami tactics and the strategy of indirect approach are likely to continue, and so will further attempts to soften the United States' posture, to Finlandize West European attitudes, and to play on U.S.-West European divergencies (or "contradictions").

There may however be more to it than "more of the same." The Soviet attitude to what it sees (and always has seen) as a protracted conflict remains patient and cautious, but "more of the same" does not offer it the prospect of a strategic breakthrough, particularly as it sees that its own aggressive actions are beginning to cause anxieties in adversaries and potential victims, anxieties which lead them to react, however timidly. The détente line as a politically disarming tactic may have exhausted its usefulness. One can sense the growing irritation in the Soviet press about countervailing (anti-Soviet) tendencies appearing on the world scene, irritation which has resulted so far in verbal huffing and puffing, warnings and threats.

To what extent the tactics of soft-sell through détente may be replaced by intimidation (which has always been in the background even when the threats were not credible) depends at least partly on Western reactions. If this intimidation is seen to be ineffective, it will be counterproductive, but if the West is frightened, fear may lead to the rationalization of cowardice. This remains a question of Western political will and nerve.

The same applies to the Eurocommunists. The Soviet Union knows that it cannot persuade them ideologically, but it does not have to "excommunicate" them as long as it can impress them with Soviet might, which is for them a stronger and more realistic argument. Eurocommunists continue to support most Soviet foreign policy actions and are careful not to challenge the Soviet Union too provocatively.

China is accused with great vehemence of supporting the reactionary elements in Third World countries. In this context the term reactionary (like the term fascist) covers a multitude of sins, the worst of which is the lack of sympathy for the Soviet Union. The intensification of Sino-Soviet polemics is both an indication and a consequence of the deepening of the conflict. The tone of these polemics is more stringent than ever, and the political clashes extend to all the countries with whom the two Communist giants have any contact.

We are a long way from the time when Brzezinski and Huntington wrote in their book *Political Power: USA/USSR* (1964): "The United States is ill-prepared for protracted struggle with its enemies; the Soviet Union is ill-equipped for protracted disagreement with its friends." Since then the Soviet and Chinese friends have become enemies. But the United States is still "ill-prepared for protracted struggle." Brzezinski and Huntington also wrote that in the Soviet Union "Marxism-Leninism can evolve into a more effective doctrine of domestic control," a less perspicacious prophecy.

The relation between ideology and Soviet policies is a perennial subject, analysed to the point of exhaustion in the past; but it seems that the question still continues to exercise curiosity. The old duality of ideology versus Realpolitik, and hackneyed formulations about the role of ideology being primordial as against power motives and national considerations or vice versa in Soviet external conduct still recur regularly in articles and books. New debates on these subjects are occasioned by current developments in East-West relations, by discussions among Soviet dissidents (between, say, Solzhenitsyn and Sakharov, or Medvedev and Shafarevich), or simply by the emergence of new generations of analysts.

As Pierre Hassner remarked, "the same crude dichotomies between ideology and power have re-emerged intact after a generation in current debates about détente, the significance of Soviet arms policies, Soviet attitudes toward change in Western Europe, and the source of Soviet conduct in Africa." Although many analysts, like Lowenthal and Brzezinski, pointed out twenty years ago that the two factors are interdependent, attitudes toward the problem continue to be polarized between that which sees ideology as the ultimate source of Soviet conduct and that which sees in it nothing but post hoc rationalization of other basic drives. Thirty years ago Kennan described the problem as one of interaction between Marxist-Leninist ideology and the "circumstances of power," even though he argued that the former provided "a highly convenient rationalization" for the "instinctive desires" of the Soviet leaders. Recently, however, he came to the conclusion that "the rhetoric of revolutionary Marxism" is today just a "verbal smokescreen" for traditional nationalist Russian foreign policy.

Where then do we stand now vis-à-vis this eternal question? Is the end of ideology in the Soviet Union in sight? If the answer is yes, what are the implications for Soviet foreign policy? If the answer is no, and ideology continues to play a role in Soviet conduct, even if it is changing, how would this change affect the Soviet leaders' concerns with the power of their party and their empire? Would it imply in either case that the Soviet challenge to the West might become easier to manage?

One of the sources of confusion in the controversies about the role of ideology is the lack of a clear distinction between the significance of ideology's particular and general features. To be concerned with the first aspect is to deal with the modification or abandonment of specific tenets of the Marxist-Leninist gospel, be it the "dictatorship of the proletariat" or the "withering away of the state." Doctrinal change of even the most cherished particular tenets is compatible with the preservation of ideology. It is only the modification of the general features of ideology which might spell a basic change of its character or presage its demise. Such general features include the utopian perspective of Marxism, its soteriological and chiliastic nature, and a belief in the scientific character of its historical laws. As long as these general features of communist ideology are preserved, any alterations of its particular features can be rationalized. Dialectics is always at hand to reinforce the dogma "when the prophecy fails." Indeed, specific parts of a utopian doctrine must change in confrontation with the reality of historical development if ideology is to survive. Otherwise the credibility gap could grow too wide even for true believers. But the ideology survives in spite of the credibility gap; it does not depend only on the existence of true believers. Those who say that ideology is "nothing but rationalization" do not ask what role rationalization performs in the maintenance of ideology, why there is a need for rationalization rather than the abandonment of ideology, in short, how pertinent is the relationship between ideology as rationalization and ideology as a motivating force. Even for an individual, motivation and rationalization can be mutually reinforcing mechanisms; this is even more the case with respect to political processes in society, and particularly in Soviet society where power rests on doctrinal authority. The crux of the matter is that ideology is a necessary part of the system because it provides the principles of legitimacy and imposes a general framework for the perception of reality. Thus, inevitably, it also conditions Soviet attitudes toward foreign policy.

In order to grasp the nature of the evolution of Soviet foreign policy it is not enough to analyse the changing foreign policy situation. It is necessary to be aware of doctrinal evolution in the Soviet Union, the current state of ideology there, which is a related but distinct problem, and their specific relation to power and other factors. To treat the problem as if it were only one question is to oversimplify it to a point where wrong conclusions about foreign policy inevitably follow.

Those who dismiss ideology as "nothing but rationalization"

stress the pragmatic character of Soviet policies; but this overlooks the Leninist distinction between short-term considerations (which impose limitations on policies) and long-range ideological goals. In a certain sense, all politics, ideological or not, tend to be concerned first of all, with short-term considerations. But there is a difference between policies which appertain to nothing else, and those which take long-term considerations, ideological or other, as their frame of reference. To confuse the two as pragmatic in the same sense is to misunderstand the character of Soviet policies in the past and, I would argue, also at present.

It is this indiscriminate use of the word pragmatism vis-à-vis both Soviet and Western foreign policies, and the existence of many preconceived notions about Soviet realism, which account for most of the erroneous expectations generated by Western political leaders and commentators. This was the case with regard to the treaty of Brest Litovsk, the Stalin-Hitler Pact, Yalta, and détente. Throughout this period, all too many voices in the West have been ready to disregard the persistence of the ideological factor in Soviet foreign policy. No amount of official avowals would induce most Western politicians to treat Soviet ideological utterances seriously. When confronted with a myriad of Soviet assertions which contradicted American assumptions about détente, the usual Western pattern of reasoning was to explain them away as mere "ideological rationalizations" or "ideological rhetoric." The additional stock argument was that they were for home consumption only, even though they were also addressed to foreign communists.

Henry Kissinger provided the grand premise for this type of Western self-deception. He assumed that what he imagined to be the rules of the game in détente were also binding on the Soviet Union. According to him these rules precluded: a) "attempts by either country to achieve a position of predominance either globally or regionally," b) "any attempt to exploit a policy of détente to weaken our alliances," c) the exploitation of "relaxation of tension . . . as a cover to exacerbate conflicts in international trouble spots."

These rules were based on the Declaration of Basic Principles of Relations Between the USA and USSR, signed in Moscow in May 1972 and on a similar document signed in Washington in June 1973. They solemnly proclaimed that neither of the two powers would try "to obtain unilateral advantage at the expense of the other."

Illusions about Soviet pragmatism die hard and so does wishful thinking about the Soviet approach to détente. After Yalta there was a disenchantment when it finally dawned upon Western observers that Stalin's use of the word democracy did not coincide with Western usage. Now there was another painful discovery of the obvious, that Brezhnev's use of the concept of détente differed from the Western one. It is still assumed by many that the Soviet leaders accepted (in fact) the Western 'rules of the game' in détente. Zbigniew Brzezinski complained in May 1978 that the Soviet Union had violated its "code." This presupposed of course that the signing of the pieces of paper by the Soviet Union in Moscow, Washington and Helsinki amounted to its having seriously accepted such a code.

Just as on past occasions, there was no dearth of voices in the West warning against such interpretations of current Soviet policies. Innumerable doctrinal and ideological pronouncements were explicit about the Soviet attitude to peaceful coexistence. In fact, Soviet words matched Soviet deeds in anti-Western policies and propaganda. They were of course incompatible with Soviet diplomatic declarations, but there was nothing new in this: Soviet policies in the past always displayed such duality when engaged in diplomatic "soft-sell" during periods of "offensives of smiles."

Now that the period of bourgeois euphoria about détente is over, it is interesting to recall how Soviet political commentators tried to persuade the Western New Left that the Soviet Union remained faithful to its revolutionary ideology. Here is the American "independent Marxist" journal, *Science and Society* (Spring 1978), describing how Eduard Batalov explained in his book *The Philosophy of Revolt*[1] that the ideological *angst* of Western radicals is groundless:

> The problem of violence, according to Batalov,[1] exposes the New Left's lack of grasp of the correlation of class forces. Certainly in our epoch revolutionary transformations have thus far been carried out only by means of violence. But a premature outbreak of violence incites an overwhelming reaction from the right. Consequently, this question must be handled with extreme tactical skill and must be based on a careful analysis of class alignments and forces. . . . Many New Leftists use guerrilla warfare, the revolutionary method *par excellence*, as a pretext for attacking "Soviet revisionism" and détente—even though no other country has been a more consistent supporter of authentic guerrilla movements. Détente submits capitalism to two pressures, the external one of socialism and the internal one of the working class. Détente favours the liberation of people from imperialism, and helps consolidate socialism.

Even if ideology is only an inhibiting or exacerbating factor, it plays a role in important specific cases. It is difficult for instance to

1. Eduard Batalov, *The Philosophy of Revolt* (Moscow: Progress, 1975).

imagine that a pragmatic approach would maintain the present structure of Soviet agriculture, a source not only of domestic but of international weakness for Soviet leaders. Whatever the historical roots of the Sino-Soviet conflict may be, its character would be different without the ideological dimension which makes it not just a clash between national interests and powers but a contest that also affects the legitimacy of the respective ruling parties.

Ideological evolution during six decades of Soviet history can be summarized as a reluctant retreat, without abandonment, from the utopian and universalistic claims of Marxist doctrine. The content of the doctrine has been undergoing constant modification in line with the dual impulses which come from the intractable reality on the one hand and from the needs of legitimation of power on the other. There is, of course, nothing historically extraordinary in the reluctance to retreat from universalist pretensions of a doctrine. Even in a period of decline Byzantium stuck obsessively to its imperial claims of Christian universality. So did Rome faced with the Reformation. Tribal religions evolve into universalistic ones, as history testifies, but there is usually no reverse evolution in places which claim to be the *fons et origo* of such universal doctrines, and the same applies to the secular ideology of Communism. There is usually only a fragmentation through splits—into Christian churches, Islamic sects or national Communist parties—each one adapting the universal doctrinal truths to local conditions. This is the one proposition on which all Communist parties in this polycentric age agree in theory, but the Soviet Union continues to emphasize the universal validity of its own interpretation of Marxism against those who deny it.

In spite of sociological parallels drawn by Crane Brinton, Jules Monnerot and S. F. Kissin, communism is not a religion; it has no transcendental concern. Certain social and political consequences follow from this. The promise of utopia is not the same as the promise of paradise; utopia is to be realized on this side of the Great Divide. Therefore the legitimacy of churches, even where Christianity was a state religion, was a different problem from the one faced by Communist parties in power. The latter cannot accept the separation of the church (the party) from the state. The legitimacy of those in power depends on the construction of a Communist society with its utopian features, not on attending to the spiritual (theistic) needs of the faithful.

It is not surprising therefore that this part of Marxist doctrine has undergone modifications in the Soviet Union. The Communist utopia has been postponed ever since Lenin wrote his *State and Revolution,* but it has never been abandoned as unrealizable. From War Communism and the first party program, through Lenin's "Dictatorship of the Proletariat," Stalin's "sharpening of contradictions under Socialism," Khrushchev's "State of All People" and the promise of Full Communism within two decades in the third party program (1961), and finally to Brezhnev's "Developed Socialism"— all these doctrinal formulas testify to the same problem: power needs legitimacy, legitimacy needs utopia, utopia cannot be realized, so it has to be at the same time preserved and constantly postponed. But, needless to say, the state has not withered away and is no longer expected to, the party has become not only de facto but also constitutionally the state's alter ego, classes are officially on the way to extinction, yet social and political hierarchies flourish in all their rigidity.

That is not, of course, how *Pravda* sees it. In its editorial article "The Strength of Our Ideology" (24 August 1978) *Pravda* says:

> Marxist-Leninist ideology of the working class which triumphed and became firmly established forever in the motherland of October is an ideology of genuine humanism and of social justice, of socialist patriotism and internationalism, of freedom, equality and brotherhood of nations ... Marxism-Leninism has become the ruler of the minds of all advanced humanity. This has been in many respects helped by the active ideological and theoretical work of the Communist and workers' parties and their increasingly strong ideological cooperation. Mentioning this in his speech at the ceremonial meeting in Prague in the spring of this year, the General Secretary of the Central Committee of the CPSU, Chairman of the Presidium of the Supreme Soviet of the USSR, Comrade L. I. Brezhnev said: "Today Marxist-Leninist ideology occupies an *avant-garde* position in the world's social thought. It is a focus of passions, it attracts various social movements. This is to a very great extent the outcome of the common creative activity of our parties, the result of the influence of the richest practice in building a new world."
>
> The growing influence of real socialism, of communist ideals in the consciousness of working men is the most important factor in the ideological struggle between the two social systems at the present stage. As the 25th Congress of the CPSU indicated, the problems of the ideological struggle are coming more and more to the fore in present conditions, and the truth about socialism is a mighty weapon in this struggle. In cooperation with other fraternal parties, the CPSU is doing its best to make the example of victorious socialism radiate more and more brightly, to make the magnetic attraction of Marxist-Leninist ideology grow ever stronger.

Soviet Foreign Policy: Looking Back to the Future

Reading *Pravda* regularly (which for my sins I have done for decades) teaches one how to perceive its emphases. They reflect, without fail, Soviet leaders' concerns, however inverted or camouflaged in form, and the above example is no exception.

There can be little doubt that after sixty years of doctrinal acrobatics, Soviet ideology is showing strains; its credibility is wearing thin. It is no longer a living faith, but only a ritual code and a mental straightjacket. From the point of view of the mechanism of party power it is necessary, a kind of ballast which cannot be thrown out. But ideology is a source of strength which is now becoming a source of weakness. Internally, even the attenuated utopian perspective necessitates the continuous flaunting of the reality principle. Externally, Soviet ideology has lost most of its persuasiveness and is more and more frequently forced to confront polycentric ideological challenges within the international Communist movement. What was once a source of unqualified support is now often a drag and an embarrassment. Revolutionary romanticism is dead in the Soviet Union. The Soviet ideology has therefore lost almost all power of attraction for the idealistic radicals abroad (they have to use Cuba as a substitute). The political sex appeal of the Soviet Union is increasingly based on crude power and the rise of the Soviet empire coincides with its fall as an ideological Mecca for communism.

All this cannot but have some negative repercussions, not only for the general image of the Soviet Union, but also for its performance in specific areas of international relations. The long-term implications are yet to be assessed, but the present consequences can be discerned even though they are contradictory and not quite clear. Soviet Leninist strategy and Soviet Leninist ideology have somehow gotten out of joint. Now, ideology is an asset which can hardly tip the scale.

Politically the Soviet Union has almost achieved a state of splendid isolation. Its so-called allies in Eastern Europe are unreliable satellites. It has always been preoccupied by the spectre of two-front confrontation. Stalin avoided this by helping to deflect the Japanese Imperial drive southwards (during his conversation with Matsuoka, when he told him: "We are both Asians"). But after the war the Soviet Union managed to frighten the West sufficiently to provoke the creation of NATO, and it is no exaggeration to say that Stalin was the architect of German rearmament. Thirty years later the flagrant ambiguity of Brezhnev's détente combined with the Soviet arms drive and expansionism provoked the very situation the Soviet Union feared most: a tendency towards a two-front strategic confrontation. Brezhnev cannot claim the entire credit for the American-Chinese rapprochement and the Sino-Japanese Treaty, but he has a major share in it. Even if there is no complete symmetry because Sino-

American rapprochement and the Sino-Japanese Treaty are not military alliances, it is nevertheless clear that in both cases the Soviet Union is the losing party. It cannot prevent the United States from playing the China card or Japan from supplying technology and economic assistance to its hated neighbour instead of to the Soviet Union as it had once hoped. On the other side, the Soviet Union is hemmed in by the Western alliance. A policy which succeeds in mobilizing one way or another as adversaries the U.S., Western Europe, Japan, and China is no great political achievement, even though it can be defended on all fronts in the ideological struggle. And indeed the Soviet Union is now involved in such an ideological struggle with China and the West, not to mention Eurocommunism, Albania, and parts of the Third World.

This poses three questions for the future. One: How will this dynamic of Soviet expansionism be affected by the fact that ideology no longer helps it? Two: Soviet expansionism provokes countervailing coalitions, while Soviet self-centred ideology is finding few supporters abroad. In view of the gap between the traditional Soviet strategy and the debilitation of its ideological appeal, might the Soviet leadership in the future be taking a higher-risk strategy to compensate for its internal and external frustrations? Three: If the Soviet Union tries to break its "splendid isolation" (as China did when Chou En-lai started its ping-pong diplomacy to make up for the self-inflicted wounds of the Cultural Revolution) what political and military strategy can it conceivably adopt? If one were to look at the political and strategic developments in the world through Soviet eyes, one would be struck by a number of ideological juxtapositions and political dilemmas facing the Soviet Union at present. One would notice that the Soviet Union has now abandoned its previous perspective on the Third World. As *Kommunist* (No. 11, 1978) put it,

> There is no sufficient basis . . . for calling the developing countries a "Third World" which allegedly has a parallel existence with the captalist and socialist worlds. To determine the common features of developing countries it is necessary to take as a starting point two fundamental observations: the division of the contemporary world into two opposite socio-political systems and the historical significance of our epoch as a period of transition from capitalism to socialism. This predetermines the objective impossibility for the liberated countries to develop in a "third" direction.
>
> Among developing countries there are already states which are following the capitalist path and states which have chosen the socialist orientation . . . some developing

Soviet Foreign Policy: Looking Back to the Future

countries associating with the world socialist system and some others joining the developed capitalist countries.

Among the former group, *Kommunist* lists Angola, Congo (Brazzaville), Ethiopia, Afghanistan, Madagascar, South Yemen, Benin, Tanzania, Algeria, Libya (neither Iraq nor Syria is mentioned). Among the latter group are Egypt, Iran, Kuwait, Saudi Arabia, Somalia, Sudan, Pakistan, Sri Lanka, and Bangladesh.

It is clear that the inclusion in one or another group is determined by Soviet political interests and hopes, and not by any Marxist, social, or economic criteria. Some of these countries have full-fledged Communist regimes, others are included in the "progressive" group simply on account of their pro-Soviet foreign policies. What matters to the Soviet Union are the strategic and geopolitical opportunities they may be providing and, in this respect, Afghanistan, South Yemen and Ethiopia (after its reconquest of Eritrea) are offering particularly good prospects as the staging ground for pressure on the Persian Gulf riparian states with their access to oil, the jugular vein of Western industrial economies.

Looking through Soviet eyes, one would certainly not imagine that the Soviet Union was committed to the international status quo; one would know that it was ideologically against the status quo and striving to change it. Unlike most of his Western colleagues the Soviet observer would be at least as much concerned with Soviet geopolitical strategy as with its military stockpile, which is almost the only focus of Western perceptions. He would realize that both intentions and capabilities depend on opportunities and temptations which are exploited by strategic and tactical foresight.

The foreign policy record is indubitably positive from the Soviet point of view. The Soviet Union has managed to achieve the status of a super-power and has registered many gains in the Third World. It has even managed, in spite of détente, to avoid the stigma of ideological betrayal, the stigma which it now pins on China for her "bed-fellowship" with the imperialists.

The overall achievement has been summarized by a Polish commentator in *Trybuna Ludu* (14 August 1978) as follows:

> In the long-run the attitude of the capitalist countries to détente . . . is determined and will be determined in future by objective circumstances. As far as the United States is concerned there are several. But I will limit myself to the enumeration of only a few of them.
>
> 1) The change in the balance of power between the socialist and capitalist systems. During the more than 30 years since World War II there have been substantial shifts

in the political, economic and military correlation of forces between East and West [in favour of the former] . . .

2) The inability of the United States to win the strategic race with the Soviet Union. In spite of great arms expenditures in the USA, the doctrine of "assured" strategic superiority over the USSR has ended in fiasco . . .

3) Changes in the world political configuration. The emergence of about 100 new states after World War II, despite their political differences, has generally weakened the capitalist countries. On basic questions of war and peace many new states supported the concepts of the socialist countries . . .

4) The West has not won the Cold War. It has not achieved the goals of its policy, it has not "contained Communism", nor reversed the progressive social and political changes in the world . . .

Although this points to real developments, it is far from being the whole picture. The postwar balance sheet of East-West relations is undoubtedly marked by Western strategic backsliding, but the Soviet advance has been accompanied by so many unwanted occurrences which complicate both the power and the ideological perspectives that the prospect of the triumphal Soviet march into the radiant future is less than certain.

Internally, the erosion of ideological momentum spells long-term trouble for party legitimacy and position. Soviet economic performance is on the decline; nationality problems are on the rise. The handling of any one of these problems would intensify the difficulty with at least one of the others, while immobilism would render future action on them even more difficult.

Externally, it is enough to read the fifth page of *Pravda* (dealing with foreign affairs) to see that the self-congratulatory exultation on its editorial page is bunkum. In the short period of summer 1978 it was filled with indignant outcries against almost everybody, as well as warnings and threats to the United States and China, Japan and Pakistan, France and Germany, Yugoslavia and Romania, Iran and North Yemen, Egypt and Saudi Arabia. The list can be extended. The Sino-Soviet dispute has reached the high point of absurdity. The Soviet Union accuses China of persecuting the dissidents, of violating human rights, of using show trials against political opponents, of practising "legal farces" against those "suspected of dissatisfaction." Such high-minded sentiments, expressed in the Soviet press shortly after the trials of Orlov, Ginzburg and Shcharansky, are not only directed against what *Pravda* (27 August 1978) calls "reprisals from above" in China. Similar indignant denunciations are also regularly made against the abuse of human rights in Great Britain and the United States. One article condemns a "War against Dissidents" in the U.S., another compares the strengthening (by four thousand men) of the much dwindled British army to the Nazi military build-up in the thirties, a third cavils sarcastically on the misuse of psychiatry in capitalist countries, and so forth. Country after country and personality after personality, from Chile to Israel, from Santiago Carrillo to Zbigniew Brzezinski, become targets of Soviet obloquy.

The unrelenting castigations of all and sundry make the black-list longer and longer. Today it is Fukuda who is attacked for getting ready to sign the "anti-hegemony clause" in the Sino-Japanese Treaty; tomorrow, Hua Kuo-feng for visiting Rumania, Yugoslavia and Iran. Even Albania has not escaped censure, although its split with China was seen as opening promising possibilities for the Soviet Union. But if dogmatic Albania was sternly rebuked, so were the "revisionist" Eurocommunists. The Spaniards like Azcarate are already beyond the pale, but even the more accommodating Italian communists get stiff lessons in elementary Leninism. Thus *Kommunist* (No. 10, 1977) reminded them of Gramsci's words that "not a single revolutionary movement can be dictated to by a national assembly," that the problem of power cannot be decided by "arithmetic majority," that this basic problem of revolution "cannot be decided by voting" but must transcend "the framework of the formal principles of bourgeois democracy."

Clearly, ideological struggle in the Soviet Union has become a matter of *defense de tous les azimouths*. And this, I suppose, is as good an indication as any that, contrary to the historical reflections of the *Trybuna Ludu* commentator, not everything is for the best for the Soviet Union in the worst of all possible imperialist worlds. It may even suggest that some waves of the future may never reach the future.

It is not political meteorology but political geology that must be kept in mind in answering the three basic questions for the future posed earlier:

1. Contrary to Western wishful thinking, the weakening of the Soviet ideological dynamic does not in the short run diminish the danger of Soviet expansionism. It obviously weakens the New Soviet Class in some respects; yet this only increases the need to strengthen its legitimacy by compensating for the emergent weakness. Intensified ideological education is unlikely to be very effective. There are also objective limits (mentioned above) to the promotion of "consumer satisfaction" or of Russian nationalism. The only compensatory factor which can avoid the need for facing the dilemmas of internal reform

would be external expansion. Only foreign policy successes can somehow compensate the proverbial "man in the street" (or "the man in the queue") for his ideological, national and economic frustrations. Conversely, only foreign policy failures can seriously put the problem of Soviet internal reform on the agenda. But this proposition does not easily enter into Western policy calculations. In the absence of general war (which is undesirable in the nuclear age) defeats like those of 1905 or 1917 are unlikely, but if the containment of Soviet expansionism will not produce revolutionary situations it may well frustrate its effect in compensating for internal Soviet failures and thus open the way for pressures for reform.

2. The Soviet Union's foreign policy problem for the early part of the 'eighties is how to exploit the (probably temporary) advantages which have resulted from its military build-up and from American and Western neglect to maintain their own strategic superiority. Unless the Soviet military ascendancy brings about politico-strategic gains the reaction it is bound to engender will make it futile in the long run. All the factors enumerated above point to the probability that the next Soviet leadership will try to avoid such an outcome and that it will strive to change the balance of power further in its favour. It will have to avoid the risk of general nuclear conflagration, but it may well hope that by using its increased might prudently it can achieve further political and strategic advances, if the Western powers continue to display cowardice and confusion.

3. The area between Pakistan and the Balkans remains the "soft underbelly" of the West from the Soviet strategic point of view. New Soviet gains in this region may well endanger Western Europe and bring about its eventual "Finlandization." The political strategy of the Soviet leaders will of course be to continue to try to prevent the cooperation of their enemies (as they see them), even when their own acts make such cooperation more necessary (or even more likely). Whether the dire Soviet warnings intended to prevent the British from selling the Harriers to the Chinese or similar Soviet threats will be effective now and in the future remains to be seen, but undoubtedly they will continue. The prospects for Soviet political and strategic advances in the 'eighties will depend ultimately on the Western resolve in resisting them. At present this does not look impressive, but if it were strengthened in the face of danger, the Soviet Union would have no choice but to focus on its own internal weaknesses. Such a retreat may lead to fundamental changes in the international scene (also in view of the rise of China), with the eventual need for some surprising shifts in alliances. But this is unlikely to happen before the new millenium is upon us.

Klaus Mehnert

Sino-Soviet Relations

Three questions will be asked in this paper: How are Sino-Soviet relations today? What about the future? And what about the outside world?

The answer to the first question is very simple. Sino-Soviet relations are very bad. They were bad while Mao was alive and they have remained bad under his successors. We do not know whether these men contemplated any change in the relationship. All we know is that they continued in Mao's vein after they had taken over the reins, following the arrest of the Gang of Four on October 6, 1976.

With the benefit of hindsight it is clear that there was little chance of the Gang of Four assuming power, so the question is irrelevant what the Four would have done had they been victorious in the struggle for Mao's mantle. There are, however, no serious indications that they would have steered a pro-Soviet course. Counting the lines in the anti-Soviet articles of *Peking-Rundschau* (the German equivalent of *Peking Review*), in the first four issues of the month of June in four consecutive years, I found—in round figures—these results:

1974	1210 lines
1975	900 lines
1976	2730 lines
1977	1570 lines

This might mean that in June 1974, when Teng Hsiao-ping was still at the beginning of his second rise, there was an average number of attacks on the USSR. In 1975 when Teng and the Four were more concerned about each other than about the "Polar Bear," the figure dropped to 900. In 1976, with the Four at the zenith of their power (Teng had been eliminated for the second time), the figure trebled. In June 1977 the new men, including Teng, were interested in building their own power base, paying less attention to the conflict with the USSR; the curve dropped.

Another indication of the Four's attitude is offered by the journal *Historical Review*, one of their pet mouthpieces. When the Four had a monopoly over the media, from 1974 until their fall, this journal paid an extraordinary amount of attention to Russian (or Soviet) topics: more than two dozen articles treated the history of the border issue alone, some going far back into antiquity. Whether Saint Petersburg or the old Moscow or the new Moscow, the Polar Bear always appeared as the aggressor; in this respect the USSR occupied "the place of Hitler's Germany" in the words of the *Historical Review* of May 1976. No doubt the general reader in China, especially the history-minded one, now knows infinitely more about the history of the regions bordering on the USSR than ever before.

The main event of publication in China since the new men came to power was Mao's *Volume V*, which includes a selection of speeches and articles of his first eight years in power, 1949-1957. The editors, with Mao's official successor Hua Kuo-feng at their head, have stated explicitly that the documents are edited, hence it was up to them to decide which documents and which passages of documents to include. It would have been easy for them to eliminate all traces of Mao's criticism of the USSR, which would have freed their hands in case someday they should want to improve relations with their Soviet neighbor. But they did the opposite. Here are a few examples: Mao's speech on the *Ten Relations* (1956) had reached the outside world years ago in a version which contained no hostile words against Moscow. The version published in *Volume V*, however, includes quite a few. (Presumably Mao made these remarks in his 1956 speech but had them stricken in order not to offend the USSR when the transcript was prepared for distribution among party leaders.) Thus Mao had poked fun at those Chinese who wanted to copy everything the Soviet Union did and were later forced to make somersaults when the Soviet road proved wrong. Many Soviet people, he had said, were arrogant and held their noses very high. About some Chinese noses he remarked sarcastically that to them, "every Soviet fart smells sweet."

On the other hand, a number of documents in which the USSR had been praised for its friendship toward China were missing in

Volume V. In these documents, which had reached the West by various means, there were originally to be found frequent expressions of gratitude toward the USSR, such as "reliable ally," "enormous help," and "unbreakable friendship." The Communist party of the USSR was called "the most progressive, the most experienced, the best prepared from the point of [Marxist] theory," and "a model for the future;" and Khrushchev, whose name was one of the most negative in the Chinese vocabulary for two decades, had been addressed as "Dear Comrade." All this was now eliminated.

Thus fortified by Mao's *Volume V*, the new Chinese leaders stepped up their attacks against the Kremlin, which culminated in the six page long article in *People's Daily* of November 1, 1977, covering thirty-five pages of *Peking Review* (November 4, 1977, No. 45, from which the following quotations have been taken). Entitled *Chairman Mao's Theory of the Differentiation of the Three Worlds as a Major Contribution to Marxism-Leninism*, the article offers the most detailed exposition of the Chinese view of the world which, as is known, to the Chinese consists actually of three worlds. The first is that of the two superpowers, the USA and USSR; the second comprises the industrialized countries which lie outside the U.S. and Soviet borders; the third is more or less identical with what we call the Third World and includes China.

Here one remark must be inserted. Since his early days in the revolutionary struggle it was Mao's strategy to determine, at any given moment, who was the number one enemy and to unite against him with all who were willing to do so, even though they may have been enemies too. Mao united with Chiang Kai-shek against the Japanese, when they were the worst enemy; he even helped to free Chiang after he had been captured by his opponents on the "double twelfth" (December 12, 1936) because he needed him as an ally against the Japanese. With the Japanese defeated, Chiang Kai-shek became the primary enemy, and again Mao united with all who were willing, such as the democratic and liberal groups in China. A year after Chiang Kai-shek had withdrawn to Taiwan, America—in the Korean War—became the number one enemy, and help was appreciated from every quarter, even from the USSR. America lost its number one enemy position with the events in Vietnam. Who has taken its place now?

The November 1, 1977, article is quite clear on this point (*Peking Review*, p. 22): "The conduct of the Soviet Union in international affairs is quintessential imperialism and hegemonism, without a trace of socialist proletarian spirit. Nor is that all. Of the two imperialist super-powers, the Soviet Union is the more ferocious, the more reckless, the more treacherous, and the most dangerous source of world war."

With this question settled, the task is to unite with all forces that are willing to share the Chinese view. All liberation forces opposed to Soviet imperialism are by their very nature potential allies of China. "In present-day Europe, national wars against large-scale aggression, enslavement and slaughter by a super-power [i.e., the USSR] are not only possible and probable; they are inevitable, progressive, and revolutionary." And, of course, "the national war which these countries wage against such invasion and annexation is a just war and ought to enjoy the support and assistance of the international proletariat" (*Peking Review* p. 32).

Thus, by implication, the European NATO armies are progressive, revolutionary, and deserving of the support and assistance of the international proletariat.

For those readers of the *People's Daily* article who might think that, after all, the ideological ties among all communists should be stronger than differences arising from strategic considerations, the Chinese authors have this word of advice: "We must . . . start from reality and not from abstractions" (p. 11). The reality is the position of the USSR as number one enemy, everything else is abstraction. To fortify this dictum, Stalin is quoted: "The logic of facts is stronger than any other logic" (p. 15).

The line of the November 1 article has been repeated over and over, in the speeches before the National People's Congress in Peking and before the United Nations in New York as well as in discussions with foreign statesmen. Although the article was signed by the editors of the *People's Daily*, it obviously reflects the policy of the top leadership.

Thus the picture on the Chinese side is clear. And on the Soviet side? All those who discussed the Sino-Soviet issue in the USSR during the last years of Mao's life found the Russians deeply worried about the situation, pinning their hopes on a change after Mao's death. For them, Mao was the arch villain; hence they hoped that once Mao was out, there would be improvement. As a result, Moscow moved very cautiously when Mao's death became known. When the Kremlin's telegram of condolences came back undelivered because it had been addressed to the Central Committee of the Chinese Communist Party, which insists on not entertaining any relations with the CP of the USSR, Brezhnev remained undaunted. He sent a telegram of congratulations when Hua was installed shortly afterwards as Chairman of the party and did not grumble publicly when it too was promptly returned.

Toward the end of November 1976 the Kremlin dispatched to Peking one of its Vice-Ministers of Foreign Affairs, Leonid Ilyichev, for ostensible border negotiations but probably to sniff the post-Mao Peking air. Moscow remained quiet when it led to nothing. When

Moscow's leading party review, *Kommunist*, published a summary of the year's events in its last issue for 1976 (no. 18), China was not even mentioned, although some of the most momentous events had happened there. Issues 3 and 4 for 1976 of the quarterly *Voprosy Dalnego Vostoka (Problems of the Far East)*, never reached the subscribers; probably they were destroyed because they included anti-Peking materials, whereas the English edition came out abnormally thin.

Obviously, nothing was being done to annoy the Chinese in public. Hopes were revived about allegedly pro-Moscow Chinese leaders. One Soviet diplomat who had participated in the Sino-Soviet border negotiations in Peking told me about that time that he placed his hopes on a certain man in the Chinese top echelon (whose name he mentioned) because he had heard him saying friendly and encouraging words to the Soviet chief delegate during a reception. But this was the same Chinese whom I had heard making some of the strongest anti-Polar Bear statements during a German state visit.

Finally, in May 1977, the Kremlin must have come to the conclusion that there was not the least indication of a turn in the Chinese position. It fired its first serious post-Mao blast at the new Chinese leadership in Peking under the pseudonym of I. Alexandrov, which is employed whenever Moscow wishes to make an important point. From then on the polemics became mutual, frequent, and bitter, as they had been for many years.

The official answer to the *People's Daily* exposition on the Three Worlds of November 1, 1977, came in *Kommunist* in March 1978 (no. 5, pp. 89-100). It was called *How Mao's Successors Fight Against Socialism and Its Allies. Peking's Latest "Theory" of Collusion with Imperialism* and began with the angry accusation that the Chinese had seen fit to publish this slanderous article precisely at the time "when the Soviet People and all progressive mankind celebrated the sixtieth anniversary of the Great October Revolution" (p. 90). This article, *Kommunist* said, was one of the worst anti-Soviet statements of the Maoists and one of the most wicked manifestations of contemporary anti-communism. In it the "concept of the three worlds" was no longer presented as just one of Mao's ideas but as a complete theory of Maoist social-chauvinism. (Two semantic comments: Mao's successors are now called Maoists, just as Peking gave the name Khrushchevites to Khrushchev's successors, even though they had overthrown him; and Peking's anti-Moscow label "social-imperialism" returned as "social-chauvinism" from Moscow to China.) *Kommunist* called the Three Worlds' article a "fig leaf" which was supposed to cover the pro-imperialist position of the Chinese leadership and a danger for peace, democracy, and socialism because it showed that the forces of the world reaction had found helpers—Mao's successors. The Soviet review appealed to all those who treasured peace and progress, liberty, and national independence to rally against the ideology and policy of Maoism, the reserve force of imperialism (p. 100).

At about the same time, in the spring of 1978, Leonid Brezhnev was visiting Siberia and the Soviet Far East, making patriotic speeches, addressing, among others, units of the Army (March 31) and the Navy (April 7) and pledging "immediate defense against any aggression." (Full texts in *Kommunist*, 1978:6, pp. 13-28.)

The warnings to Peking culminated in a fourteen column *Pravda* article on June 13, 1978, signed again by I. Alexandrov. Its ominous title was *The Policy of Peking—A Threat to Peace* (sounding even more forceful inasmuch as *mir* means both peace and world, hence a threat to peace and a threat to the world). In fact, the new Alexandrov article was a threat to China because, so *Pravda* wrote, Peking was pushing toward war, forming a united front with the imperialist forces. At length the article mentioned warlike Chinese statements and accused Peking of aggression against Burma, India, Vietnam and Indonesia, of organizing the overseas Chinese against the governments of the countries in which they were living, and of working for collusion with Washington. Zbigniew Brzezinski was mentioned as the villain of the piece and was accused of trying to form an anti-Soviet bloc of Asian countries with China against the USSR, the latter accusation being an echo of Chinese complaints that Moscow attempted an anti-Chinese bloc under the guise of an Asian security pact.

Those were mild tunes compared to the furioso which began exactly two months later. On August 12, 1978, China and Japan signed a peace and friendship treaty. For years Moscow had warned the Japanese that a treaty with the "hegemony" clause in it would be most detrimental to Japanese-Soviet relations. But finally a Japanese government had summoned the courage to sign. The same day the Kremlin broadcast the news as well as its anger—restrained against Japan, violent against China. During the two months following the signing of the treaty and up to its ratification by the Japanese Diet on October 16 (the date up to which the present paper is carried), there has not been a day without attacks, usually numerous, against China in the Soviet press and radio.

First we might mention the Soviet accusations against China which are more or less identical to simultaneous Chinese accusations against the USSR, what one might call the "You too!" line. The Soviets say about China: that it is the one and only true hegemonist and expansionist country, conducting aggressive wars (against India 1962) and demanding territories outside its own borders (10.5 million square kilometers). China is a danger to the peace of the world and

Sino-Soviet Relations 37

to the security of its neighbours. It is wooing the Third World (not quite without success, especially in Africa where "some leaders lack political experience and show a careless attitude" toward Peking), but its aim is to dominate these countries and to use them for its own purposes. China's economic aid is wicked, for China builds factories for countries which do not have the raw materials for them, forcing them to import these from China and thus "to finance China's industry." China is unreliable as a giver of economic aid; in Africa it promised the building of 300 projects in the 1960s of which only one third have been completed. China broke its economic agreements with Albania and Vietnam as soon as it did not like their policies. (Here especially the Chinese might cry "You too!", remembering the summer of 1960 when the Soviets withdrew their experts from China from one day to the next.) China wants to become the gendarme of Eastern Asia (the Chinese have pointed out for a long time that Russia is the gendarme of Eastern Europe). The Chinese are liars (both have called each other "Dr. Göbbels"). The Chinese have invaded the Balkans where they have never been before in order to stir up trouble (the Chinese have accused the Soviets for a long time of doing exactly the same thing in Asia's "Balkans," Southeast Asia). The Chinese are responsible for the border incidents and the Chinese say the opposite. No human rights for the unfortunate people of China! Terrible treatment of the national minorities! (Daily Soviet broadcasts are telling the non-Han population in the border areas, especially the Uighurs and the Mongols, how badly treated they are by the Chinese and how happy is the life of their ethnic brethren in the USSR, just a few miles away. And the Chinese radio does more or less the same in reverse.)

There are also what one might call one-way accusations. One of them concerns the overseas Chinese. Moscow accuses China of using them as its fifth column in southeast Asia. At the same time China is forcing the overseas Chinese bourgeoisie to invest large sums of money in China, about 100 million U.S. dollars yearly; and of the 500 million U.S. dollars which overseas Chinese are sending yearly to their relatives in China "the lions's share goes to the Chinese treasury." To squeeze these relatives even more, the Chinese government has opened shops in which goods are sold only to those who have received foreign currency. (I remember the first such shops in Moscow, called Torgsin, back in the early thirties, as well as the outraged cries of Soviet citizens, continuing to this day, about the way in which the Soviet treasury appropriates the lion's share of the foreign currencies which they get from relatives abroad.)

Soviet broadcasts beamed to China frequently mention the good deeds done to China in the past, as long as the relations were friendly and China was on the right path. Did not the USSR supply China with a vast arsenal of weapons during the war against Japan, including 800 planes? ("You did," Peking would reply, "but to whom did you give them? To Chiang Kai-shek! And against whom did he employ them? Against us, the Communists!") Never should the workers and soldiers of China forget this and never should they let themselves be used against the Soviet Union. The workers especially must beware because the Chinese government intends to export them for exploitation in Hong Kong and Macao.

"China is the 16th member state of NATO" is a frequent statement. China is playing into the hands of the imperialists; it is madly rushing about to obtain weapons from the imperialists, thus tying itself to them hand and foot. At the same time China is sending arms abroad, especially to Cambodia where there are also "thousands of Chinese advisors." China is cooperating with all the reactionaries in the world, as shown by the recent visit of the Chilean Foreign Minister in Peking, at the same time attacking progressive countries such as Cuba. Anti-Sovietism being the core and almost sole object of China's foreign policy, Peking stops at nothing to further its ends. It is even betraying Taiwan for a friendly smile from America (as it is betraying Hong Kong for the sake of the foreign currency it obtains there).

The situation is, however, not entirely hopeless. Moscow's China watchers are keenly interested in any sign of power struggles in Peking; they look especially for indications of a conflict between Teng Hsiao-ping and Hua Kuo-feng and point at any evidence in this connection, for example at the changes in the cabinet during Hua's Eastern European trip. They discern, in fact, not only the Teng and the Hua lines but also a third group which is not siding with either, headed, they think, by the defense minister. This is also the reason why, in broadcasts in Mandarin, the armed forces are warned of impending new purges, while the appeals to the masses voice the slogan: China's economy was doing well while relations with the USSR were good; China's economy is in a dreadful state since relations went bad.

During the last twenty years much has been written, including works by the present author, on the causes of the Sino-Soviet conflict. There is no reason to recapitulate. But we should try to assess how much validity these causes have for the future. We will discuss them one by one.

IDEOLOGY

For Mao, I believe, differences in ideology were the main source of his conflict with the Soviet leaders. I see two main differences.

Firstly, Mao saw the revolution as an unending process because only by ever new upheavals could stratification, the ensuing petrification of society, and the emergence of a hierarchy and a "New Class" be prevented; while the Kremlin considered the revolution to be completed, with the party leaders in the role of guardians of the now inevitable movement toward a classless society, an attitude which made them fearful of the change and evolution that Mao believed to be essential.

Here I shall not dwell on the curious fact that Mao, on October 31, 1975, told his German guest, Chancellor Helmut Schmidt, for the first time about the influence of a fourth German on his thinking: Ernst Haeckel (the first three being, of course, Hegel, Marx, and Engels). I have discussed this point in the chapter "Hegel und Haeckel" in my *Kampf um Maos Erbe*, (*Struggle for Mao's Heritage*, Stuttgart, 1977). Haeckel was a latter-day Darwin whose idea of eternal evolution of the universe was echoed by Mao more than once, especially in his speech of March 1958 (quoted by Stuart Schramm in *Chairman Mao Talks to the People*, New York, 1974, p. 110). Here Mao described the evolution of billions of years in a breathtaking vision, compared to which the ideas of the Soviet leaders sound more than pedestrian. No wonder the Chinese consider Mao's thesis of the revolutions needed after the victory of the revolution as his "main contribution to the treasure house of Marxism-Leninism."

The second difference is closely related to the first: Mao was a passionate egalitarian. He wanted a society of equals, and he was right in noticing the absence of equality in the USSR. The drive for equality excludes material rewards for achievements, because an achievement-rewarding society cannot be a society of equals; on the contrary, it will divide the people into rewarded achievers and unrewarded non-achievers. Therefore to Mao equality had priority over achievement, while in the USSR, which has rewarded achievement ever since the early thirties, a pyramid structure of society has emerged, with the high achievers on the top. Quite apart from other points of difference, these two alone made a reconciliation or a compromise between Mao and the Soviet leaders impossible. Mao's attitude toward the Kremlin was comparable to Martin Luther's irreconcilable conflict with the Vatican.

The situation is different for Mao's successors. They are pragmatists rather than ideologists, and they are willing to forego equality for the time being if they can achieve their goals. Their priority is to make China a modern industrialized state by the year 2000 and for this they need, as they well know, material rewards to stimulate achievement. It is along these lines that their innovations have moved, most noticeably through the introduction of entrance examinations for the universities to ensure the admission of well-prepared students, whereas Mao insisted on political consciousness as a prerequisite. For Mao, the redness of the heart was decisive. Teng Hsiao-ping, the driving force in the new team, says that it makes no difference what color a cat is as long as it catches mice.

As far as ideology is concerned, I suggest that the gap between Moscow and Peking has been narrowed, and the cause of conflict reduced.

THE FRONTIERS

Theoretically there are two issues: First the 1.5 million square kilometers of territory east of the Stanovoi Mountains which the tsarist empire acquired from China by the treaties of 1858 and 1860. But this area is not under discussion; a statement by the Soviets to the effect that they are not responsible for a regrettable act of the tsars and that the issue is now closed because of the population situation would, I think, satisfy the Chinese.

At stake however is the delineation of the present border itself, in Central Asia as well as along the Amur and the Ussuri, especially the question to which side the many river islands belong. This is a relatively minor issue, except at one point. Where the Ussuri flows into the Amur, a pointed triangle is formed because the two rivers meet at an angle of 45 degrees. This triangle is completed by a body of water, the Channel of Kazakevitch. The Chinese claim the Amur and Ussuri to be the border, hence the island between the Channel of Kazakevitch and the confluence of the rivers as theirs, while the Russians insist on the island being theirs south as far as the channel. The island in itself is not important; the problem arises from the fact that north of the confluence lies a Soviet city, Khabarovsk. Were the Chinese to get the island, they would stand almost in the center of Khabarovsk. It is hard to imagine that the Soviets would agree to such a solution. Thus, the frontier question reduces in the last analysis to the difficult question of the Kazakevitch island.

TRADITIONAL HOSTILITY

While at present very strong indeed, hostility is, historically speaking, stronger in Russia than in China. The Chinese, to be sure, have had since ancient times a well founded fear of invasions from the North; and against them they have built one of the most astounding structures in history, the Great Wall. But this hostility existed for thousands of years, long before the Russians. The Russian fear of

China, on the other hand, is deeply embedded in the fabric of Russian history and culture. It is misplaced inasmuch as it derives from the "Tartar Yoke" (13th to 16th centuries) which was imposed not by the Chinese but by the Mongols who had conquered China at the same time. But the Russian sentiments were well expressed by the poet Yevgeni Yevtushenko when he called Mao a Genghis Khan with atomic bombs in his quiver. The enormous population of China, its famous inscrutableness, the daily challenge to Moscow's position as the center of the Communist universe, the endless conflicts with China in every capital and about every political issue on this globe, as well as the lingering bad conscience of possessing vast tracts of Asia at a time of decolonization—all this has created the complex of fears and suspicions which permeates most Russians, even non-Communists. There are some who may, on the contrary, see in a Chinese assault on the Soviet Union a hope for liberation from the Bolshevik yoke (Andrei Amalrik in *Can the Soviet Union Survive until 1984?*); and the Asian peoples of the USSR might again have different feelings. But for the ethnic Russians the China trauma is well nigh universal.

To this trauma one more dimension has presumably been added in recent months although it has been absent so far from the anti-China propaganda—the fear that Chinese economic development might progress much faster than anybody had imagined. The present writer who has spent four weeks in China (from the middle of September to the middle of October 1978, after visiting China twice in 1977) has been much impressed by the drive for the industrialization of China (the "four modernizations") with the help of the West including, of course, Japan. Two aspects of this development must cause apprehension in the USSR: the serious possibility that China will become much stronger in the next two decades than it would have become if the chaotic conditions prevailing until 1976 had continued, and secondly that this dramatic rise will occur in close cooperation with the West. For the Russians it must be truly alarming to see the speed with which China and the West are rushing toward each other.

The hitherto almost complete silence of the Soviet mass media concerning this development might indicate that the leaders in Moscow are stunned by it and do not yet know how to treat it. Some day they will have to tell their people about it, and it is easy to predict the reaction: profound apprehension. Soviet citizens are being taught from childhood on that the economy decides everything. If this is so, then the creation of economic ties of such magnitude between China and the West must also produce political ties of similar magnitude and of long duration. This means that the hope for a shift in Peking's orientation from the West toward the USSR in the foreseeable future will be seriously diminished.

WORLD LEADERSHIP

For centuries the Russians have displayed a messianic urge; they called their country "the Third and final Rome," and they see themselves as the home of the Third (and also final) International. For the Soviet leaders Russia and Communism are identical, and only by following in their footsteps can mankind reach a happy state. The Chinese, on the other hand, have always been ethnocentric; to them the Middle Kingdom was the world, the rest being uninteresting. Communism has added, to be sure, a strain of messianism, but this is a new phenomenon and may not last very long.

The objection of the Chinese to Soviet foreign policy is therefore directed against Soviet imperialism rather than against Soviet messianism. In other words, Soviet messianism is, in their eyes, just a cloak for Soviet imperialism. As long as the Chinese are at odds with the Soviet Union, they will resent and fight Soviet expansion at any point of the globe, especially close to home, that is, in Asia. Their policy toward Japan and toward Southeast and South Asia shows this clearly. It may well be that here lies the core of the Sino-Soviet conflict and that the Chinese fear of Soviet rule over a vast portion of the globe will prevent indefinitely any real détente between the two red neighbors.

The Sino-Soviet conflict is primarily a conflict between the two countries; not even the American CIA has been accused of having fabricated it. But this conflict does not exist in a void. Like everything else, it is interdependent with the rest of the world. At the moment, two such links with world affairs stand out.

First, China is determined to become a modern industrialized power by the year 2000. Its leaders are well aware that for this purpose they need modern technology, know-how, and experts from abroad. In the first period after Mao's victory they had no choice but "to lean" toward the USSR, in Mao's graphic phrase, because they were deeply at odds with America and thus with most of the West. Now they lean toward the West, and they will continue to do so for the foreseeable future because the West has more to offer in the fields which matter. The West can provide billions of dollars, yen, and marks which the USSR cannot; the West has the better and more flexible technology; the West has very little inhibition about supplying China with modern know-how (while the Soviet Union has); the West today poses no threat to China and her borders.

Second, the Chinese stepped over their shadow in 1971/72, greeting Kissinger and Nixon in their capital and establishing close (if unofficial) relations with Washington. They did this at a time when their fear of the USSR was at its height (following the border clashes with the Soviets in 1969) and they did it because they believed America to be a tiger and thus a suitable ally against the Polar Bear.

In the following years, however, their enthusiasm for the new connection waned. Especially they feared that the U.S. was too much concerned with Moscow, too willing to listen to the Kremlin's honeyed words on détente, and that it was getting soft in its determination and strength—in short, that it was changing from a tiger to a paper tiger. If ever China should come to this conclusion, the question would arise: while dragon and tiger would be a good team against the Polar Bear, dragon and paper tiger would not. Would it not be wiser under these circumstances to improve relations with the bear?

It seems that Washington has understood this. The Brzezinski visit to China in May 1978, the increasingly apparent willingness of America to allow the shipment of armaments from Western countries to China, the bogging down of the SALT II negotiations, the general cooling of the American-Soviet dialogue—all this has helped to allay the Chinese fears of American "collusion" (a favorite Chinese term in this context) with the USSR.

The European countries are militarily infinitely weaker than the U.S., yet they have been less nervous about Moscow becoming angry due to their usually excellent relations with China. While the members of the European community have many quarrels among themselves, none of them has any consequential conflict with Peking. This is appreciated by the Chinese, as their frequent visits to the "Nine" and to their headquarters in Brussels indicate. For the Bonn government, to take one example, it is valuable to deal with a country which speaks incessantly of European and German unity and with which it has not a single worrisome problem. The case is similar for other European governments.

The governments of the Third World countries do not wish to get entangled in the Sino-Soviet quarrel, even though some of them feel closer to Moscow than to Peking or vice versa. With most of them, anyone is popular who professes to be in favor of Third World liberation movements as do both Moscow and Peking. The Third World leaders in general cannot be interested in the prolongation of the Sino-Soviet conflict because it absorbs money which otherwise— theoretically at least—might go into economic aid for them. But they also realize that rivalry between the West and the East forces them to compete—by the use of aid and credits—for the good will of the Third World and that a similar rivalry between Peking and Moscow is also to the benefit of the Third World.

In conclusion, the high degree of open hostility between the USSR and China has led both countries to adopt policies and positions which will be difficult to reverse—difficult, but not impossible. Even deadly enmities can be overcome, as the pact between Germany and the Soviet Union in 1939 has shown. To be sure, that pact existed only briefly, but long enough to change the world. In politics, neither love nor hate should be taken as permanent. Nor are leaders immortal. Chinese leaders will be closer to the West than to the Soviet Union as long as they feel that this is advantageous to their cause. This is true today. But it is neither a matter of principle nor an immutable fact.

The many "on the one hand—on the other" statements presented in this paper may sound somewhat ambiguous. But we have been dealing with countries that profess to believe in dialectics. Why should we not use some of it when describing and measuring their mutual relations?

Jan F. Triska

Soviet-East European Relations

ON PREDICTIONS

Carl J. Friedrich of Harvard used to say that predictions of scholars are irrelevant and immaterial because (1) no one acts on them, and (2) they are soon forgotten. What matters, he said, is the plausibility of predictions when they are made, how sound they sound.

I agree. One's assessment of the future depends on one's assessment of the present. If the analysis of the present appears sound, predictions become credible. In other words, assumptions about future outcomes are more important than the actual forecasts. They can be judged on their own merits.

For this reason, I will make my assumptions about Soviet-East European relations as explicit as I can, as I go along. To be able to do that (and given the development of those relations to date), I have cast my analysis in the frame of reference of political economy. At the present time, both the USSR and Soviet-controlled Eastern Europe (East Germany, Poland, Czechoslovakia, Hungary, Romania and Bulgaria) face severe economic problems. Three acute shortages are emerging—in energy, labor force and materials. They will affect negatively industrial and agricultural production and the balance of trade. A significantly lower GNP and overall economic slowdown may be the result, and this process may have adverse socio-political consequences. Economic trends, conditions and developments thus offer a useful conceptual medium in which to analyze the major contexts, domestic and international, of future Soviet-East European relations.

FROM THE PAST TO THE PRESENT

Eastern Europe is not known for its political stability. The network of small states was supported by France and England as a bulwark against Germany after World War I, a *cordon sanitaire*—a tier of independent states to separate Germany and Russia and thus "a stabilizing factor" in Europe. Eastern Europe failed in that role, as it failed after World War II to maintain its independence from the USSR. Both Nazi Germany and the Soviet Union viewed Eastern Europe as a power vacuum, which it was, and moved in.

The East European countries differ in size, historical and cultural experience, political orientation, nationality, language, level of economic development, resource endowment, and economic performance. They thus have little in common and do not particularly like each other. They share, however, dependency on the outside world; left to their own devices, they would be hard pressed to survive economically. Politically, they have never been natural allies; and when three of them—Czechoslovakia, Romania, and Yugoslavia—did enter into a coalition, the Little Entente, the alliance broke up without a whimper when threatened for the first time.

The area underwent two radical, systemic transformations since it was established sixty years ago: when Nazi Germany came to control it and when the Soviet Union wrested control from Nazi Germany for itself. All the other major changes in Eastern Europe were reformist, intra-system modifications and/or regime changes within the established political systems. The defection of Yugoslavia from Soviet control in 1948 came closest to systemic transformation. The break resulted in a trade-off: Yugoslavia gave up Soviet protection for greater internal stability. To that end, Marshal Tito opted for some sharing of power with selected domestic groups and institutions, but there was no radical change in the Yugoslav socio-political system. Similarly, the Stalinist consolidation process which followed in Eastern Europe—a savage offensive of terror against Titoism, reformism, and nationalist tendencies—was simply a dramatic, preventive increase in the intensity and scope of Soviet controls over East European leaders, policies, structures, cultures and groups.

After Stalin's death in 1953, the change in Soviet leadership led to a change in Soviet policies toward Eastern Europe. Khrushchev, supported by Mao Tse-Tung and Tito, was ready to relax Soviet controls in Eastern Europe and to bestow more autonomy on the respective European leaders. At the 20th Congress of the CPSU in 1956, Khrushchev proclaimed the right of each socialist country to work out its methods of building socialism with reference to its particular historical, economic, and social conditions, "to build its own road to socialism." What exactly did he mean?

The Polish and Hungarian crises in 1956 were attempts to find out, and while the Polish de-Stalinization of Gomulka proved to be compatible with that of Khrushchev, the Hungarian way of Nagy was not. The Hungarian revolution, a nationalist, anti-Soviet uprising, was brutally suppressed and a strong Communist leadership was reinstated. No systemic change resulted either in Poland or in Hungary. Similarly, when Albania broke with the Soviet Union in the Sino-Soviet dispute in the early thirties and Romania broadened its autonomy after 1963, the two countries altered their policies, not their systems. And when, following the Soviet lead in the 'sixties, Soviet bloc countries—minus Yugoslavia and Albania but including Romania—turned to the problem of economic development, they began to reform their economic systems. What social conditions would best guarantee the optimum outcome of sound socialist economic innovation? Poland, East Germany, and Bulgaria opted for minor economic reforms, essentially within their established social order. Hungary moved gradually and quietly but with determination toward making cultural, social, and even political conditions more compatible with the spirit of its more ambitious economic reforms. Romania, with its emancipated foreign policy, experimented only cautiously with reform of its economic order. It was Czechoslovakia that might have changed not only leadership and policies but the dominant culture and social structure as well in an authentic socialist transformation. The Soviet occupation in 1968 brought an abrupt halt to this process. Leaders as well as policies were brought back to the pre-1968 conditions, but no change in political system took place.

After the initial shock, the Soviet invasion of Czechoslovakia was interpreted in Eastern Europe as a restoration of status quo ante—a Soviet intervention coping with a specific situation as well as a general warning to others in Eastern Europe. Then the Polish leaders raised consumer prices in 1970 and again in 1976. Major consumer riots followed in both cases. The 1970 uprising cost the Party leader, Gomulka, his job. In 1976 the new Party leader, Gierek, kept his job because he promptly reversed policy.

In the first half of the 1970s, East Europe's trade with the West expanded rapidly. Facilitated by détente, this trade boom was based on fears of East European leaders of decline in the growth rates of their GNP's. Massive imports of advanced Western technology would reverse this trend, and consumer goods would increase popular satisfaction as well. By 1975 the volume of Eastern Europe's trade with the West exceeded $35 billion, surpassing Soviet trade with the West by some seventy percent. However, while imports increased sharply, exports lagged behind, in part because they were not marketable in the West and in part because of the Western recession. As a consequence, East European countries had to borrow hard currency. By the end of 1976, indebtedness on the part of Eastern Europe reached the sum of (estimated) $31.4 billion, or more than one hundred times the traditional East European trade deficit of the mid-fifties. The cumulative trade deficit increases were as follows: Romania, 10 percent; Bulgaria, 180 percent; Hungary, 200 percent; Czechoslovakia, 450 percent; East Germany, 680 percent; Poland, 2,920 percent; and the USSR, 580 percent.)[1] According to an Associated Press report, Eastern Europe and the USSR owed international banks and Western governments about $47 billion by mid-1978.[2]

Volume of East European Trade with the West[3]
(Turnover in billions of U.S. dollars)

	1965	1970	1975
Poland	1.1	1.9	9.2
Yugoslavia	1.6	3.4	7.9
East Germany	1.2	2.5	6.3
Romania	.6	1.4	3.9
Czechoslovakia	.9	1.6	3.8
Hungary	.7	1.2	2.9
Bulgaria	.4	.5	1.5
East Europe	6.5	12.5	35.5

The Western trade bonanza ushered in a period of economic well-being unsurpassed in Eastern Europe's socialist history. To increase political cohesion and stability, a policy of consumer prosperity appeared to be a sensible and, under the prevailing

1. Jan Vanous, "The East European Recession: Did It Come from the West or Was It Sent from Russia with Love?," Discussion Paper No. 78-8 (University of British Columbia: Department of Economics, 1978).
2. San Francisco *Chronicle*, June 28, 1978, p. 29.
3. Ivan V. Matousek, "Eastern Europe: Political Context," in *East European Economies Post-Helsinki,* Joint Economic Committee, Congress of the United States (Washington: United States Government Printing Office, 1977), pp. 3-11.

conditions, viable alternative. A relatively high standard of living also made up for political deprivation. Eastern Europe was now treated by the West, for all practical purposes, as a recognized, permanent Soviet sphere.

The terms of Soviet trade with Eastern Europe through the Council of Mutual Economic Assistance (hereafter CEMA) had changed little in the 'seventies, in spite of the changes in world prices, some of which, as in the case of oil, were dramatic. In 1975, however, violating the spirit if not the letter of CEMA pricing arrangements, the USSR initiated a major increase in CEMA foreign trade prices, especially of oil (sales of which account for 12 percent of Soviet exports to Eastern Europe) reportedly by 130 percent.[4] But the price of oil on world markets rose by 400 percent. The Soviet price increase thus appeared moderate, even if it was used to help persuade East Europeans to participate more heavily in joint Soviet-East European projects in the Soviet Union, such as the Orenburg natural gas pipeline from the Southern Urals to the Czechoslovak border.[5] Without Soviet restraint in the price hike, East European economies (with the exception of Romania's) could have been seriously and perhaps permanently damaged.

However, the USSR increased prices of raw materials exported to Eastern Europe by 8 to 50 percent and the prices of all fuels by about 100 percent, or on the average of about 40 percent.[6] Since in the 'seventies about fifty to sixty percent of East European foreign trade had been with the Soviet Union and since fuels are economic staples, the Soviet price increase affected East European economies sharply.

The East European economic slowdown brought about jointly by the trade deficits with the West, higher Soviet prices, and a lack of substantial Soviet credits, lowered growth rates of national income in Eastern Europe again in 1975/76 by 33 percent in Czechoslovakia, 33 percent in East Germany, 45 percent in Hungary, 33 percent in Poland, and 9 percent in Romania. Bulgaria's growth rate was up 14 percent in 1975, chiefly because of its trade deficit with the West, but down 12 percent in 1976.[7] For this reason, in 1977, the USSR finally relented and increased its lending to Eastern Europe by about 87 percent from the 1976 level, thus bailing it out, temporarily, once again.

4. Martin J. Kohn, "Developments in Soviet-East European Terms of Trade, 1971-1975," in *Soviet Economy in a New Perspective*, Joint Economic Committee, Congress of the United States (Washington: United States Government Printing Office, 1976), p. 69.
5. Ibid.
6. Vanous, p. 9.
7. Ibid., p. 11.

EAST EUROPEAN ECONOMIES

After World War II the Soviet political-institutional framework and the Soviet mode of economic organization were installed in Eastern Europe. Their questionable legitimacy has complicated the problems of social management ever since.[8] Eastern Europe was turned into a Soviet dependency. To suit the needs of Soviet economy, East Europeans had to build steel mills to process Soviet iron ore, had to buy Soviet oil and natural gas, and ship their industrial goods to the USSR.

By about the mid-sixties, however, Soviet economists began to advise the East Europeans that this pattern of relationship would have to change, that Soviet raw materials might no longer be abundant, and that they should start reorienting their economies to new suppliers.[9] The subsequent sharp rise in world oil prices underlined the Soviet warnings. Since then, the USSR has tried to limit its raw material ties with Eastern Europe in favor of trade with the West. This is understandable. Not only did the world market prices of raw materials become very attractive, but the needed Western technology was superior to that of East Europe. Ample hard currency could now be obtained for Soviet oil and other raw materials.

As encouraged by their Soviet advisers, the East Europeans began to turn for satisfaction of their needs to the industrial West. To their surprise, they were welcomed there by businessmen, firms and corporations attracted by the opportunity of entering new and presumably lucrative markets. With both sides eager, East European-Western trade grew by leaps and bounds. In the process, East European economic development, modernization and quality of life began increasingly to be tied to Western imports. But because East European exports lagged behind Western imports, the trade became rapidly lopsided. To be able to do business with the East Europeans, the West had to grant large credits. This process became even more unfavorable to Eastern Europe when the West was hit with economic recession. The already small quantity of East European exports dwindled. As a consequence, and with the sudden 1975 Soviet price rises, East European economies slid into recession in 1975/76. Only the 1977 Soviet credit grants temporarily saved the day.

Not all the East European economies have faced the same economic problems. Poland, Bulgaria and East Germany have been hit the hardest. They will probably have to reschedule their debts with the West, perhaps even before the early 'eighties, which may

---

8. Walter D. Connor, "Social Change in Eastern Europe," *Problems of Communism*, 26:6 (1977), p. 31.

9. Marshall J. Goldman, "Autarchy or Integration," in *Soviet Economy*, p. 89.

hurt future Soviet credit-worthiness in the West. At the same time, their need for new Soviet credits will be the most substantial. Czechoslovakia, Hungary and Romania will have their economic problems as well, but compared to Poland, Bulgaria and East Germany, these will be less drastic in the short run.[10] Given the slowdowns in the rate of growth in Eastern Europe, which prompted the borrowing in the West in the first place, all the East European countries will face difficulties in improving their proverbially low productivity.

The most pressing problems Eastern Europe will face in the near future are how to restore the economic imbalance created by existing obligations, especially the large hard currency indebtedness, and how to improve the efficiency of production. With reference to the first problem, East Europeans plan to increase exports rather than to restrict imports. This, however, depends on their ability to produce competitive, high-quality goods in sufficient quantity, as well as on the economic conditions and commercial policies of the West.

With reference to the problem of improving efficiency of production, the quality of industrial labor is so poor within the East European organizational and systemic set-up that little can be expected to be accomplished in the future. It is true that in the short run an increase in the supply of consumer goods and services does lead to an increase in the effectiveness of labor, chiefly in the form of increases in labor productivity. Increased labor productivity in turn leads to a further increase in the supply of consumer goods. But a lower investment rate leads to lower capital stock and consequently to a lower level of national income, which limits the consumer goods supply.[11]

Moreover, a critical shortage of manpower is threatening to cut the labor supply still further. Compared to the 'fifties, population growth in Eastern Europe slowed noticeably in the 'sixties (from 9.1 per thousand average annual rate of growth to 7.6 per thousand). While Czechoslovakia and Hungary remained below the average, the GDR in 1970 had 1.3 million inhabitants less than in 1950.[12] As a consequence, the overall growth of the labor force has slowed in the 'seventies in Eastern Europe and a shortage of labor is becoming serious. Since in some East European countries, notably the GDR, Czechoslovakia and Hungary, the labor force reserves have been exhausted and people of retirement age and women are already working, the employment of foreign labor has been initiated. Compared to the numbers of *Gastarbeiter* in Western Europe, the

10. Vanous, pp. 18-24.
11. Ibid., p. 15.
12. Friedrich Levcik, "Migration and Employment of Foreign Workers in the CEMA Countries and Their Problems," in *East European Economies*, p. 459.

numbers of foreign workers in Eastern Europe is still modest—some 150,000 in 1977. An estimated 70,000 Poles, Hungarians, Bulgarians and Yugoslavs (and Turks) work in the GDR, some 38,000 Poles, Hungarians, Russians and Yugoslavs in Czechoslovakia, about 50,000 Bulgarians, Czechoslovaks, East Germans, Poles and Hungarians (and Yugoslavs) in the USSR.[13]

Renewed emphasis has been placed on technological innovation and on reducing the share of labor-, material-, and fuel-intensive products in output.[14] But since East European economic performance can really be improved in the longer run only by overcoming systemic obstructions to increased productivity—a step which has not been taken in the past (with the possible but not really significant exception of Hungary) and is unlikely to be seriously contemplated in the future—the future looks bleak.

Although Eastern Europe is approaching a structure of economic activity close to that of Western Europe, per capita productivity seriously lags behind that of Western Europe in spite of exceptionally high rates of investment.[15] This is due in part to chronic East European ailments—inadequate incentives; worker apathy induced by disguised unemployment; poor consumer goods and services; housing scarcities; inefficient agriculture, and so on. In part, however, the problems are new—growing labor shortages due to a slowdown in population growth; rising consumer expectations after years of neglect and unfulfilled promises; disappointing technological progress; large hard currency trade deficits; and rising cost of imported raw materials.

There is no reason to doubt that these problems, old and new, will persist in some combination in the future because, with the exception of the last two, they are of a systemic nature, pertaining to the East European socialist system of economy and its organization of production. They will not go away short of drastic systemic change. Eastern Europe is thus highly vulnerable. Because the economies of the East European countries are in chronically poor shape, they are dependent, with the exception of Romania, on both the Soviet Union and the industrial West.

The Soviet Union is still the dominant major trading partner of most of Eastern Europe, accounting for more than half of the total (Soviet-controlled) East European trade-over. Over the years East Europeans have come to depend on the huge Soviet economy in imports, exports, and credits. Soviet cutbacks in resource transfer

13. Ibid., pp. 463-464.
14. Paul Marer, "Economic Performance, Strategy and Prospects in Eastern Europe," in *East European Economies*, p. 564.
15. Thad P. Alton, "Comparative Structure and Growth of Economic Activity in Eastern Europe," in *East European Economies*, p. 261.

and price increases would slow down their economic growth rapidly and critically, as would Soviet reluctance to continue buying expensive, poor quality goods and obsolete equipment.

But since the early 'seventies, East European economic growth has depended also on imports of Western capital goods and industrial materials. A cutback on those imports, which are approaching half of the East European total foreign trade turnover for any reason—such as lack of new credits, Western recession, bad harvests in Eastern Europe—would affect drastically the recipients' economic well-being. Serious production slowdowns would be inevitable.[16] Yet East European borrowing simply cannot be maintained at the 1974-1977 levels.[17] The amounts are too large relative to the recipients' ability to pay.

Most East European countries are thus approaching an economic crisis. If the USSR will indeed supply only 75 percent of East European oil needs in the late 'seventies and early 'eighties, the East Europeans will have to increase their oil imports from the Middle East and, unable to step up domestic production and improve industrial efficiency, to slow their economic growth.[18] If this economic slowdown should be coupled with cutbacks in Western imports, as it may, Eastern Europe will face another deep recession.

This scenario, to which poor harvests in Eastern Europe would contribute materially, will call for ample Soviet aid. Once again the Soviet Union will be asked for help above and beyond its normal assistance. Above-plan deliveries of raw materials, including additional deliveries of oil; permission to continue running trade deficits with the USSR; reduction in the resource allocations required to invest in joint projects located in the USSR; and hard currency credits will be essential.[19]

Future East European economic well-being will depend on trade with both the Soviet Union as well as with the West: on Soviet trade for staples—fuels and raw materials, a market for East European industrial goods, and for credit; on Western trade for modernization, oil and the amenities of life—industrial products and consumer goods—as well as for markets. Both trade fronts will be critical because of East Europe's traditional heavy dependence on foreign trade as well as because of the built-in domestic economic liabilities. East Europeans wish to increase exports rather than to restrict imports; this they may be unable to do. If imports have to be

16. Joan Parpart Zoeter, "Eastern Europe: The Growing Hard Currency Debt," *Problems of Communism*, 27:2 (1978), p. 1351.

17. Vanous, p. 14.

18. John R. Halberstroh, "Eastern Europe: Growing Energy Problems," in *East European Economies*, p. 395.

19. Zoeter, pp. 1361-1362.

cut, which is probable, the growth rates of consumption will decrease rapidly. This would be a political calamity. Yet Eastern Europe is being pushed in this direction.

East Europe's double dependency is approaching a welfare status. Its freedom of maneuver is limited. If the industrial West should decide, as it well may, not to send good money after bad, there is nothing the East Europeans can do short of a substantial Soviet subsidy. If the USSR cuts its supplies, credits, and imports from Eastern Europe, on the other hand, it will be breaking a long-standing tacit understanding with its loyal allies, for whom leisure on the job has been part of the agreement. Where does Eastern Europe stand in Soviet priorities?

THE SOVIET ECONOMY

The Soviet Union has been at peace for over thirty years. It has become a rough strategic equal of the United States. The Soviet economy may have its weaknesses, but it is the world's second largest. Over the past quarter-century the Soviet economy has produced an impressive rate of growth in total national product and in per capita consumption; and it is still largely self-sufficient and thus fairly isolated from world economic ills. To this extent the balance sheet of power has been changing in the Soviet favor. Moreover, the USSR is the only major industrial nation in the world that is self-sufficient in energy. Its hard currency earnings for oil amounted to $3.2 billion and for coal to almost $400 million in 1975. Before long the USSR will also be a large net exporter of natural gas. True, future growth in energy supply depends on development of resources in difficult, environmentally hostile West Siberia and the Soviet Far East. The Soviet Union may not meet its 1980 oil and gas goals, but by then lags in other parts of the economy will probably occur, preserving the balance between energy supply and requirements.[20]

At the same time, the Soviet economy will continue to slow down even under the most favorable assumptions. The effectiveness of capital investments will probably continue to diminish; manpower increments will shrink; labor productivity, given the expected slowdown in growth of consumption, will decrease further; after peaking in 1980, oil production growth will begin to lag;[21] and ailing agricultural output, repressed inflation, formal and informal rationing,

20. Emily E. Jack et al., "Outlook for Soviet Energy," in *Soviet Economy*, pp. 460-462.
21. Holland Hunter et al., "Assessment of Alternative Long Range Soviet Growth Strategies," in *Soviet Economy*, pp. 211-212.

black markets, rising prices for consumer products, and so on, will probably continue. The long-term pressures for substantial changes will likely persist: to raise the technological level of the economy; to avoid repetitive and costly crises in agriculture; to improve the quality of consumer goods and services; to increase the technological transfer from the West; to shift and utilize resources effectively.[22]

Thus, while a long-term slowdown is very likely to continue and, if anything, get worse, major institutional and social groups, encouraged by past promises, will undoubtedly press for more: the military to expand strategic and conventional forces to continue to deter the increasingly sophisticated Western forces; the economists to modernize the deteriorating economy; the planners to increase the diminishing manpower supplies to keep up with the growing military and civilian needs; the political leaders to increase Western technology imports to avoid risky economic reforms; and the consumers for material incentives in order to raise productivity.

Given these many pressures and the state of the economy, will the Soviet Union turn to foreign trade, this time en masse? It is not clear as yet whether, having recognized "the growing worldwide economic interdependence" in the Helsinki agreement—and, more importantly, trying to alleviate its increasingly troubled economy— the USSR is indeed moving from autarchy to interdependence. Some Western economists argue that it is. Marshall Goldman, for example, claims that, while "no one move by itself has been that far-reaching, . . . the totality of these processes in recent years" has been impressive. In the years to come, growing Soviet interdependence "may eventually bring about a qualitative change in the USSR."[23] Holland Hunter and others, on the other hand, maintain that the large Soviet economy will be hard-pressed to respond in any meaningful way to the benefits that can flow from a sustained, significant participation in the world economy. Trade is still only a small item in the Soviet economy, which, except for trade with Eastern Europe, is still essentially autarchic.[24]

It is true that in the last ten years the USSR has been more involved in foreign trade than ever before. Current Soviet leadership has favored increasing foreign trade, particularly with the West, on the assumption that trade can speed up the pace of Soviet modernization, development, and growth. The Soviet Union will be hard-pressed, however, to maintain in the future the high growth rates achieved in foreign trade in the recent past. Problems such as large hard currency trade deficits, uncertain agricultural output, limited demand for Soviet exports in the West, Western recession, balancing

22. John P. Hardt, "Summary," in *Soviet Economy*, p. xxxiv.
23. Goldman, p. 95.
24. Hunter et al., p. 212.

domestic priorities and requirements, and so on, will impose restrictions.[25]

As to the transfer of technology and sophisticated products, and machinery and licenses from the West to the Soviet Union, its impact is uncertain. Though undoubtedly beneficial to the Soviet economy, it may not do for it as much as the Soviet leaders have hoped.

Even if the rate of technology transfer from the West should increase in the future, its total impact on the economy may be limited. In particular sectors of the Soviet economy, however, when patiently and successfully integrated, high technology imports result in important gains. Capital productivity rises considerably, and output growth is significant.[26] As a consequence, selective grafting of Western high technology on particular sectors of Soviet industry may be beneficial.

The USSR may be the world's second largest economy, but it is not an economic super-power; its impact on the world economy and vice versa is still minimal. For better or worse, the stern Soviet system, isolated from exogenous influences in the past, has been protected even against advantageous and profitable outside effects and influences. The Soviet economic system has not changed in any substantial way since Stalin's day, and its priorities, with a few relatively minor exceptions, remain the same. The Soviet leadership has shied away from economic experimentation and reform because of its short-run economic costs and potential political dangers, and has opted instead for a concerted infusion of Western technology and consumer products. The Soviet leadership, present or future, will probably act prudently and minimize change. The choices are difficult, and risks are attached to innovation. Maintenance of the status quo will continue to frustrate popular desires and will be expensive in growth of productivity; but, experience tells the leadership, it does not cause social and political turbulence. Imports of technology and consumer goods make postponing of difficult decisions feasible—as long as the USSR can afford it. Hard currency for that purpose is at a premium. And this is where Eastern Europe (together with the military, the economists, the planners, and the consumers) enters into Soviet priority calculations.

THE MILITARY: THE WARSAW PACT

Before 1970 the East Europe Warsaw Pact members contributed to military spending a lower share of their GNP than the USSR. Since 1970,

25. Jack Brougher, "U.S.S.R. Foreign Trade: A Greater Role for Trade with the West," in *Soviet Economy*, pp. 691-692.
26. Hunter et al., p. 212.

however, the rate of growth in military spending has been higher in Eastern Europe than in the USSR. Eastern Europe now spends more on defense than any country of the world with the exception of the USSR and the United States (or about one-fifth of the United States' military expenditure.)[27] East Europe's contribution to the Warsaw Pact expenditures is thus quite meaningful.

Given the Soviet commitment to modernization and integration of the Warsaw Pact forces in the next five years (a 30 percent increase in battle tanks, a 25 percent increase in tactical aircraft, a 50 percent increase in artillery, and a 10 percent increase in troop strength), the impact of the military on the East European economy will be much greater than in the past.[28] The military will be taking energy, manpower, materials, and investment funds from both industry and agriculture. As conditions get worse, the East European countries' ability to upgrade the increasingly expensive Warsaw Pact military machine will become critical. Given the well-established Soviet priorities in this respect, the Warsaw Pact forces will get most of their wants, thereby adding another heavy burden to the members' economies.

SOCIO-POLITICAL CONDITIONS IN EASTERN EUROPE

Social conditions in the seventies have been changing in Eastern Europe almost as dramatically as economic conditions. The socialist economies are maturing, social mobility is declining, and the population is becoming aged, urbanized, and middle-class. Workers, the political mainstay of the Communist party-state governments, are growing restless. They feel threatened by the new emphasis on high productivity, which violates their tacit, long-standing agreement with their governments to a trade-off of political support for labor peace in the factory.[29] After thirty years, such an understanding may be difficult to replace. Strikes, work stoppages, and slowdowns have taken place in Poland, Hungary and Czechoslovakia. When Romanian workers struck in August 1977, at the Jiu Valley Coal Mines, workers in Bucharest, Braila and the Tirgu Mures honored the strike with slowdowns and stoppages. While all these strikes were settled peacefully, they showed a degree of widespread worker dissatisfaction unusual in formerly docile Eastern Europe.

    27. Thad P. Alton et al., "Defense Expenditures," in *East European Economics*, pp. 273-274.
    28. John Erickson, "European Security: Soviet Preferences and Priorities," *Strategic Review* (Winter, 1976), p. 40.
    29. Vanous, p. 18.

As a consequence, worker incomes are rising; labor unity is growing; private savings are larger than ever before; 1980 estimates call for increasing ownership of consumer goods (cars, refrigerators, washing machines, etc.); and popular expectations, high already, are rising. If, due to deteriorating economic conditions, the growing gap between consumer expectations and social reality gets much wider as it appears likely, negative social attitudes toward the political systems may reach critical proportions. The 1970 and 1976 consumer riots in Poland; the East Berlin October 1977 anniversary riot; the widespread consumer restlessness in Romania following the March 1977 earthquake and the government decision to increase the investment rate; and the Bucharest riot of June 1977, may be samples of things to come.

Moreover, social and political dissent is widespread in Eastern Europe (with the exception of Bulgaria). The Czechoslovak Charter '77 group, the Hungarian New Left, Polish dissidents in the civil rights movement and the Workers' Defense Committee, East German student unrest, and so on, are again examples of the intellectuals' and workers' more visible dissatisfaction and proliferation of an increasingly vocal negative social and political outlook among segments of the East European population.

FUTURE SOVIET-EAST EUROPEAN RELATIONS

Energy, material, and manpower shortages will negatively affect industrial and agricultural productivity and the balance of trade in Soviet-controlled Eastern Europe. With the exception of Romania, East Europe's annual rate of growth of national income may fall even lower, to about 3 percent at best. (The figures for 1976 were 5.2 percent for the USSR, 2.6 percent for Czechoslovakia, 3.7 percent for East Germany, 3.5 percent for Hungary, 6.6 percent for Poland, 6.6 percent for Bulgaria, and 10.5 percent for Romania.)[30] This adverse economic development, exacerbated by large military spending, will place new constraints on Soviet relations with Eastern Europe. The temptation to lower economic support of Eastern Europe will be growing with the increasing demand of Soviet domestic claimants for diminishing scarce resources. Some observers think that the USSR will have no choice but to decrease its economic support of Eastern Europe in direct proportion to its diminished economic capability. Walter Connor, for example, argues that "it is by no means clear that the USSR, ... constrained by the spectre of slow-down and retrench-

30. Ibid., p. 40.

ment, will provide the material wherewithal for the East European regimes to moderate the (destabilizing) tension;" and, he maintains, "the USSR would readily move to restore order by use of force."[31]

I disagree, for two major reasons. First, in the post-Stalin past but especially since 1968, Soviet leaders have appeared sensitive to the socio-political consequences of the decline in welfare in Eastern Europe. They have pumped funds to help leaders to satisfy workers' and consumers' demands in order to maintain social tranquility. Soviet-financed "buy-offs" have temporarily appeased socio-economic dissatisfaction—especially in Czechoslovakia, Poland and East Germany—and have temporarily solved East European leaders' major political problems. And the Soviet Union has sanctioned East Europe's gigantic increase in trade with the West, cooperation with the European Economic Community, joining with capitalist corporations to form ongoing joint production relationships,[32] private ownership of multi-family dwellings, legal advantages for small business and private agriculture, and a multitude of other measures designed to reduce the social effects of the economic recession.

Soviet leaders have learned that economic hardships in Eastern Europe can lead to social unrest and political crises, which may have to be put down by force. In a region such as Eastern Europe, crises tend to be contagious. Military interventions are costly and a last resort, not to be undertaken lightly. The Soviet leaders' agonizing vacillation, before August 21, 1968, whether or not to invade Czechoslovakia illustrates the point. Moreover, armed interventions can be avoided by prudent policies based on established, sensible relations.

Second, besides Cuba, the six East European Soviet-controlled states are the only real military and political allies the Soviet Union has. They contribute heavily to Soviet defense—in expenditures, men, weapons, and geographic location—and they defend Soviet policies in international forums. They assist substantially in Soviet military and foreign aid to developing nations and, according to news reports, are now "joining the Soviet drive for more influence in Africa [by] pouring money, technology, weapons and military training into the area." They also act as "surrogates in areas where the Soviet Union does not want to become directly involved."

> East Germany is reported to be setting up security police organizations in Angola, Mozambique, Benin and South Yemen and is training glider pilots, maintaining military vehicles and providing youth organizations with "premilitary" training.

31. Connor, p. 32.
32. Goldman, p. 94.

Poland is building a power station in Libya and has promised Nigeria 300 geologists and technicians.

Czechoslovakia is lending Ethiopia $46.5 million to modernize and expand a variety of industries.

Hungary is lending Tunisia $35 million—mostly for agricultural development—and is exporting whole factories to "lessen dependence on former colonial powers."

Bulgaria is expanding Mozambique's Limpopo Valley irrigation area from 75,000 to 785,000 acres and is building a hydroelectric dam at Massingir.

Romania is providing experts to help find and export gold and precious stones in the Central African Empire and to help find lead ore in Kenya and oil in Nigeria.

Western experts say that East Germany apparently is taking care of Africa's badly wounded, just as it once provided hospital space for wounded North Vietnamese.

Some Western analysts see strong signs that staunchly pro-Soviet East Germany is becoming Russia's main helper in a long-range move to build influence in Africa.

There is adequate evidence, one West German Africa expert says, that Moscow and East Germany are teaming up "so that East Germany becomes active in areas where the Soviets don't want to burn their fingers."[33]

East European governments invest capital and manpower in joint projects on Soviet soil; and, to alleviate the Soviet labor shortage, some of them may assist in stepping up Soviet employment of East European labor in the future.

Eastern Europe may be a Soviet dependency, but it "represents a relatively high degree of interdependence for the Soviet Union."[34] Soviet interest in maintaining the viability and durability of this interdependence is bound to be high in the future because the relationship is indeed a two-way street. Eastern Europe has been a Soviet economic liability and promises to be more so in the future. But it has been a Soviet political and military asset and, with imagination and skill, can be put to new, important political-military tasks in the future, at home and abroad.

In terms of priorities, Soviet defense-related production has

33. Stephen Miller, "East Europe's Big Plunge into Africa," San Francisco *Chronicle*, June 30, 1978, p. 14.

34. Goldman, p. 89.

been traditionally superordinated to agricultural and consumer goods production, whatever their importance for higher labor productivity and the population's real income. By the same token, Eastern Europe must be viewed as a Soviet high priority item, worthy of priority investment.

I would thus expect that prudent Soviet decision-makers, given the anticipated constellation of economic deprivations in Eastern Europe, will do their utmost to grant substantial credits to needy East European countries even when pressed very hard at home. And while marginal corrections in this direction or a hard bargain or two cannot be ruled out, as in the case of the 1975 Soviet price rise, significant deviation from direct subsidization of Eastern Europe, however persuasive the arguments in terms of the Soviet Union's own priorities, will probably not be viewed as a viable option. Soviet stakes in Eastern Europe are just too high.

Eastern Europe may be a Soviet dependency, but it does have a leverage against the USSR. It would be presumptuous to view the relationship as interdependent; the Soviet Union does control the six states and Soviet use of force in Eastern Europe, as a last resort to restore law and order, cannot be ruled out. But the content of that dependency is much changed since Stalin's and even Khrushchev's times. With Soviet credits, East Europeans will try to maintain and, in some cases, step up their trade relations with the West. To the extent of their dependency on Western imports, described earlier, the East Europeans will be less dependent on the Soviet Union. It would be contrary to Soviet self-interest to insist that they should not. On the other hand, future Soviet neglect would be worse than past exploitation. It would be dangerous for the socialist system in Eastern Europe; it would cripple Soviet political and military allies; and it would diminish the stature of the Soviet Union as a superpower.

On the other hand, should the USSR withdraw from Eastern Europe, an unlikely event, the liberated states would probably find themselves prey to a myriad of forces they could not deal with. The sheltered economic life they are accustomed to would be shattered and with it, probably, their social and political systems. Once again they would revert to the status of a tempting power vacuum, ready for a new suzerain.

East Europe's proverbial instability is structural. A prudent superpower would, and should, act as a stabilizing influence there. On the record it is still doubtful that even with a longer learning experience the USSR will discover how to govern it properly.

Of course, material support, economic well-being and consumer satisfaction do not tell the whole story. There is more to life in Eastern Europe than securing apartments, driving cars, or owning refrigerators, TV's, and washing machines. East Europeans still do not appear "to accord [their] regimes a basic confidence and/or legitimacy based on qualities *other* than material effectiveness."[35] This issue the East European leaders will have to work out for themselves, as Kadar apparently has in Hungary. But consumer satisfaction would, without doubt, make the task easier.

And finally, what about the consequences of the stepped-up Soviet subsidy to Eastern Europe on the Soviet Union itself? Given the future Soviet economic deficiencies, the traditional tight constraints, the fairly rigid system of priorities, the leaders' sustained dislike for substantial economic reforms, and the *very* limited number of options, Soviet freedom of maneuver will be circumscribed—with one possible exception: foreign trade.

The two major economic problems the USSR will face in the future are low agricultural productivity and investment shortage. To cope with them, to be able to raise agricultural productivity and to increase investment, the USSR has only two sectors to draw upon: consumer and military. High costs are attached to both. Decrease in the supply of consumer goods and services would decrease labor productivity. Reduced defense spending would stimulate economic growth and raise living standards but is without precedent in Soviet history. In fact, if the aggregate economic growth rate slows down, the continued Soviet arms build-up, at an estimated 4 percent increase in annual defense expenditure, may become too much for the weakened Soviet economy to sustain, and living standards may have to be lowered.[36] Add to this the fact that extractive industries (i.e., energy and minerals) will require an increasing proportion of the Soviet investment, and it becomes obvious that without stepped up foreign trade the USSR may not be able to help its East European friends.

During the 'seventies the Soviet Union has become more trade-oriented than ever before. Motivated by their need for technology, equipment and technicians, as well as hard currency earnings and export outlets, Soviet leaders have chosen the foreign trade route with the developed West with such a vigor that, "if the present trend continues, the cost of severing ties with the West will mount rapidly."[37]

While total Soviet trade in the 1971/75 period more than doubled (to about $70.5 billion,) its trade with the West more than tripled, (in 1975, Soviet hard currency trade amounted to $21.9 billion; $14.1 billion were imports, $7.8 billion exports, and $6.3 billion trade deficit,) and in spite of the traditionally close ties the USSR has with

35. Connor, p. 32.
36. Hunter et al., p. 214.
37. Goldman, p. 95.

Eastern Europe (56.3 percent of Soviet trade in 1975,) trade with the West now accounts for 31 percent of the total Soviet trade. This is the "big reserve" for Soviet economic development, the Soviet "central economic problem" as Leonid Brezhnev put it.[38]

It is in the nature of foreign trade that once the policy commitment has been made, demands for trade increase. This has been true of Soviet imports of grain, bauxite, complex technology (parts, experts, updating processes); Soviet exports of raw materials, tractors, insurance, chemicals, machine tools; the Soviet network of overseas banks (in London, Zurich, Singapore, Beirut,); Soviet heavy investment in oil tankers and the merchant fleet; the Soviet decision to build the Baikal-Amur Railroad, which will open up raw materials in East Siberia.[39]

The ongoing Soviet involvement in foreign trade will not be very problematic *if* the Soviet leaders can stomach the growing Soviet dependency on the outside world. Economic interdependency is easy to enter into from a position of strength, as in Eastern Europe; and with minor exceptions Russian leaders have traditionally avoided it in the West. But the stakes have never been so high before. Legitimate domestic needs combined with justified East European demands will push the leadership further in a direction which it had elected earlier.

Judging from their statements at the 24th and 25th CPSU Congresses in 1971 and 1976, the Soviet leadership is committed to an increased role of foreign trade to speed up development of natural resources and to advance industrial production. Such a step would substantially change the role of Soviet foreign trade, "from a subsidiary source for supplementing domestic production to an active force to improve the functioning of the Soviet economy, using the criteria of comparative advantage," as some Soviet economists advocate.[40] Foreign trade would no longer function as a dog's tail (and everybody, of course, knows that "even a very active tail cannot move a large dog,") but as a butcher shop full of meaty bones.[41]

To be able to increase its purchases in the West, the USSR would have to increase exports. Given the liabilities of its economic system, it may not be able to export machinery and equipment, which the Soviet leaders would prefer. (In 1974 less than 5 percent of Soviet exports consisted of manufactured goods.)[42] It may, therefore, have to step up exports of raw materials. To do this, it would have to rely

38. Brougher, p. 678.
39. Goldman, p. 91.
40. Brougher, p. 685.
41. Hunter et al., p. 213.
42. Paul Ericson, "Soviet Efforts to Increase Exports of Manufactured Products to the West," in *Soviet Economy*, p. 710.

even more on Western assistance jointly to develop and speed up its resource development, in particular the extractive industries, especially in Siberia and in the Soviet Far East. Strong resistance to such a step would come from many sources—the military, the ideologues, many bureaucrats, and many leading economists. And, indeed, a rapid pace of foreign trade growth would involve risks. Dependence on foreign goods and services may develop; foreign recession or inflation may affect the domestic economy; foreign trade partners may apply political pressures; foreign influences of all sorts may penetrate Soviet territory. And yet, the constraints posed by probable future Soviet economic performance—slowing growth rates; increasing ratios of capital inputs to outputs when capital is diminishing; and rising defense and manpower needs—may leave the policy-makers no choice.

*Col. William F. Scott and
Harriet Fast Scott*

Military Stance and Outlook

Without military power, the Soviet Union today simply would be another developing nation. Soviet industries produce few manufactured goods, other than weapons, that are desired by or available to other nations. Food production is marginal. Each year tens of thousands of tourists from the West visit the Soviet Union to admire not the achievements of Soviet science, industry, or the arts, but the buildings, paintings, operas, and ballets from the tsarist regime of Imperial Russia. Only its armed forces, particularly its strategic nuclear forces, have given the Soviet Union superpower status.

This status has been achieved at a cost. In the immediate post-World War II period, while millions of Soviet citizens faced starvation and millions more were without homes, the Kremlin leadership embarked on a massive program for the development and production of both atomic and hydrogen weapons, as well as jet aircraft and bombers. This emphasis on the production of arms has continued up through the present.

Before looking into the future of Soviet military power, first let us review the current position of the Soviet armed forces. These forces cannot be mirror-imaged with those of the United States or with any other non-Communist nation; they have a military doctrine and strategy that is difficult for most Westerners to understand. Their organizational structure is unique. Their system of obtaining military manpower is different from that of the NATO nations. There are similarities in arms, since weapons are developed along specific scientific principles and not in accordance with an ideology.

BASIC DOCTRINAL AND STRATEGIC CONCEPTS

Any examination of the Soviet armed forces, especially with respect to its future posture, requires an appreciation of Soviet military doctrine and strategy. In the United States and other Western nations, expressions such as military doctrine and military strategy may have very general meanings. In the Soviet Union these terms have precise definitions. As explained by Soviet spokesmen, "Military doctrine is a system of views on the nature of war and the methods of waging it, and on the preparation of the country and army for war, officially adopted in a given state and in its armed forces."[1] Military doctrine is charged with answering the following basic questions:

> What enemy will have to be faced in a possible war?
>
> What is the nature of the war in which the state and its armed forces will have to take part, what goals and missions might they be faced with in such a war?
>
> What armed forces are needed to complete the assigned missions, and in what direction must military development be carried out?
>
> How are preparations for war to be implemented?
>
> What methods must be used to wage war?[2]

In contrast to military doctrine, Soviets define strategy as a component of military art "which investigates the principles of preparing for, and waging war as a whole and its campaigns. . . . Strategy is common to and unified for all branches of the country's services, since war is waged, not by any one service or branch of the Armed Forces, but by their combined efforts."[3] The armed conflict

---

1. A. A. Grechko, *Voorushennyye Sily Sovetskovo Gosudarstva* [Armed forces of the Soviet state], 2nd edition (Moscow: Voyenizdat, 1975), p. 340.

2. Ibid., p. 341.

3. S. N. Kozlov, *Spravochnik Ofitsera* [The officer's handbook] (Moscow: Voyenizdat, 1971), p. 68.

will be conducted "primarily by military-political and military-strategic considerations, conclusions and generalizations which stem from the conditions of the specific situation. Consequently, war, armed combat, is governed by strategy, not doctrine."[4]

Soviet military doctrine in the late 1970s, which is establishing guidelines for the 1980s, had its origins in the 1950s. As the Soviet leadership successfully tested ballistic missiles at intercontinental ranges, a series of secret seminars was being conducted to examine what impact this new weapons system might have upon a future war.[5] Studies generated by these seminars concluded that missiles and nuclear weapons would be decisive factors in any major conflict. The party leadership accepted this conclusion and called for further studies to determine how the nuclear weapon and missile would affect each service and service branch. These studies, prepared by "the Minister of Defense, his deputy, commanders of military districts"[6] and other senior military personnel, were known as the "Special Collection" and were published in a highly classified version of *Military Thought*, beginning in January, 1960. [7]

On January 14, 1960, in the same month that publication of the "Special Collection" began, Nikita Khrushchev delivered a speech before the fourth session of the Supreme Soviet of the USSR. In the course of this speech he stated that any future war would begin not as in the past by invasions of frontiers, but by rocket strikes deep in the interior of a nation. He claimed that Soviet rocket sites had been constructed, in duplicate, that rocket troops had been formed, and that even in the event of a surprise attack the Soviet Union would be able to retaliate.[8]

In October 1961, almost two years after Khrushchev's speech and one year before the Cuban missile crisis, the then Soviet Minister of Defense, Marshal R. Ya. Malinovskiy, specificially referenced Khrushchev's speech of January 1960 and further explained:

In this report, a deep analysis of the nature of modern war, which lies at the base of Soviet military doctrine, was given.

4. Ibid., p. 78.
5. M. V. Zakharov, ed., *50 Let Vooruzhennykh Sil SSSR* [50 years of the armed forces of the USSR] (Moscow: Voyenizdat, 1968), p. 521. See also: Oleg Penkovskiy, *The Penkovskiy Papers* (New York: Doubleday and Company, Inc., 1965), p. 251.
6. Oleg Penkovskiy, *The Penkovskiy Papers* (Garden City, N.Y.: Doubleday, 1965) p. 251. It is recognized that the authorship of these papers is open to question. Based on over 15 years of research in this area, we find that the chapters attributed to Penkovskiy in this book are generally accurate and check with other sources.
7. Ibid., p. 251-58.
8. N. S. Khrushchev, "Disarmament for Durable Peace and Friendship," address delivered at the Fourth Session of the Supreme Soviet, USSR, January 14, 1960, *On Peaceful Coexistence* (Moscow: Foreign Languages Publishing House, 1961), p. 146.

One of the important positions of this doctrine is that a world war, if it nevertheless is unleashed by the imperialist aggressors, will inevitably take the form of nuclear rocket war, that is, such a war where the main means of striking will be the nuclear rocket weapon and the basic means of delivering it to the target will be the rocket.[9]

The new military doctrine demanded a new military strategy. An unclassified version was revealed in the summer of 1962, approximately two months before the Cuban missile crisis, when *Military Strategy*, edited by Marshal of the Soviet Union V. D. Sokolovskiy, appeared on sale in Moscow bookstores. This book was in accord with the military trends found in the "Special Collection" and the concepts expressed by Marshal Malinovskiy in his speech before the 22nd Party Congress in 1961. The Cuban missile crisis of October 1962 had no major effect upon the Soviet military doctrine and strategy which had been formulated and disseminated earlier. The guidelines for the Soviet armed forces, emphasizing strategic nuclear forces, already had been established. Later editions of *Military Strategy* with extensive revisions showed no basic changes.

The ouster of Nikita Khrushchev in 1964 apparently did not alter the new direction which had been planned for the Soviet armed forces. In 1965 military journals announced that a series of books, called the "Officer's Library," would be published by Voyenizdat. One of the announced purposes of this series would be to explain further the revolution in military affairs to all officers.[10] Seventeen books in this series were published between 1965 and 1973, describing to Soviet officers the guidelines that the armed forces were to follow. The authors, in the main, were noted military spokesmen from the General Staff and the senior Soviet military academies. Among the best-known works in this series were *Tactics* and the

---

9. R. Ya. Malinovskiy, "Report to the XXII Congress of the CPSU." For an English translation, see: Harriet Fast Scott, *Soviet Military Doctrine; Its Continuity—1960-1970* (Menlo Park, California: Stanford Research Institute, Strategic Studies Center, 1971), p. 87.

10. Soviet leaders adopted the slogan, "the revolution in military affairs," to impress upon both military personnel and the Soviet population the importance of the new military doctrine, which had resulted from the introduction of nuclear weapons and missiles in the Soviet Armed Forces. For a discussion of the revolution in military affairs and the "Officer's Library," see Harriet Fast Scott, *Soviet Military Doctrine: Its Formulation and Dissemination* (Menlo Park, California: Stanford Research Institute, Strategic Studies Center).

third edition of *Military Strategy*.[11] The final book of the series, *Scientific-Technical Progress and the Revolution in Military Affairs*,[12] appeared after the signing of SALT I.

In the early 1960s, Soviet military doctrine and strategy were based on the assumption that if nuclear war did take place all of the missiles would be launched as quickly as possible, before their sites could be attacked. After the all-out nuclear strikes, war might continue with any weapons available.

By the mid-1960s nuclear weapons for tactical use had been introduced into all Soviet forces. At the same time, theater forces were in the process of being strengthened and Soviet strategic nuclear forces were reaching parity with those of the United States. The increase in nuclear forces, both at the strategic and tactical level, provided the Soviet leadership with a capability the United States had achieved in the early 1960s, that of flexible response. Marshal A. A. Grechko, Minister of Defense at the time, expressed a Soviet version of flexible response by stating that "in certain circumstances, the possibility is admitted of units and sub-units *(chasti i podrazdeleniya)* conducting combat actions with conventional weapons."[13] Since that date, this expression has been repeated, almost word for word, in major Soviet writings on military concepts.

THE PROJECTION OF SOVIET MILITARY POWER

In the beginning of the Soviet state, Leon Trotsky urged that the Red Army be used to support worldwide revolutionary movements. Stalin supported a more cautious policy, that of building socialism first in one country. Stalin's policies prevailed and the Soviet Union became, if not a Communist nation in the sense its early theorists had hoped, a major world power. Now, with its military super-power status, the Kremlin leadership appears to be adopting policies that may put the Soviet Union on the same course that Trotsky proposed.

11. V. G. Reznichenko, ed., *Taktika* [Tactics] (Moscow: Voyenizdat, 1966). This work, written by the staff of the Frunze Military Academy, was nominated in 1968 for the Frunze Prize, an annual award for military writings; V. D. Sokolovskiy, *Voyennaya Strategiya* [Military strategy] (Moscow: Voyenizdat, 1968). This book was nominated for the Frunze Prize in 1969. For an English translation, see: V. D. Sokolovskiy, *Soviet Military Strategy*, 3rd edition, edited with commentary, by Harriet Fast Scott (New York: Crane, Russak and Company, 1975).

12. N. A. Lomov, *Nauchno-Tekhnicheskiy Progress i Revolyutsiya v Voyennom Dele* [Scientific-technical progress and the revolution in military affairs] (Moscow: Voyenizdat, 1973). General Lomov was formerly a professor at the General Staff Academy and later a consultant to the Institute of the USA & Canada. He was a consultant at the time he edited this major work.

13. A. A. Grechko, *Krasnaya Zvezda*, 27 November 1969.

In 1974 Marshal Grechko advised Party members that:

> At the present stage the historic function of the Soviet Armed Forces is *not* restricted merely to their function in defending the Motherland and the other socialist countries. In its foreign policy activity the Soviet state purposefully opposes the export of counter-revolution and the policy of oppression, supports . . . national liberation struggle, and resolutely resists imperialist aggression in whatever distant region of our planet it may appear.[14]

This statement was in accord with the build up of Soviet forces for projecting military power and presence that began in the 1960s. The Soviet naval infantry, comparable in some ways with the United States Marines, was reconstituted and the construction of small helicopter carriers completed. By the mid-1970s, Soviet air transport capabilities were receiving attention, and a new class of carriers, with advanced VTOL (vertical takeoff and landing) aircraft on board, were being deployed.

Methods of fighting small wars in distant areas were receiving close attention. In 1977 a major Soviet military text, prepared by faculty members of the Soviet Academy of the General Staff, the Frunze Military Academy and the Lenin Military-Political Academy, described how:

> . . . . our military cadres are obligated to study thoroughly problems connected with local wars of today and make practical conclusions; and carefully take them into account in all daily activities in training and educating personnel of subunits, units, and ships.[15]

Nuclear weapons remain the decisive weaponry for major wars but, at the same time, studies must be undertaken for other types of military actions.

> . . . . Military thought carefully studies questions of waging nuclear war, the use of various means of mass destruction, various aspects of military actions in local wars, and gives corresponding recommendations.[16]

---

14. A. A. Grechko, "The Leading Role of the CPSU in Building the Army of a Developed Socialist Society," *Problems of the History of the CPSU*, May, 1974. Translated by FBIS, May, 1974.

15. D. A. Volkogonov et al., *Voyna i Armiya* [War and the army] (Moscow: Voyenizdat, 1977), p. 256.

16. Ibid., p. 217.

Political instructors in the Soviet Armed Forces now teach enlisted personnel the internationalist responsibilities of the Soviet people and how these have been met in the past. "Volunteers" in Spain and China during the 1930s are glorified in dozens of books. In the mid-1960s Soviet texts only mentioned that assistance was given to North Korea in the early 1950s. But in 1978 Soviet writers stated that Soviet air divisions were sent to China and that five Soviet Ground Force divisions were prepared to march into North Korea should the situation there worsen.[17]

The emphasis given at the end of the 1970s to the necessity for projecting military power and presence was concealed under a variety of slogans, such as "proletarian internationalism," "internationalist duties," "prevention of the imperialists' exporting counterrevolution," and the like. Only rarely did Soviet theorists express an actual requirement to project military power. Instead, support of "just" liberating wars, which would result in more favorable conditions for building communism, was stressed. All of this ostensibly was to prepare the Soviet armed forces, as well as the Soviet people, for the possibility of active Soviet participation in distant military conflicts. The Soviet leadership may have recognized that abstract terms such as building forces to support "proletarian internationalism" might not have major appeal for their own people, struggling to support a massive defense burden that takes almost twenty percent of their gross national product. Another slogan, "preventing the imperialists from unleashing war," is also used.

This justification stemmed from Krushchev's famed "revisionist" thesis presented before the 20th Party Congress in 1956. At that time Khrushchev stated that war is no longer "fatalistically inevitable" since the "mighty forces" possessed by the Soviet Union could prevent the imperialists from starting a nuclear war.[18] As the Soviet military buildup continued, Soviet spokesmen wrote that the enormous military power of the socialist states made possible not only the prevention of world nuclear war, but also "the prevention of local wars unleashed by the imperialists."[19]

Prevention of local wars is a critical issue, according to Soviet spokesmen, since such wars might lead to world nuclear war. Therefore, in the interests of peace, the Soviet Union must have forces trained and equipped to prevent the imperialists from stop-

17. S. A. Tyushkevich, *Sovetskiye Vooruzhennyye Sily* [The Soviet Armed Forces] (Moscow: Voyenizdat, 1978), p. 378.

18. N. S. Khrushchev, "Report to the Central Committee of the Communist Party of the Soviet Union to the Twentieth Party Congress, February 14, 1956," in *On Peaceful Coexistence* (Moscow: Foreign Languages Publishing House, 1961), p. 10.

19. See, for example: N. Ya. Sushko et al., *Marksizm-Leninizm o Voyne i Armii* [Marxism-Leninism on war and the army] (Moscow: Voyenizdat, 1965), p. 5.

ping or suppressing national liberation wars or exporting counter-revolution into countries which the Soviet Union has assisted in "liberating."

Only since the early 1970s, after the Soviet Union had built up its strategic nuclear forces and theater forces to massive levels, did the Soviet leadership give major emphasis to the external function of its armed forces. For without strategic nuclear forces and theater forces, the Soviet Union's ability to project military power would be of little consequence. With such forces now to provide for the security of the Soviet base, the Soviet projection of military power will be a dominant feature of international affairs in the 1980s and beyond.

COMMAND STRUCTURE AND ORGANIZATION OF THE SOVIET ARMED FORCES

Many mistakes about the capabilities and possible utilization of the Soviet armed forces are made by Western analysts because they do not understand how Soviet forces are controlled and organized. For example, a number of Western writers have asserted that Soviet forces could not wage a sustained non-nuclear war in Europe because they lack logistical support. It is made evident by their articles that these writers are not aware that a central Soviet organization provides logistical and quartermaster support to all Soviet military services. When this fact is considered, the combat-to-support personnel ratio in Soviet forces is approximately the same as in United States forces.

Official Soviet documents state that the armed forces of the USSR include the Strategic Rocket Forces, Ground Forces, Troops of National Air Defense, Air Forces, Navy, the Tyl (rear services), staff and troops of Civil Defense, and Border and Internal Troops. Two of these components, Border Troops and Internal Troops, are not under the command of the Ministry of Defense. Border Troops are part of the KGB (Committee of State Security) headed by General of the Army Yu. V. Andropov, who also is a Politburo member. It was Andropov's Border Guards, and not troops under the Ministry of Defense, who fought the Chinese in 1969 at Damansky Island. Internal Troops are under General of the Army N. A. Shchelokov, Minister of Internal Security. Both the Border Guards and Internal Troops are armed with tanks, armored personnel carriers, light aircraft, and helicopters. Border Guards, in addition, have their own fleet, with heavily armed vessels carrying depth charges.

This organization suggests that the Soviet leadership has not subscribed to the United States concept of mutual assured destruction. Troops of National Air Defense are the second largest Soviet service, providing defense against attack both by manned aircraft and missiles. Civil Defense troops are another major component of the Soviet armed forces. In contrast, the United States has neither a viable civil defense program nor an air defense for the hemisphere.

Overall control of the Soviet armed forces lies with the Council of Defense, chaired by the party's General Secretary. Top members of the Politburo, including the Minister of Defense, are members of this council and they consider Party requirements for military support. Since the Soviet armed forces have been responsible for elevating the Soviet Union to its new position as a super-power, military matters are of the utmost importance. Lenin's paraphrase of Clausewitz, "war is a continuation of policy by other (violent) means," guides their actions. All military decisions first of all are Party decisions. As Soviet spokesmen aptly state, the Party leadership determines the most important question of our day: "Is there or is there not to be a thermonuclear war?"[20]

The party has taken many measures to assure its control over the military. Military leaders are provided funds only for certain direct operating costs. Funds for weapons procurement, research and development, construction of new facilities, and related activities are handled outside of the Ministry of Defense. In order to lessen the possibility of a secret conspiracy by the military leadership, the first three deputies of the Ministry of Defense have individual direct access to the Politburo, without going through the Minister of Defense. The Chief of the Main Political Administration of the Soviet Armed Forces is responsible directly to the Central Committee and not to the Minister of Defense. This organization serves as a further control mechanism over the military. Other party and KGB controls exist throughout the military system.

Should a war take place involving the Soviet Union directly, the present Council of Defense would again become the State Committee of Defense (GKO). As during World War II, top members of the Politburo would serve on this body, which would have the power to issue edicts having the force of law. At this level political, military, economic, diplomatic, and other functions necessary for waging war are brought together.

Below the State Committee of Defense would be the General Headquarters of the Supreme High Command, generally referred to as Stavka of the VGK. As during World War II, the Chairman of Stavka would be the party's General Secretary, who also would be the Supreme Commander-in-Chief. This would bring about "a further centralization of leadership and a merger of the overall

20. M. P. Skirdo, *Narod, Armiya, Polkovodets* [The people, the army, and the commander] (Moscow: Voyenizdat, 1970), p. 96.

leadership of the country with the strategic leadership of the Armed Forces."[21] Stavka is a small organization without any staff of its own; its working agency is the General Staff of the Ministry of Defense. It is a general staff in the traditional sense, directing and coordinating the efforts of all five of the Soviet services, and is responsible both for planning and for development of future concepts.

Soviet writers of the 1970s discuss how Stalin and the General Staff directed the war fronts during World War II.[22] Reports went to Stavka three times daily, describing the activities of units down to divisions. Stalin would then dictate orders directly to the senior officer from the General Staff who would relay the new directions directly to the front commanders. In the view of present-day Soviet spokesmen, this system provided a high degree of centralization thereby making possible extreme flexibility and an ability to react swiftly in critical situations. A similar command center would be established in any future war.

The development of computers significantly increased the call for "growing centralization of direction." Soviet military theoreticians note that "the broad introduction into the work of the General Staff . . . of automatic systems of direction of weapons and troops permits the more operational solution of the complicated tasks of directing the armed forces in peace and in war."[23] During World War II Stalin had to talk with his front commanders by telephone, and the positions of troops had to be plotted on maps. With reconnaissance satellites gathering information, with television scanners portraying the conflict at ground level, with communications systems of all types passing data directly into centralized banks of computers, electronically displayed, the Supreme Commander-in-Chief of the Soviet armed forces could control the strategic battle directly from his command post, even to the point of selecting targets and releasing individual missiles.

Soviet military theoreticians have described how in past wars strategic maneuver was accomplished by the movement of bodies of troops from one area of military action to another. In nuclear-rocket war, they argue, strategic maneuver will be accomplished by retargeting strategic missiles.[24] There is no reason why this cannot be

21. Sokolovskiy, *Voyennaya Strategiya*, p. 359.

22. See, for example: S. M. Shtemenko, *The Soviet General Staff at War*, (Moscow: Progress Publishers, 1970), and M. P. Skirdo, *Narod, Armiya, Polkovodets*, pp. 109-116.

23. *Sovetskaya Voyennaya Entsiklopediya* [Soviet military encyclopedia], vol. 2 (Moscow: Voyenizdat, 1976), p. 513.

24. V. V. Larionov, "New Means of Fighting and Strategy," *Krasnaya Zvezda*, April 1964. For an English translation, see William R. Kintner and Harriet F. Scott, tr. and ed., *The Nuclear Revolution in Soviet Military Affairs*, (Norman-University of Oklahoma Press, 1968), p. 41.

accomplished from a central control point, and in a matter of minutes.

Strategic planning for the Soviet services, accomplished by the General Staff, must provide for the following tasks: the strategic nuclear offensive, military operations in land theaters, defense of the country from nuclear rocket strikes, and military actions in naval theaters.[25] Responsibilities for these tasks are charged to the five services, with assistance from the Troops of Civil Defense, the Tyl, Border Guards, and Internal Troops. It is unlikely that these basic missions will change radically in the foreseeable future, although they might be modified. The assignment of tasks cuts across service lines.

The Strategic Rocket Forces, assigned all land-based missiles with ranges in excess of 1,000 kilometers, have major responsibilities for conducting the strategic nuclear offensive. Although the Soviet leadership has given a large share of the strategic nuclear offensive task to the nuclear submarine component of the Navy, as well as the long-range aviation arm of the Air Forces, primary reliance still is given to land-based missiles. Such missiles have greater accuracy than submarine-launched ballistic missiles, and hence would be the primary component of a counterforce first strike seeking to destroy an opponent's forces. Hardened missile sites, as well as mobile missiles that could be concealed in large buildings or in caves, will serve as the basis of the Soviet assured second strike.

Soviet writers have asserted that, in the event of a nuclear war, the Strategic Rocket Forces would provide assistance to the Troops of National Air Defense. The specific type of assistance is never spelled out, although it is given in the context of "frustrating the criminal plans of the aggressor" when it has been determined that he is prepared to launch a nuclear strike. This would appear as a plan for a preventive strike, or "launch on warning."

The 1,600 Soviet ICBM's permitted under the SALT I agreement may be reduced somewhat if SALT agreements discussed in the mid-1970s are approved. At the same time, however, accuracies and payload would be increased. New agreements might place the Soviet ICBM launchers at 1,400, but these would provide combat-ready missiles carrying between 6,500 and 9,200 warheads. Numbers of United States missiles are expected to remain at 1,054, with 2,154 warheads. The Soviets continue to produce new generations of ballistic missiles, regardless of the international situation, and arms control negotiations are not likely to stop or to affect significantly Soviet efforts to continue improvement in their land-based missile systems.

25. I. Kh. Bagramyan, ed., *Istoriya Voyn i Voyennovo Iskusstva* [History of war and military art] (Moscow: Voyenizdat, 1970), p. 499.

Soviet Ground Forces, the largest single component of the Soviet armed forces, have the major responsibility for conduct of operations in land theaters. Soviet strategists maintain that multimillion man armies will be required in any future major conflict, regardless of whether the war is fought with nuclear or conventional weapons. The Ground Forces are divided into four branches: motorized rifles, rocket troops and artillery, tanks, and troop air defense. Airborne troops are considered as a strategic reserve of the High Command but are closely associated with the Ground Forces.

Although Soviet spokesmen since the early 1960s have asserted that their forces are prepared for war either in a nuclear or nonnuclear environment, this fact was not fully appreciated until the October, 1973 Mideast War. At that time it was found that the military equipment with which the Soviets provided the Arabs was designed for a nuclear battlefield.

Tactical missiles, with ranges of less than 1,000 kilometers, are considered by Soviet strategists as the primary firepower of the Ground Forces. Numbers of such weapons, the SCUD and FROG, are estimated at 500 and 650 respectively whereas comparable United States weapons, the Pershing and Lance, number 108 and 48. Soviet scientists have been called upon to reduce the weight and size of their tactical missiles, while increasing their maneuverability, range, and accuracy.

Soviet spokesmen assert that tanks will remain the primary strike force in land warfare and that the 1973 Mideast War disproved the theory that the tank's days are numbered. Considering the 45,000-plus tanks in the Soviet inventory, the future of the tank is of major importance. Tank strength of United States forces, in contrast, is approximately 5,500. The Soviets recognize that tanks are vulnerable to precision guided munitions (PGM's),[26] of which the United States forces possess over 130,000, as compared to approximately one-quarter that number held by the Soviets. The combat machine of the motorized rifle troops is the armored personnel carrier called the "BMP," referred to as the tank's "partner" on the battlefield.[27] This is considered as "the best means for overcoming contaminated areas and rapidly using the results of nuclear strikes." The BMP has speed and maneuverability beyond the capability of any comparable United States military vehicle.

Soviet surface-to-air missile systems were tested and proven during the 1973 Mideast War, and new missiles and attendant guidance systems are in production. In 1977 the Soviets had 4,200 such missiles in units, compared with 435 in the United States.

26. Grechko, *Vooruzhennyye Sily Sovetskovo Gosudarstva*, p. 197.
27. John M. Collins, *American and Soviet Military Trends* (Washington: Georgetown University Press, 1978), p. 52.

Additionally, the Soviet Ground Forces are protected against air attack by 8,700 anti-aircraft guns, as contrasted with 531 in United States forces.

The Soviet Ground Forces are manned by approximately 1,700,-000 personnel in line organizations, with over 750,000 in support. In contrast, the United States Army has 471,000 in combat units, with 310,000 in support.

Troops of National Air Defense consist of approximately 600,-000 personnel and are charged with defending the nation from nuclear and other means of strategic attack. Strategic defensive forces of the United States, in contrast, number approximately 37,000. Current Soviet planning calls for this service to be "renovated," and automated to the maximum extent possible. Its interceptor aircraft and surface-to-air missiles, providing defense against manned aircraft, are being supplemented with anti-space defense weapons. Although the SALT I agreement limited the number of antiballistic missile sites, Soviet officers in 1976 were informed that it would be necessary to be able "to repulse strikes not only of aerodynamic but also of ballistic means of attack."[28]

Antirocket defense, which will become of greater importance in the 1980s, is defined as follows:

> PRO (antirocket defense)—a component part of PVO, designated for detecting, intercepting, and destroying enemy ballistic rockets in the trajectory of their flight and creating jamming for them. PRO fulfills its mission with the help of antirocket and special jamming equipment.[29]

Soviet anti-satellite weapons became of increasing concern to the United States in 1977, after it was revealed that the Soviet Union had successfully completed testing of this weapons system. According to Soviet definitions:

> PKO (airspace defense)—a component part of air defense (PVO), designed for destroying the enemy's cosmic means of fighting, which are being used for military purposes (in the capacity of a carrier of nuclear weapons, for carrying out reconnaissance, and so forth) in their flight orbits. Special spaceships, satellite fighters, and other flying apparatuses are the basic means of PKO.[30]

---

28. G. V. Zimin, *Razvitiye Protivovozdushnoi Oborony* [The development of antiair defense] (Moscow: Voyenizdat, 1976), p. 192.
29. P. I. Skuybeda, *Tolkovyy Slovar' Voyennykh Terminov* [Explanatory dictionary of military terms] (Moscow: Voyenizdat, 1966), pp. 348-349.
30. Ibid., p. 351.

Soviet scientists are working on ballistic missile systems of many types, including lasers and satellites. Another problem for strategic defense will be posed by cruise missiles. Since cruise missiles have existed in one form or another for several years, the Soviets are working hard to develop defenses against the low altitude cruise missile before the United States deploys it in the early 1980s.

The Soviet Air Forces have three major components: long-range (bomber) aviation, frontal aviation, and transport aviation. In the latter part of the 1970s this has been one of the most rapidly developing of the Soviet services, in the process of acquiring new equipment. Production of Soviet bombers, fighter bombers, and fighters is currently greater than 1,000 per year, twice that of the United States. The famed bomber, "Backfire," will be supplemented by an even more advanced aircraft in the early 1980s. Although Soviet transport aircraft lagged behind the West throughout the 1960s and into the first half of the 1970s, the fleet will be receiving the wide-bodied IL-86 in considerable numbers by 1980, and this force will significantly enhance the ability of the Kremlin leadership to deploy its airborne divisions at great distances.

Primary emphasis will be given to frontal aviation. The lead that NATO previously possessed in ground-support aircraft is being challenged, and strikes by tactical aircraft such as the variable-wing "Fencer" can be launched against NATO targets from Soviet bases. Frontal aviation also includes combat helicopters which, Soviet theoreticians believe, will be a primary antitank weapon. Another major advantage of helicopters, according to the Soviets, is that they can carry out an attack across nuclear-contaminated areas.[31]

The Soviet Air Forces support, to some degree, all four of the tasks assigned to the Soviet armed forces. Long-range aviation is a part of the Soviet strategic nuclear troika. At the same time this component, as well as frontal and transport aviation, may participate in operations in land theaters. Frontal aviation also supports the strategic defense forces, if required, and the Air Forces as a whole may support actions in naval theaters.

The Soviet Navy's growth since the early 1960s has been astounding. Priority for its buildup had to wait until the Soviet strategic nuclear forces were able to neutralize the strategic capability of the United States, and until theater forces were able at least to contain both the NATO military forces and China.

Soviet spokesmen claim that the nuclear submarine force, armed with ballistic missiles, is the Navy's primary arm.[32] This force

---

31. V. I. Zemskov, *Vidi Vooruzhennyky Sil i Roda Voysk* [Services of the armed forces and branches] (Moscow: DOSAAF Publishing House, 1975), p. 30.

32. Lomov, *Nauchno-Teknicheskiy Progress*, p. 111.

probably will continue to be larger than that of the United States. The straits near Denmark and Turkey and in the Far East have made it traditionally difficult for the Soviet Fleet to be supplied and maintained in the world's oceans, even when political conditions were such that Soviet warships were allowed to navigate the straits unhindered. Soviet strategic nuclear forces are now such that no nation dares to close these straits to Soviet ships. Additionally, the Soviets have worked hard to provide the Navy with the supply ships and techniques to maintain combat vessels in the open seas for long periods. This capability, together with access to ports in underdeveloped countries, has made the Soviet surface fleet a major instrument for the projection of military power and presence. Soviet writers assert that the USSR is becoming a major sea power with an ability to gain and maintain influence in all parts of the world.

The Navy also possesses a large force of land-based bomber and reconnaissance aircraft. New carriers have been designed for helicopters and VSTOL aircraft. It is highly unlikely that the Soviet Navy will build large super-carriers such as those possessed by the United States; rather, advanced VSTOL aircraft for small carriers are being developed.

The Soviet naval infantry (the Soviet approximate equivalent of the United States Marines) has been promised "better, improved equipment" which should include new types of "air-pillow" (surface effect) vehicles[33] able to lift naval infantry from their ships to the beaches. The naval infantry, although relatively small, could be effective in establishing beachheads in Third World areas or in accomplishing important but small missions alone.

These five Soviet services are the major combat elements of the Soviet armed forces. They are supported or supplemented by 800,000 to 1,400,000 personnel in other military components.

Civil Defense, Soviet spokesmen claim, "has taken on great importance in modern war for protecting the population, industrial objectives, and cities from weapons of mass destruction and other forms of air raids."[34] Civil Defense Troops are scheduled to receive improved equipment—although Soviet spokesmen do not indicate what type. Approximately 100,000 military personnel are now assigned to civil defense duties, with many more hundreds of thousands of reserve personnel having civil defense mobilization assignments. Soviet spokesmen remind us that "the Soviet state and its civil defense are religiously carrying out Lenin's behest: *The first productive force of all mankind is the worker, the toiler.* If he

33. Tyushkevich, p. 463.
34. Ibid., p. 471.

survives, we shall save and rebuild *everything*."[35] Contemporary writers assert: "The strength and firmness of Soviet civil defense are the invincible strength and firmness of the Soviet socialist system."[36]

The *Tyl* (rear services), often overlooked in Western estimates of Soviet military forces, currently are being improved with respect to mobility and provision of more rapid and complete service to the combat arms.[37] Building and Construction Troops, numbering several hundred thousand, have participated in many of the large construction projects demanded of the Soviet armed forces, from digging missile silos to helping with the construction of the BAM (Baykal-Amur-Mainline Railroad). Soviet engineers, signal troops, road troops, chemical troops and the like are considered as Special Troops, providing support to the Soviet armed forces as a whole. Border Guards and Internal Troops, also have been promised new equipment. These forces are formed into nine special military districts around the borders of the Soviet Union. Internal Troops are found throughout the nation, assisting the militia and guarding labor camps and special installations.

In the event of a nuclear missile attack, the Tyl, Building and Construction Troops, Special Troops, Border Guards, and Internal Troops would be in a position to assist the Troops of Civil Defense and regular military units maintain order and re-establish control. The United States does not have forces that would provide a similar capability.

SOVIET MILITARY FORCES AND THE ECONOMY

In 1978, Soviet spokesmen reported that in the 1970s "increased efforts" were being made in the United States to develop "mobile missiles, the B-1, Trident, and cruise missiles." These Western measures to build up their armed forces "naturally, have forced, and are forcing, the Soviet Union to necessary retaliatory measures."[38] Therefore, it follows that the Soviet Union must increase the power of its armed forces; in fact, this is viewed as the "sacred duty" of the party and the people and "as the most important function of the socialist state."[39]

35. A. S. Milovidov, *Filosofskoye Naslediye V. I. Lenin i Problemy Sovremennoy Voyny* [The philosophical heritage of V. I. Lenin and problems of contemporary war] (Moscow: Voyenizdat, 1972), p. 333.
36. Ibid., p. 337.
37. Tyushkevich, p. 471.
38. Ibid, p. 442.
39. Ibid, p. 443.

For this purpose the economic strengthening of the state is essential. The Soviet authors assure their military readers that the pattern of growth as shown in Table 1 will be maintained.[40]

Table 1

Kind of Product	1965	1970	1975	1980 (plan)
Electric Power billions of kwh	507	740	1038	1349-1380
Coal, millions of tons	578	624	701	790-810
Oil, millions of tons	243	353	491°	620-640°
Steel, millions of tons	91	116	141	160-170
Rolled metal, millions of tons	71	92	115	115-120

° Including condensed gas.

The course taken by the party at the 25th Party Congress was aimed at assuring the constant strengthening of the economic and military might of the USSR. The next Congress should be held in 1981. Due to lead-time in weapons production, weapons of the 1980s are already being manufactured, and the weapons of the 1990s are almost certainly now on the drawing board. The military may be confident, since Brezhnev has almost doubled basic industrial production in the 13 years between 1964 and 1978, that their needs will be met. It should be noted that the military play an important role in the development of each five year plan. The past Deputy Director of GOSPLAN, V. M. Ryabikov, was a General Colonel, although this was not known until his death. In all probability a general officer continues to hold this position. One out of every six rubles in the Soviet Union is spent, directly or indirectly, for defense, and defense costs tend to dominate Soviet economic planning.

Some Western analysts believe that the Soviet economy cannot support a continued buildup of military forces and equipment. They feel that there is such a demand for housing and consumer goods in the Soviet Union that the Party leadership cannot risk the displeasure of the population. Such analysts may not be aware that during the 1930s when Stalin's forced collectivization of agriculture was underway, and many millions of people were in forced labor camps with millions more dying of starvation, Soviet weapons production increased as shown in Table 2.[41]

40. Ibid., p. 445.
41. Zakharov, *50 Let Vooruzhennyk Sil SSR*, p. 193.

TABLE 2

Types of Weapons	Yearly Averages: 1930-1931	Yearly Averages: 1935-1937
Aircraft	860	3,578
Artillery	1,911	5,020
Tanks	740	3,139
Rifles	174,000	397,000

Soviet spokesmen are concerned specifically with the need to improve agriculture production in order to create reserves of food. Defense needs also call for further development of transportation. The BAM Railroad will provide an alternate line to the Far Eastern area, and for that reason, railroad troops of the Soviet armed forces are engaged in its construction.

Regardless of what goals will be met, defense industries in the Soviet Union will, as in the past, receive first priority. The Soviet people still are reminded of the views of M. V. Frunze, written in the 1920s:

> Before each new beginning—economic, cultural, etc.,—the question must always be asked: How will the results of this enterprise be found in assuring the defense of the country? Isn't it possible, without damage to peaceful needs, to arrange it so that certain military tasks can also be assured of achievement?[42]

MILITARY MANPOWER

As a result of the extremely low birthrate during World War II, Soviet military manpower was significantly affected in the early 1960s. Between 1959 and 1963, the personnel available in the primary military age group, 19-21, dropped from over six million to a mere three million.[43] Correspondingly, there was a decrease in the birthrate as this group married and raised families. In a ripple effect, this will result in a decrease in the number of 18 year olds available for military service in the late 1980s. The birthrate has a significant impact upon the Soviet armed forces. A professional group of

---

42. Tyushkevich, p. 446.

43. Murray Feshbach, "Population," *Economic Performance and the Military Burden of the Soviet Union* (Washington: United States Government Printing Office, 1970), p. 68.

Military Stance and Outlook 83

approximately 1,000,000 regular officer personnel, plus 250,000 to 400,000 warrant officers and extended service enlisted personnel compose the permanent cadre in the armed forces. The remainder of the force consists of approximately 4,000,000 conscripts who serve for two years (Navy—three years) on active duty beginning at age 18 and then are "discharged into the reserves," where they remain until age 50.

The Soviet Union today has a policy of providing military training for every male. Universal military service was first introduced in 1939. In 1967, a new law lowered the age of induction from 19 to 18 and reduced the period of service from three to two years. To compensate for the shorter period of service, compulsory "beginning" military training was introduced in the 9th and 10th grades for 15 and 16 year olds. At 17, all males must register for call-up and at this time they receive assignments for training in various military specialties determined by the government. This training is carried on both by vocational type schools and by the paramilitary sports organization, DOSAAF. Such training is designed to make the conscript more effective in specified tasks soon after entering service.[44]

The primary task of the professional cadre of the Soviet armed forces is to train the youth of military age. Had the three year period of service been maintained, the size of the call-up force would have grown until it exceeded 6 million by 1970, assuming that about 80 percent of the age group was to make it possible to provide military training to "almost all" males,[45] without alarming the West with a sudden increase in military manpower.

Universal military service now is specified in the new Soviet Constitution which was adopted in 1977. Thus, the system of military training as described above will continue through the 1980s and beyond. It should be noted that only eight years of education was required until the mid-1970s. This, combined with the fact that "beginning" military training in the 9th and 10th grades was not fully implemented until about the same time, leaves much room for improvement over the next decade.

Military indoctrination of Soviet youth was expanded in 1967, when military-sport games, called *"Zarnitsa,"* were introduced for 12-15 year old boys and girls. These games were so successful that in

---

44. A. G. Gornyy, *Spravochnik Po Zakonodatel'stvu Dlya Ofitserov Sovetskoy Armii i Flota* [Handbook of legislation for officers of the Soviet army and navy] (Moscow: Voyenizdat, 1970), pp. 43-44.

45. Sokolovskiy, *Voyennaya Strategiya*, p. 309. In all three editions of *Military Strategy* the observation is made that reducing the period of military service makes it possible to train more people. Soviet spokesmen assert that almost all males are called up for active military duty.

1972 "*Orlenok*" military-sport games were introduced for 16-18 year olds. By the mid-1970s approximately 25,000,000 boys and girls were taking part in these games each year.[46] This mass military indoctrination program is reminiscent of the Hitler youth program of the 1930s.

Professional officer training and education is given in eighteen military academies, which correspond roughly to staff and war colleges in the United States. The most senior of these is the Academy of the General Staff, with a course length of two years. Course lengths at the other academies range from three to five years. The curriculum at these academies is being upgraded to accommodate the better educated officers who are now being commissioned.

But the Soviet Union faces problems. The first is the consistently lower birth rate for the Slavic majority; in comparison, minorities, particularly those in Central Asia, are increasing. As much as 25 percent of the available manpower in the 1990s may come from the non-Slavic Central Asian and the Caucasus republics whose basic language may not be Russian. However, since "beginning" military training is given in Russian and since movies, television, and radio bring a common language to all parts of the Soviet Union, it is not believed that those conscripts having Russian as a second language will pose major problems. Such techniques can largely eliminate language barriers, but cannot overcome cultural differences. What effect the decline of the Slavic majority will have on the character of the armed forces remains to be seen.

By discharging approximately 2,000,000 men each year into the reserves, where they remain until age 50, the Soviet Union probably has the world's largest trained military manpower reserve base. The military commissariat system, and the internal controls exercised through the KGB, MVD, and other agencies, make it possible for the military leadership to keep track of its reserve personnel without much trouble. Within a matter of days it should be possible to mobilize an additional 5,000,000 to 6,000,000 personnel, all of whom would have had active duty service within the preceding three years.

IMPACT ON THE SOVIET MILITARY OF SOCIOLOGICAL AND POLITICAL FACTORS

As a result of two or more years on active military duty, the Soviet male population should be well-indoctrinated in Party ideals. Young call-ups, as General Secretary Brezhnev explained:

46. See: V. Nikolayev, "'Zarnitsa'—School of Courage," *Voyennyye Znaniya* 5 (May 1974), p. 19, and L. Pesterev, "The Combat Examination—Orlenok," *Voyennyye Znaniya* 6 (June 1974), p. 23.

... come into the soldiers' family, not having gone through the school of life. But they return from the army as men, who have passed through the school of self-control and discipline, receiving technical and professional knowledge and political training.[47]

As part of the work force of the 1980s and 1990s, these young men will be called on to continue "building communism" in the Soviet Union. As in the past, soldiers will be required to help bring in the harvest (55,000 military trucks were provided in 1976 for the Kazakhstan harvest, for example), and build apartment houses, roads and bridges.

Vietnam was a watershed for the Soviet Union. The victory of the North Vietnamese encouraged the Soviets to believe that the Western democracies lack the will to stop so-called national liberation movements, especially those backed by the USSR and the socialist community. Soviet spokesmen assert that Western nations were "forced" to sign international agreements and agree to détente because of Soviet military power—or, as they say, because the "correlation of forces" has become favorable to the USSR. In the future, the Soviets will attempt to play on this theme in luring the Third World into the socialist camp. The Kremlin is seeking influence and a presence in those nations that have strategic significance.

As Kremlin spokesmen explain, one of the uses of détente is to create a favorable climate for wars of national liberation. Just as the Soviet Union supplied North Vietnam and the Viet Cong with aircraft, rockets, tanks, artillery and ammunition, and also trained officers of the North Vietnamese forces in Soviet military schools, there are now students in Soviet schools from countries which may be the Vietnams of the future. Not all will be successful, since Soviet training of revolutionary groups in the past has backfired more often than it has succeeded. Yet, with the prestige achieved by the Soviet Union as a result of its military might, revolutionary leaders now more than ever are looking to the Soviet Union. Soviet military and other specialists have been and will be sent as advisers to many of the countries receiving Soviet military aid, especially if the countries are of strategic importance to the Soviet Union.

The Kremlin will push for disarmament simultaneously with advances in new armaments for the armed forces. SALT II may be followed by SALT III and perhaps SALT IV. SALT has proven to be a very useful platform from which the Kremlin can address the world in general and the United States in particular, reminding all of its superpower status. But when SALT ceases to perform this useful function, it

47. Tyushkevich, p. 450.

will be dropped. Slowness of the United States in coming to an agreement in 1978 on SALT II has evoked this tirade from Soviet party-military spokesmen:

> Imperialism does not intend to give up its positions. It is trying to wreck the process of détente and return the world to times of the 'cold war'. High circles of military leaders, representatives of the military-industrial complex, pro-fascist and Zionist elements, revanchist circles are constantly galvanizing myths of a 'Soviet threat', 'Soviet military advantages', and increasing the scale of anticommunist propaganda.
>
> .... The nature of imperialism has not changed; it has not lost its aggressive essence. The Soviet Union is being forced to strengthen its Armed Forces.[48]

CONCLUSIONS

Military doctrine, which lies at the base of Soviet military planning, calls for the armed forces, the population, and the entire nation to be prepared for the eventuality of a nuclear rocket war. The military doctrine of the state is the military policy of the Communist party. Although this doctrine was fully explained in the Soviet press in the 1960s, its implications were not widely grasped, at that time, by Western analysts. Worldwide publicity given to the provisions of SALT I made people aware of the relative strategic nuclear levels of the Soviet Union and the United States. The Soviet civil defense program, another result of Soviet military doctrine, did not become generally known in the West until the mid-1970s.

In the mid-1960s Soviet military doctrine was modified to take into account the necessity for the Soviet Armed Forces to be prepared to fight with or without the use of nuclear weapons. This modification brought about an increased capability to fight a conventional war and anticipated the buildup of theater forces, first along the Chinese border and then in Eastern Europe.

Once Soviet strategic nuclear forces had achieved parity with or surpassed those of the United States, and its theater forces had reached a comfortable margin of superiority with respect to NATO, the Kremlin leadership began to emphasize a new external function for its armed forces. This function, the projection of military power and presence to Third World areas, may be the dominant feature

48. Ibid., p. 454.

of international relations in coming years. New equipment will be required for the projection of military power, but it is unlikely that the Soviet leadership will develop the kind of massive forces for this purpose that the United States used during World War II and afterwards. Soviet power projection is made possible by its strategic nuclear forces and, to a lesser extent, by its theater forces. With their backing, the Kremlin would not expect to encounter more than token or light opposition if its forces actually were deployed into a Third World battlefield.

For the future, the greatest military advantage the Soviet Union has over the United States may be the quality and quantity of its military manpower. The Soviet officer corps, numbering between 800,000 and 1,000,000 with the support of 150,000 to 200,000 warrant officers and sergeants, provide a cadre force. Each year approximately two million Soviet youth enter the armed forces to serve a minimum of two years active duty, and another two million are discharged into the reserves. As a result of this cadre force, universal military training, and the reserve program, the Soviet Union could increase its armed forces from approximately 5,000,000 to 10,000,000 within a matter of days. In contrast, the small officer corps and volunteer force of the United States, numbering approximately 2,000,000, would require months to double in size.

Power, once achieved, is seldom relinquished willingly. The prestige of the Soviet leadership is based to a great extent on the super-power status their armed forces have achieved for the nation. Even the average Soviet citizen appears to take pride in seeing that leaders of foreign nations visit his country to ask for arms or to sign international agreements. Whatever the cost may be in economic or social terms, the continued support and buildup of the Soviet armed forces will be maintained. The momentum of military drive has not yet run its course.

Joseph S. Berliner

Economic Prospects

The economist's task is somewhat easier—perhaps deceptively—than that of other participants at this conference because of that grand summary measure of overall economic activity, the Gross National Product. What should one make of the fact that in the last quarter century the Soviet GNP has grown at an annual rate of about 5.1 percent?[1] One basis of evaluation is to compare that figure to the growth rate of other countries and, in this respect, Soviet performance is to be considered rather satisfactory as economic systems go. The Soviet economy has grown more rapidly than the United States (3.8 percent) and at about the same rate as the major countries of Western Europe. It has been far surpassed only by Japan (9.6 percent), but Japan has surpassed all other economies as well.[2] Moreover, the political leadership has made good use of their

1. *Soviet Economic Problems and Prospects*, Joint Economic Committee, Congress of the United States (Washington: United States Government Printing office, 1977), p. 2. Except where otherwise noted, the quantitative data in this paper are taken from this source.

2. U.S. Bureau of the Census, *Statistical Abstract of the United States: 1975* (Washington: 1975), p. 381. The period is 1950-1972 for the U.S. and Japanese growth rates.

growing national output. Dr. Schroeder has found the increase in per capita consumption to have been about 4 percent per year since 1950.[3] That is a most creditable rate of improvement in living standards, certainly higher than that experienced by most of the citizens of the West during the same period. To be sure, that rapid increase followed the long period of depressed living conditions during the strife-torn 'thirties and the war-torn 'forties. Nevertheless, that increase is certainly rapid enough to have been consciously experienced by the population as a steady improvement over a considerable period of time.

One must not ignore leisure in such matters. It is one thing to be better off because one has worked harder, but it is quite another thing to have both more goods and more leisure. On the basis of recent data compiled by Feshbach and Rapawy, it appears that the number of hours per year worked by the average Soviet worker declined by about 18 percent over a quarter century, or almost 1 percent per year.[4] Thus not only has the worker's standard of living been increasing, but he has been working less time to obtain it.

A nation that acquires more butter must normally give up something else like guns, but the expansion of the Soviet GNP, has been sufficient to acquire both. During the past fifteen years military expenditures have been rising at about the same rate as the GNP, accounting for about 11 to 12 percent of all output.[5] In the U.S., by contrast, military expenditures presently consume about 5.4 percent of total output, and even at the peak of the Vietnam War rose no higher than 8.2 percent of total output.[6] Soviet military capacity has expanded greatly both at home and abroad relative to that of potential antagonists.

If this were a complete depiction of the recent past—which it is not in one crucial respect—the Soviet leaders would have good reason to believe that the economy has performed well under their stewardship. The missing piece of the picture is the trend. For while the average growth rate of the GNP has been about 5 percent, the

---

3. Gertrude E. Schroeder and Barbara S. Severin, "Soviet Consumption and Income Policies in Perspective," in *Soviet Economy in a New Perspective*, Joint Economic Committee, Congress of the United States (Washington: United States Government Printing Office, 1976), p. 622.

4. Murray Feshbach and Stephen Rapawy, "Soviet Population and Manpower Trends and Policies," in *Soviet Economy*, p. 135, 138. Their results imply that between 1950 and 1975 the number of hours worked by the Soviet non-agricultural worker declined from 2,132 to 1,737. That is a decline of 18 percent, or about 0.8 percent per year.

5. *Soviet Economic Problems and Prospects*, p. 1.

6. U.S. Central Intelligence Agency, *Handbook of Economic Statistics: 1977* (Washington: 1977), p. 41.

trend over the period has been distinctly downward. In the decade 1951-60 the growth rate was 5.8 percent. In the following decade it declined to 5.1 percent. And in the quinquennium 1971-75 it fell further to 3.7 percent. The continuous decline in the growth rate is the dominating note in the prologue with which the past introduces the economic future. Perhaps the best way to consider possible futures is to examine the principal causes of the decline in the growth rate and the prospects of their reversal.

THE LABOR FORCE

First, the record of the past holds out the prospect of a sharp decline in the rate of increase of the labor force during the remainder of the century. The labor force grew at an appreciable annual rate in the period 1951-75; during that period the increasing supply of labor helped maintain the growth rate of output rather than contribute to its decline. But the decline in the fertility rate dating from about 1960 portends a decline in the number of new, young workers who will enter the labor force each year from the late 1970s on.

A number of measures might be taken to cushion the effect of the decline in the annual crop of new workers. One is to keep older workers from retiring at the stipulated age and to bring some retired workers back into the labor force for a few more years. To the extent that this is done by withdrawing past privileges (e.g., by arbitrarily raising the retirement age or reducing the size of pensions) it would be politically risky and would have a negative effect on morale. A more popular way of accomplishing this would be to eliminate the present limit on the income that a retired worker may earn; this is a measure that is very likely to be adopted.

When faced with a similar problem in his time, Khrushchev introduced the educational reform that required secondary school graduates to serve in the labor force for a period before being admitted to higher education. The measure succeeded in increasing temporarily the number of new entrants to the labor force, and it had some positive appeal to older people who regarded it as proper that young people learn what it is like to be a worker before entering a life of intellectual labor. The reasons that the reform was eventually ended are instructive. Factory managers found that there was no great advantage in the influx of unenthusiastic young people marking time until they got out of their obligatory service and back into comfortable educational institutions. And the academic community, led initially by the mathematicians and then the physicists, protested the educational and scientific loss of those precious young years in the lives of talented students and succeeded in having exemptions introduced, the list of which got longer and longer.

A final source of increased labor is housewives. However, the labor force participation rate of married women is already extremely high and it is doubtful whether many more could be enticed into the labor market. Even if they were, there might well be concern about the long-term effects of that development on the fertility rate and therefore upon the labor force a decade and a half from now. The present problem, indeed, springs from the decline in fertility that is a consequence, to some extent, of the high female labor participation rate. The low rate of population growth is a source of considerable concern, not only because of its consequences for the future labor force but because of its broad social and military implications; makers of population policy would argue for measures to decrease the female labor participation rate in order to encourage Soviet women to have more children. The pressure for short-term increases in the labor force is likely to dominate, however, so that the net pressures are likely to favor increases where possible in the female participation rate.

One feature of the demographic situation that has elicited much interest is the differential fertility between the Slavic republics and the non-Slavic republics in Central Asia and the Caucasus. If there is indeed concern among the Russians in the political leadership about the impending minority status of the Russians in the total population of the USSR, a policy to increase the female labor participation in the non-Slavic republics would "kill two birds with one stone." It would help relieve the labor shortage and it would tend to diminish the fertility rate of non-Slavic women. Such a policy would, however, aggravate the regional maldistribution of the growth of the labor force which is already concentrated in the non-Slavic republics. From the national point of view it would be desirable for the new workers in the non-Slavic republics to move to labor deficient areas in Siberia and the Western regions of the USSR. Most observers agree that the possibilities of such a large scale migration are very slim. If the workers refused to move, the State would be under great pressure to shift the regional allocation of investment to the workers, which would further increase the economic weight of the non-Slavic republics. Given this background, a policy to increase the female labor participation rate in those republics would aggravate the nationality problem from the point of view of the Slavs by requiring an even greater shift of new investment to those republics in order to employ the increased number of women.

NATURAL RESOURCES

It is the normal experience of developing nations that the quality of the resources employed in the expanding economy eventually diminishes. The effect of those diminishing returns on the rate of growth then depends on the extent to which they are offset by the discovery of new resources, by capital investments, by technological progress and by international trade. The two sectors in which the resource problem has been most evident in the USSR are agriculture and petroleum.

The virgin lands opened for cultivation by Khrushchev were the last large remaining area for the expansion of agriculture in the USSR. Even those lands were regarded as of marginal quality because of the variability of the rainfall, but the program did succeed for a time in meeting the growing need for grain. In the present decade, however, large scale imports of grain provided dramatic evidence that the demand of the expanding economy for grain has threatened once again to overtake the supply. The size of the growing demand was itself the result, in part, of the improving level of living. As real income rises, the proportion of meat to other foods desired by the consumer tends to mount rapidly, and an expansion of livestock production sharply increases feed grain requirements. The economy has thus become increasingly vulnerable to variations in weather conditions, and the heavy grain imports in recent years have been costly in terms of foreign exchange.[7]

The postwar history of the petroleum industry exemplifies the race between the exhaustion of resources and the discovery of new ones. For a quarter of a century the Ural-Volga oil fields provided the bulk of the crude oil of the nation, but many of the wells are approaching exhaustion. The opening of the new West Siberian fields has taken up some of the slack, and they now account for all of the annual growth of production. But these fields have also begun to show signs of incipient depletion. At this time there appear to be no large new fields on the horizon to take up the slack once again.

The prospects are somewhat in dispute in the West. CIA analysts cite evidence that the normal depletion process has been aggravated in the USSR because of techniques that have increased the rate of current output at the expense of the long-run total output of the fields. The forecast is that by the mid-eighties, rising Soviet domestic oil consumption will catch up with declining production, which will mean the loss of the valuable foreign exchange earnings of recent years due to petroleum exports. The USSR may even be compelled to import petroleum.[8] Forecasts of this kind, however, are highly conjectural. The Soviets may be more successful than anticipated in conserving oil, and the newer fields may prove to be more prod-

---

7. David W. Carey, "Soviet Agriculture: Recent Performance and Future Plans," in *Soviet Economy*, pp. 575-595.
8. *Soviet Economic Problems and Prospects*, pp. 6-8 and *passim*.

uctive than anticipated. In the long run, more new fields may be found. Under the best of circumstances, however, the petroleum prospect is more likely to contribute to the further decline in the growth rate rather than to the reversal of that decline.

Among the measures employed by developing economies to offset the decline in the quality of resources is the application of increasing quantities of capital. It is in the issue of the prospective role of increasing capital that some of the thorniest problems of the future will have to be confronted.

CAPITAL

The most distinctive feature of the Soviet model of economic development is the emphasis on high rates of investment as the fuel of economic growth. The extent to which Soviet growth is investment-based may be appreciated by noting that the USSR is virtually the only major country in which the quantity of capital has grown more rapidly than the GNP itself over the long run. In the U.S., for example, the stock of capital grew at an annual rate of 1.0 percent during 1929-57, while the GNP grew at a rate of 3.0 percent. In the USSR, by contrast, capital expanded by 7.4 percent per year during 1928-66 while the GNP expanded by 5.5. percent.[9] Abram Bergson has shown that a growth model of this kind places a peculiar restriction on the uses that may be made of the nation's output. In particular, it requires that the managers of the economy devote not simply a large share of each year's output to investment, but also a growing share.[10] If the rate of investment were at the high level of 30 percent and that percentage failed to grow from year to year, for example, the growth rate of GNP would decline.

In fact, the rate of investment has increased in the USSR in the postwar period. However, it has not increased rapidly enough to maintain the growth rate of the capital stock. As a result, the annual rate of increase of the capital stock has been falling. In the period 1951-60 the quantity of capital expanded annually by 9.4 percent. In the following decade the rate of increase declined to 8.1 percent and in 1971-75 it declined further to 7.9 percent. The current five year plan provides for a further drop to 6.5 percent. This decline in the annual rate of increase of capital is one of the major reasons for the decline in the growth rate of the GNP.

One major policy alternative available to the political leadership

9. Paul R. Gregory and Robert C. Stuart, *Soviet Economic Structure and Performance* (New York: Harper and Row, 1974), p. 388.

10. Abram Bergson, "Soviet Economic Perspectives: Toward a New Growth Model," *Problems of Communism* (March/April, 1973).

is to arrest the steady decline in the rate of increase of capital by increasing the year-to-year rate of investment. Such a policy, however, entails high costs. The assessment of those costs, relative to the benefits that may be gained, is perhaps the major political task facing the Soviet leadership in the coming decade.

The costs consist of those uses of the nation's output that would have to be given up if the policy of increasing investment is adopted. The two major alternative uses of output are consumption and military. The relative shares of the three components of GNP are instructive. Roughly, consumption accounts for 57 percent, investment for 28 percent and military for 11 to 12 percent.[11] Given these proportions, consumption might appear to be the most likely candidate for trimming in favor of investment. A 10 percent increase in the volume of investment could be secured by a reduction of only 5 percent in the volume of consumption, but it would require a 25 percent decrease in military expenditures to accomplish the same result. That large difference is to some extent illusory, however, because the resources devoted to the three kinds of production are not of the same quality. In particular, the managerial, technical and scientific manpower engaged in military production is of much higher quality than that engaged in consumer goods production. The same is very likely true of the hardware; the physical resources embodied in military aircraft are of higher quality than those going into domestic refrigerators and passenger automobiles. Therefore the quantity of resources required to produce a given increase in the output of investment goods would be smaller if those resources were diverted from the military rather than from the consumption sector. For the same reason, the buildup of the Soviet military sector in the past fifteen years has entailed a greater cost, in terms of its depressing effect on the rate of growth, than is apparent from the numbers alone.

Apart from the relative magnitudes, the decision to increase the rate of investment involves weighty political considerations. Per capita consumption, like the GNP itself, has been growing continuously in the postwar period, but the annual rate of its growth has been declining; in 1951-60 it grew at 3.8 percent per year, but in 1971-75 it grew at only 2.9 percent. Any significant further decrease will diminish the resources available to the planners for maintaining worker and management incentives. The development of the resource-rich regions of Siberia and northern Russia, for example, is based on the policy of employing material incentives to induce labor and management to move to those inhospitable areas and to settle

11. Rush V. Greenslade, "The Real Gross National Product of the U.S.S.R., 1950-1975," in *Soviet Economy*, p. 277.

there permanently. And in economic activity generally, a great deal of attention is given to the search for improved incentive systems for eliciting greater effort, assuming greater risk in innovation, dismissing redundant labor and so forth. The monetary payments associated with incentive sytems must be accompanied by the production of the corresponding volume of consumer goods if they are to yield the results intended. It is therefore likely that a reduction in the annual increase in consumption large enough to produce a significant increase in investment will at the same time have a negative impact on incentives and effort. We can only guess about the magnitude of that impact. More to the point, however, the political leaders who have to make the decision can also do little more than guess about the size of the impact. They must at least entertain the possibility that the ensuing reduction in output per man may be so large as to offset the increase in output that the investment rate increase was intended to secure.

The question of incentives will be particularly salient in coming decades because of the aforementioned decline in the annual increase in the labor force. When the labor force is growing at a normal rate, a decline in labor quality because of incentive effects is offset to some extent by the increasing numbers of workers. In a period in which the labor force will not grow at all, however, an impairment of incentives is all the more costly. The growing scarcity of labor is also likely to generate an unplanned upward pressure on wages as managers compete for the services of skilled and reliable workers. Soviet experience in similar circumstances in the past provides sufficient evidence for us to expect that that will occur again. If the upward wage drift should occur in a period of planned restriction of the increase in consumer goods, the prevailing repressed inflation will increase. That would mean concretely a rising frequency of incidents in which citizens with earned cash in hand would find that the goods they had intended to purchase were not available, or that the length of the queue had grown. The consequence must be at least a further erosion of the incentive to put in extra effort for extra income. Beyond that, the effect depends on one's judgement of the intensity of the repressed inflation at the present time; this disputed question is discussed in Dr. Schroeder's paper. Some analysts regard it as of such large dimension as to constitute a major threat to financial stability. If they are correct, the consequences of adding to the inflation by an upward wage drift would be serious indeed, threatening to induce panic buying and possibly requiring such extraordinary measures as a currency conversion. Other analysts regard the degree of inflation as rather mild and not out of line with the normal experience of other countries. If they are correct, the effects of wage drift would not extend beyond the erosion of incentives mentioned above, but that negative incentive effect is concern enough.

The discussion thus far has dealt with the economic costs of reducing the rate of increase of consumption. There are, in addition, political costs. Concretely, the effects are likely to be no more serious than some additional grumbling by irritated consumers, and perhaps some occasional incidents of spontaneous political action or dissent. It is a risk the leadership would prefer not to take, but there is little reason to imagine that such manifestations could not be quickly and firmly contained. More serious is the possibility that consumer discontent would not remain isolated but might become linked to other sources of discontent, such as minority nationality issues and political dissidence. Professor Barghoorn reports in his paper on the evidence of such links already formed between discontented workers and political dissenters.

The alternative of reducing the increase in military production entails consequences that are the inverse of those of reducing the increase in consumption expenditures. The only economic costs that may be envisioned are those associated with sharp reallocation of resources in any economy. Workers are temporarily unemployed or underemployed; people trained for one production task have to be retrained to perform another; machinery and equipment are converted from one use to another and generally do not serve as well. These are transition costs, however, which eventually disappear. Offsetting these costs are the considerable benefits that the civilian economy would reap from the availability of those high quality human and physical resources presently devoted to high-technology military production.

Of the political consequences, two kinds may be identified: those associated with the foreign policy objectives of the political leadership, and those associated with the political power of the military. Since these topics are better addressed by scholars with expertise in political and military matters, only a summary evaluation will be offered here.

A significant reduction in military output, either in absolute volume or in terms of rate of increase, must be preceded by a decision to alter or postpone progress toward the military-political goals that have guided policy since the mid-sixties. I take those goals to have included nuclear superiority over the U.S.; a powerful striking force along the border with China; the capability of intervening quickly anywhere in Eastern Europe; an offensive edge in the NATO-Warsaw Pact theater; and a Navy capable of operating eventually in all the major sea lanes with appropriate onshore fueling and repair facilities. Any significant paring down of military expenditures may, at the least, oblige the leadership to forego some foreign policy objective that they might have been able to attain had the military buildup proceeded undiminished, in Africa, perhaps, or in the Middle East. The more threatening possibility is that they may be obliged to withdraw from a commitment previously undertaken, perhaps not of the dimensions of the Cuban Missile Crisis, but possibly the military defeat of an African ally because of Soviet failure to deliver sufficient military assistance. The risk of such incidents could be minimized by scaling down foreign policy objectives to a level commensurate with the reduced military capability—but even that must be regarded as a high price to pay.

Apart from the foreign policy costs, a proposal to reduce military expenditures is likely to be hotly contested in the councils of the party. It would be difficult to foretell what personal and bureaucratic coalitions will form and which will triumph, but it is probable that some political fortunes will rise and others will collapse. It is hard to imagine a policy proposal that would expose its proponent to a higher degree of political risk.

The discussion thus far has dealt with alternative ways of increasing the rate of investment. That policy is in some ways a return to the Stalinist high-investment growth model although, if the resources are obtained by a reduction of military production, it will avoid the low-consumption feature of the Stalinist model. However, that model should not be expected to reproduce the high growth rates of the past. A plausible case has been made that the stock of capital in the USSR has increased so rapidly, relative to the increase in labor, that the productivity of still further increments of capital has begun to decline.[12] Moreover, because of the resource problems discussed above, the yield on additional investments will be smaller than in the past. One of the major efforts to stabilize agricultural output is the Non-Black-Soil Zone Program in the Russian republic. The region has the highest average rainfall in European Russia but it requires heavy investments in land improvement, fertilizers, and farm machinery. The program will succeed in mitigating the impact of crop variability elsewhere, but at a high capital cost per unit of output.[13] Similarly, prospective energy and other natural resources are located far from the populated areas, often in inhospitable regions, where the costs of bringing them into production are high. Hence, a return to a high-investment strategy may succeed in arresting the decline in the growth rate, but it ought not be expected to reproduce the high growth rates of the past. There are, however, policies other than that of increasing investment that may help to raise the rate of growth. These are policies to increase the productivity of the economy.

12. Martin Weitzman, "Soviet Postwar Growth and Capital-Labor Substitution," in *American Economic Review* (September, 1970), pp. 676-692.
13. *Pravda*, February 8, 1977.

FACTOR PRODUCTIVITY

Labor and capital are the two major classes of primary resources, or factors of production, required to produce the nation's output. The more labor and capital available for use, the larger the quantity of output produced. The term "extensive growth" is often used to denote this source of economic growth. The growth of output that is not due to additional labor and capital is designated "intensive growth." There are a variety of reasons for intensive growth, but the important one for our purposes is technological progress. Loosely speaking, extensive growth derives from more machines, while intensive growth derives from better machines.

The overall growth rate of GNP may be regarded as the sum of the growth rate of factor inputs, which is the measure of extensive growth, and the growth rate of factor productivity, which is the measure of intensive growth. In terms of these measures, the distinctive feature of Soviet growth is the relatively small contribution of factor productivity to the growth of GNP. In the period 1950-62, inputs of the factors of production employed in the Soviet economy increased at an annual rate of 3.6 percent while factor productivity increased at a rate of 2.6 percent. Thus factor productivity accounted for 42 percent of the overall rate of growth of 6.2 percent. During the same period, the GNP grew in the U.S. at a slower rate, 3.4 percent, but factor productivity accounted for 56 percent of that overall rate of growth. In West Germany and France factor productivity accounted for 62 percent and 79 percent of their respective growth rates of GNP. Of the countries studied by Bergson, the country in which factor productivity made the smallest relative contribution to growth was the USSR. In absolute terms the Soviet annual growth rate of factor productivity of 2.6 percent fell just below the middle of the list.[14]

A mechanical system like an automobile may be designed to attain a high rate of speed, but then it is likely to perform poorly with respect to fuel consumption. One can modify the system to improve fuel consumption, but then the new system is not likely to perform as well with respect to speed. The Soviet economic system was designed with the end in view of mobilizing resources; that is, generating high annual rates of increase of labor and capital. It has done this very well—better than almost all other countries—but performance was obtained at the cost of low factor productivity. It was nevertheless a satisfactory system overall, in the sense that the final outcome in the form of the growth of GNP was well above average.

The source of the present problem is that the feature of the

14. Gregory and Stuart, p. 389.

system which formerly worked so well—resource mobilization—is no longer working as well, so that overall performance is declining. That leaves two courses of action: one is to repair the system so that it will do better at that for which it was originally designed; the other is to redesign the system to do better at that for which it was not designed and which it has not done well in the past.

The first part of this paper considered the possibilities of the first course of action. The general conclusion is that, with respect to labor, there are some things that can be done to augment the supply, but they cannot have a major effect. With respect to capital, there are ways in which the rate of investment can be increased, but the one which is likely to have the major economic effect—reducing military output—is fraught with political problems. Hence, the attractiveness of the second course of action. If the system could be redesigned so as to increase the growth rate of factor productivity, it would be possible to avoid having to make the difficult political choice.

TECHNOLOGICAL PROGRESS

Of the many things that contribute to the increase in factor productivity, technological progress is only one. But it is of major importance and the discussion will therefore be devoted to it alone. One may think of technological progress as the annual increase in the value of the output that can be obtained from a given bundle of resources embodied in capital equipment. Suppose a certain industry produces a new and improved model of a machine every year. The cost of producing all the models is the same, but each year's model yields a 6 percent larger net output than the preceding model. The rate of technological progress is then 6 percent per year in that industry. Technological progress in this sense has sustained the growth rate of output in the West and has been deficient in the USSR. Why has technological progress lagged in the USSR and what are the prospects for accelerating it in the future?

The Soviet sources provide a lengthy catalogue of obstacles to technological progress, three of which may be selected for discussion here. The first consists of organizational features of the economy. The crucial decisions that a manager in a market economy has to make involve uncertainty and guesswork; guesses, for example, about how much of his output the market will wish to buy. One of the virtues of central economic planning is that it eliminates guesswork. It is all worked out in advance; the manager is relieved of the marketing responsibility and can concentrate on production. The scope of managerial responsibility and authority and, therefore, autonomy is thus greatly restricted. The trouble is that while autonomy of enterprise is not necessary for the management of current production under central planning, it appears to be highly necessary for successful technological innovation. Innovation always involves uncertainty, and the greater the uncertainty, the greater the need for the authority to react quickly, to change plans, to obtain resources not anticipated earlier, and so on. In addition to the normal need for goods and services, innovating enterprises require command over research and development (R & D) resources. In the USSR, however, those resources have not been directly available to management but have been centrally controlled by the ministries. Enterprises were expected to obtain their R & D services in the same manner that they obtained their coal and other materials—through the planning system. Since planning is inevitably imperfect, all economic decisions involve risk; but the organizational structure greatly magnifies the normal risks in enterprises undertaking technological innovation. Consequently, managers prefer to avoid innovation.

The second obstacle to technological progress has been the structure of incentives. Innovation is risky in all economic systems, but innovative economies provide sufficient rewards to induce people to bear the risks. Since genuine innovation always involves a certain number of failures, the rewards for the successes must suffice to compensate for the losses due to the failures. Rewards of such large dimensions have not been provided for in the Soviet incentive structure. As is appropriate in a planned economy, material rewards have been geared toward motivating management to fulfill and overfulfill output plans, and the surest way to achieve that is to avoid the risks of production slowdown normally associated with new products or new processes. In recognition of this anti-innovation bias of the traditional incentive structure, certain special bonuses were introduced some years ago to induce management to assume the added risk of innovation. The size of these special innovation bonuses is such, however, that they barely offset the losses that innovators normally sustain because of the slowdown of regular production incident to the innovation process. The incentive structure still provides very high incomes for competent managers who overfulfill their plans regularly while minimizing their innovative activity. Those managers who have assumed the risk and effort of innovation do not earn very much more even if their innovations are highly successful.

In progressive market economies, the positive incentives for innovation are accompanied by negative incentives for non-innovation. Firms that fail to innovate tend to lose sales to the more innovative firms, with a consequent loss of profits which, in extreme cases, threatens bankruptcy or corporate takeover. This "invisible boot" is as potent a feature of the incentive structure as is the "invisible hand" of innovation profits. Since central planning provides in advance for the distribution of most enterprises' output, the latter have a virtually guaranteed market for their output and are therefore under no pressure to adopt the innovations already introduced by more progressive firms. In the absence of powerful negative incentives, the full burden of motivating innovation must be borne by the positive incentives alone.

The third obstacle to technological progress consists of barriers to the flow of technological knowledge. While there is some evidence that Soviet research people tend to treat some of their work as proprietary, on balance, the transfer of information among enterprises and among research centers within the country is probably satisfactory. The problem is the acquisition of foreign technological knowledge. The technologically advanced countries engage in a massive process of transfer of technological knowledge among themselves through such means as the travel and migration of scientists, engineers and technicians, a large volume of trade in products that convey technological information, the profit-seeking activity of multinational enterprises, the extensive volume of commercial travel by salesmen seeking to display their technological achievements in the search for new sales, and by manufacturers seeking cheaper sources of supply of components, materials, and labor skills. The USSR has hardly played a hand in that great game. The primary source of technological information from abroad has been the import of publications, a necessary source but one that is always incomplete and always out of date. Especially in high technology industries, the next generation of technology is always on the drawing boards and will not be revealed in print until it is fully in production and work has begun on the succeeding generation. Similarly, the copying of foreign technology leads inevitably to premature obsolescence. With modern electronic technology, for example, it is no longer possible to copy, since production technology is not evident in the physical items themselves. The proportion of Soviet engineers and executives who travel abroad on business thus acquiring and transmitting information is minuscule compared to the proportion of Japanese, Germans, or Americans. Thus, the typical Soviet research scientist, engineer or technician has little knowledge of the most advanced technology in his field.

Taking these three features of the Soviet economy as explanations for the lag in technological advance, what are the prospects for significant technological progress in the coming decades? The question is best approached by examining two major decisions that were designed to accomplish that end—the decision to replace enterprises by production associations as the basic units of production management, and the decision to expand the import of foreign technology.

The principal contribution toward technological progress made by the merger of enterprises into production associations is the provision for closer integration between production activity and R & D work. Most production associations are to have their own R & D facilities, so that they no longer will have to apply to the ministry to obtain access to R & D services, or to enter into contractual relations with an independent R & D institute. In some of the production associations, the R & D facility is one of the formerly independent major R & D institutes in the country. These are called "science-production associations," and the former director of the independent institute is normally the new general director of the association. Since both production and R & D are now under a single management, some of the risk previously associated with innovation may be expected to diminish. For example, if the first production run on a newly designed product is not working well, the R & D people who designed it will be called in quickly to undertake the redesign or the re-engineering because a single boss is responsible for the entire operation. In the past, the director of the producing enterprise had to appeal to the director of the independent R & D institute to send some people down to see what the trouble was.

This reform expands the degree of managerial autonomy in precisely the way that is required for the promotion of innovation. Certain problems have arisen as the merger movement got under way, but by and large, the effect of the reform is likely to be positive. The question is, however, whether that effect will be large or small. In my judgment, it will be small because it does not get to the heart of the organizational problem. The production association is still an enterprise—an enlarged enterprise to be sure, but still an enterprise—operating in a centrally planned economy. It is still dependent upon the planning system for most of its sources of supply and for the marketing of its output; and to the extent that innovation increases the possiblity that the required materials will not be quickly available or the new product will not be readily sold, the degree of risk is still very high.

The production association, moreover, operates under the existing incentive structure, and there has been neither movement toward change nor any discussion of a significant increase in the monetary incentives for innovation. There are obvious ideological sources of resistance to the kind of change that would be required. If successful innovators were entitled to a share, albeit small, of the social value created as a result of their work, the amounts might add up with awkward consequences for the distribution of income. However, there are ways in which even large innovation fortunes could be rendered consistent with the doctrine of "to each according to his work," for the contribution of innovation to the people's income may be very great indeed. The larger difficulty is that an incentive system geared specifically to the reward of innovation would, in the Soviet context, have to be operated by what are referred to as "administrative methods." This means that, as in the present system, rewards would have to be based on a schedule specifying the size of the monetary payments that would be available for innovations of various sizes. Such a system would require that the enterprise present extensive documentation proving that the new product was genuinely new and that the ultimate value to the economy of the innovation was a certain number of rubles. The size of the reward would thus depend on one's capacity to persuade some governmental official that the product was indeed innovative and that the estimates of cost-saving were correct. Even the present system with its modest rewards for innovation has generated a large amount of spurious innovation, in which enterprises make minor changes in an established product in order to try to persuade the ministry that it is new and therefore entitled to an innovation bonus. Hence, if a decision was made to increase greatly the rewards for innovation—unless it was done by some method different from the administrative method presently used—it would create the possibility of enormous abuses.

The import of foreign technology is a reasonable policy in the sense that it enables the USSR to benefit from the international specialization of labor and to share in the normal gains from trade that are available to all countries. To the extent that the Soviets have undertraded in the past, they have used scarce resources to produce goods that could have been purchased more cheaply abroad. The expansion of trade should increase the efficiency with which the country's resources are used and should therefore contribute to an increase in the rate of economic growth and an improvement in the technological level of the society. The Soviet leaders, however, appear to expect that the new policy will bring not only the normal gains from trade but that the technological knowledge embodied in the advanced imported technology will diffuse throughout industry and thus stimulate the acceleration of domestic technological progress.

The policy may indeed be expected to have this positive effect to some degree. The physical equipment itself, and the management systems training that accompanies much of it, will contribute to the transfer of technological knowledge from which the Soviets have benefitted so little in the past. But on the scale of the whole problem, that contribution cannot be expected to loom very large. It is instructive to compare the USSR with Japan in this respect. Postwar Japan engaged in a deliberate and massive import of foreign technology and in two decades rose to the technological leadership of the world. Can we not do the same thing, ask the Soviet leaders? In my judgment they cannot, for the Japanese performance derived not simply from the import of technology but from the highly innovative quality of the economic system into which the technology was imported. The import of technology can augment the technological progress of an innovative economy, but it is not a substitute for an innovative economy.

What is required to make the Soviet economy innovative? For one thing it would be helpful if Soviet industry were in as continuous contact with that of the advanced technological countries as they are with each other. The evidence of this might be the number of Soviet business executives and research personnel who are registered on a typical night in the Hiltons of the developed world. On the night that the number equals that of the Japanese, one might predict that Soviet industry was on its technological way. I put the point in this way to emphasize the political underpinning of technological progress.

The central political issue, however, is the basic structure of the economic system. By analogy to the mechanical system again, an automobile designed to maximize speed can later be re-engineered in various ways to improve fuel economy, but it is unlikely to be as successful in this respect as one that was specifically designed to maximize fuel economy. If fuel economy were the main goal, the entire mechanical system would have to be redesigned. Reforms like the production associations and new policies like the import of foreign technology are reasonable efforts to adapt the old economic system to the new objective of accelerating technological progress, but they hold promise of only limited gains. Like the bold organizational reforms of the past, such as Khrushchev's territorial reorganization of 1957 and the Brezhnev-Kosygin economic reform of 1965, their effects are weakened by the system of central planning within which they are contained.

The participants in this symposium who have considered the possibility of the introduction of a form of market socialism have generally concluded, as I have, that it is so threatening to vested interests that it is a highly unlikely alternative. If system change is ruled out, and within-system organizational reforms offer such slight promise, the economic prospect for the future looks rather somber. There is an alternative, however, that goes beyond organizational reform yet does not require the abandonment of central planning. I have in mind a modern version of the New Economic Policy introduced by Lenin when the socialist economy of his time had failed to perform satisfactorily.

Under this new-model NEP the "commanding heights" would consist of that overwhelming portion of the economy that presently operates under central planning, and it would continue to operate in the same manner. However, citizens would have the right to form small enterprises, to engage in the production of a wide variety of both producer and consumer goods and services. The scope of this lawful secondary economy would be limited in various ways: enterprises would be required to operate as producer cooperatives or on the basis of the self-management principle, and they would be limited in size. The conditions under which they might buy from and sell to state-owned enterprises would have to be specified, and the income tax system would have to be strengthened to maintain incomes within acceptable bounds.

The NEP enterprises would fulfill those economic activities in which smallness of scale and flexibility have a comparative advantage. Even before the introduction of production associations, some Soviet analysts held that the size structure of Soviet industry was excessively biased in favor of large enterprises.[15] Since the production-association reform has further increased the average size of enterprise, the case for an expansion of small enterprises may now be even stronger. They may be expected to flourish primarily in those activities, such as retail trade, restaurants, personal services, repair services, and so forth, in which state enterprise has proven to be singularly inefficient. But the potential extends much further, including small-scale and job-lot manufacturing of consumer and producer goods, construction work, industrial design, and equipment servicing. Small construction *artels*, for example, may prove to be highly efficient for small jobs, and state enterprises may prefer to employ them rather than the unwieldy state construction enterprises. The competition that the NEP enterprises would thus provide could not fail to exert a positive influence on the state sector. They might, in addition, make a particular contribution in the promotion of technological innovation, since they could operate with a degree of autonomy and flexibility that has been missing in the centrally planned state enterprise sector. Small enterprise has played a crucial role in the innovational achievements of capitalist economics and might play a similar role in a new Soviet NEP.

A new NEP would be threatening to some interests that are presently vested in the centrally planned economy, but to fewer interests than would be threatened by a turn to market socialism. For the system of central planning would continue to operate largely intact, and all existing enterprises would continue to be managed as before. The state sector would continue to be responsible as before for the maintenance of full employment. Since prices would be uncontrolled in the NEP sector, workers and consumers might regard

15. Joseph S. Berliner, *The Innovation Decision in Soviet Industry* (Cambridge, Mass.: MIT Press, 1976), pp. 33-34.

the higher prices in that sector as contributing to a lowering of their own level of living. To contain that sentiment, the planners would have to assure that the NEP sector did not "crowd" the state sector out of the consumer market. The state sector would continue to offer the standard array of consumer goods and services for sale at the conventional prices, while the NEP sector would offer higher quality goods and services at higher prices. A more serious political problem might arise as a result of worker hostility to the large incomes that would be generated in the NEP sector. The capacity of the leadership to resist such pressures would provide the test of the potential effectiveness of "economic methods;" if populist sentiment compelled the leadership to maintain income differences within excessively narrow bounds, there would be little hope of any successful economic reform.

The task of presenting an NEP reform in ideologically acceptable terms would be challenging but not insuperable. There is, after all, the great authority of Lenin as the father of the first NEP. Second, that NEP is still regarded by many Soviet people as the Golden Age of Soviet history. Third, as Donald Kelley has shown, the current concept of "developed socialism" is an idea in search of its own content. Part of that content might well be the notion that with the progress of the scientific-technical revolution, the socialist economy will become hospitable again to small enterprise, which encourages new forms of innovation and initiative. That is to say, while central planning encompasses the whole economy during the period of transition to socialism, the period of developed socialism produces new forms of enterprise that build on the basis of the planned economy sector. The dialectic is apparent in the re-emergence of the NEP on a new and higher plane.

CONCLUSION

A number of broad policy options emerge. One is a return to a Stalinist planning system and development strategy, with a sharp diversion of resources from consumption to investment and a tightening of centralized control over planning. This policy will appeal to people of reactionary temperament who believe that in the old days, with all the suffering, at least discipline prevailed, people worked hard, and the economy grew rapidly. Short of a politico-economic crisis, however, it is doubtful that such a policy would prevail; and if it did, its outcome would quickly prove to be a great disappointment to its proponents. A second option is the replacement of central planning with a form of market socialism. That policy offers the greatest possibility in the long run of accelerating significantly the rate of technological progress, but it is so alien ideologically and so threatening to vested interests that there are few prospects of its adoption. Here too, perhaps, the shock of a serious politico-economic debacle might thrust this alternative into the arena of possibility, but in such an event it appears more likely that the harsher Stalinist alternative would prevail. Third is an NEP-type reform which retains the centrally planned economy largely intact but allows for a flourishing small-scale private sector. Since it entails no retreat from central planning but, rather, the development of a new secondary economy that offers some promise of spurring new imitation and innovation, it may be entertained seriously by the post-succession leadership. Fourth is a continued progression of organizational changes which hold little more prospect of success than the reform efforts of the past. A fifth option is the sharp reduction in military expenditures, an analysis of which will serve as a convenient summary of the argument.

The reduction of military expenditures is the only option that holds the possibility of increasing the rate of growth in the short run. It would help to offset the impending decline in the rate of increase of the labor force, and it would help to hold the production of consumer goods at levels required to maintain incentives and to induce pensioners and others to return to active employment. It would release highly productive physical resources for investment purposes to augment the rate of increase in the capital stock and also release valuable scientific, technical and managerial manpower which would augment the rate of technological progress in civilian industry. Finally, to the extent that a reduction in international tension increases Soviet access to foreign technology, it would augment the rate of technological progress.

Three arguments could be advanced against this policy. First, since military expenditures absorb only 11 to 12 percent of the GNP, even a sizeable reduction would have a small impact on consumption and investment. Second, the policy would lead to a weakening of Soviet military power and would require a scaling down of foreign policy objectives. Third, it would precipitate a bitter conflict within the political leadership.

The first objection is valid, in the sense that it cautions against regarding the military sector as a boundless store within which all economic problems can be solved. However, in view of the special quality of its resources, its potential is greater than the 11 to 12 percent figure would suggest. Moreover, it is the only major sector of which the resources could be diverted to economic growth without incurring large offsetting economic costs. Finally, the policy ought not be misrepresented as one that would restore the high growth rates of the 'fifties, but should be regarded more conservatively as a way of arresting the decline in the growth rate and possibly raising it.

The second objection is also valid, but the point should be made that the scaling down of foreign policy and military objectives need only be temporary. The military program of the past fifteen years has brought the USSR to a point of reasonable parity with the U.S. in nuclear armament and of adequate capacity to promote the nation's interests vis-a-vis NATO, Eastern Europe, and China. What would need to be given up are the objectives of attaining decisive military superiority in those theaters and, more importantly, of extending military power throughout the world through the blue-ocean naval program with its accompanying requirements for widely spread shore facilities. These objectives may remain part of the long-range foreign policy program, but at present it would be unwise to pursue foreign policy objectives that are incommensurate with the nation's economic power. In the spirit of Lenin's tactical recommendation, "One step backward, two steps forward," once the economy has regained its economic strength, the march toward those long-range objectives could be resumed.

The third objection is the one on which the outcome will probably turn. The military can be expected to oppose the policy, not merely on grounds of their vested interest but also out of the conviction that it would lead to an irresponsible weakening of the nation's defense capability. Certain segments of the industrial elite would presumably support the military for the same reasons. Finally, there would be a likely ideological-nationalistic resistance to the policy. Six decades after the Revolution, military prowess has emerged as the only basis of Soviet eminence in the world. Its economic system is no longer considered a model for the developing nations, as it was a few decades ago. Its technology is nowhere in great demand. In the socialist world it has lost ideological leadership to China, Eurocommunism, and a variety of local communisms. Its literature, music, and culture, in which the nation was pre-eminent before the Revolution, have made very little impact. Hence those political leaders who regard it as important that their nation be respected in the world will be inclined to support the claims of the military.

It is perhaps sufficient to forecast what the issue will be and judicious to refrain from a guess about what the outcome will be. At the least, however, we can expect one big brawl.

Gertrude E. Schroeder

Prospects for the Consumer

WHAT HAS BEEN ACCOMPLISHED?

The first thirty years of Soviet communism, beset by war, civil strife and police terror, brought virtually none of the promised fruits of the Revolution to the people. As best one can assess these matters, given available information, consumers were little better off in 1950 than they were in 1928 or even in 1913, with the notable exception of impressive advances in communal services (education and health) from very minimal levels.[1] The second thirty years, however, witnessed remarkable gains for consumers. As conventionally measured, per capita consumption rose at an average annual rate of nearly 4 percent during 1950-1977, a gain in material goods and services of over two and a half times.[2] Sizeable advances occurred across the

---

1. Janet C. Chapman, "Consumption," in Abram Bergson and Simon Kuznets, eds., *Economic Trends in the Soviet Union* (Cambridge: Harvard University Press, 1963), pp. 238-239.

2. Gertrude E. Schroeder and Barbara S. Severin, "Soviet Consumption and Income Policies in Perspective," in *Soviet Economy in a New Perspective,* Joint Economic Committee, Congress of the United States (Washington: United States Government Printing Office, 1976) p. 622. Data given there are for 1950-1975; according to rough calculations made by the author, per capita consumption rose at about 3 percent annually during 1976-1977.

board—more and better food, clothing, housing, and both personal and communal services. The most spectacular gains were made in the availability of consumer durables, which were virtually unknown to Soviet consumers in 1950.

In more concrete terms, the daily fare of the average Russian is now far more nutritious and varied than in 1950. By Soviet measurements, per capita consumption of meat and fats rose from 26 kilograms per capita in 1950 to 57 kilograms per capita in 1977; at the same time, per capita consumption of starchy foods—grain products and potatoes—fell from 413 kilograms to 262 kilograms.[3] This shift means that the Soviet people have come a long way toward the dietary patterns of the industrialized Western nations. In 1950, consumers on the average bought only one pair of shoes per year; in 1977 they bought three. Factory-made clothing has largely replaced home-sewn garments; and, shoddy and drab though they may appear to a Westerner, the clothes provided today are much improved in style and color from the universal grayness that seemed to characterize their appearance in the early postwar years. The Soviet government has not provided data on household stocks of consumer durables in 1950, perhaps because they were so rare. Even in 1960, stocks of household durables were meager by Western standards—only 4 of every 100 families owned a refrigerator or a washing machine, for example, and only 8 of every 100 families owned a television set.[4] Private cars were the possession of the elite. By 1977, approximately two-thirds of all families owned refrigerators and washing machines, and over three-quarters had a television set.[5] About 4 percent of families owned a car.

At the same time, the Soviet government has continued to stress the importance of communal consumption by allocating steadily increased resources to education and health. The average educational attainment of the population rose from 5 years in 1950 to 8.7 years in 1977. About one-quarter of high school graduates now enter college, and the number of college graduates per 1,000 employed workers rose from 33 to 90 during 1959-77.[6] Vital rates in the Soviet Union now resemble those in Western countries. The government boasts of having more doctors and hospital beds per 10,000 population than any other country in the world and of providing education and health services to its citizens essentially free of charge.

While overall gains have been large, the rate of improvement in all categories of consumption has been slowing markedly. The

3. *Narodnoe Khoziaistvo SSSR 1922-72*, p. 372; *SSSR v Tsifrakh v 1977 Godu*, p. 202.
4. *Narodnoe Khoziaistvo SSSR 1922-72*, p. 372.
5. *SSSR v Tsifrakh v 1977 Godu*, p. 204.
6. Ibid., p. 15.

greatest gains were made in the 1950s, when per capita consumption rose on the average by 4.8 percent per year. This rate dropped to 3.5 percent in the 1960s and to 3.0 percent thus far in the 1970s. The slowdown has occurred in all major categories—food, clothing, durables and housing, as well as in health and education services. Although these statistical conclusions are based on Western measures of Soviet GNP and its distribution by sector of final demand, a persistent slowdown in the rate of improvement in levels of living is also shown by Soviet official data. Thus, real per capita incomes, a Soviet construct that includes government outlays on health and education along with individual purchases of goods and services, rose 42 percent during 1966-70, 29 percent during 1971-75 and will rise 25 percent during 1976-80, if plans are met—an unlikely outcome.[7]

It is interesting to consider to what relative level the gains of recent decades have brought Soviet consumers, compared with their counterparts in other industrialized countries. To assess this matter properly, one must make detailed comparisons of goods and services consumed, converted to a common currency by purchasing power equivalents calculated from price ratios for carefully matched goods and services. Such a comparison has been made in respect to per capita consumption in the USSR and the USA; calculations based on this study show Soviet per capita consumption in 1970 to be about one third of the U.S. level.[8] Another major study has made such comparisons between the U.S., Western Europe and Japan in 1970.[9] These combined studies suggest that per capita consumption in the Soviet Union is about half that in France, West Germany and the U.K., and perhaps somewhat over two thirds of that in Italy and Japan.

Judging from a variety of evidence, Soviet consumers are also less well off than those in most Communist countries of Eastern Europe, Czechoslovakia, East Germany, and Hungary, in particular.[10] In respect to politically sensitive comparisons of per capita

7. The Soviet measure of real per capita income is believed to overstate the rate of progress considerably. For a discussion of this measure, see: Gertrude E. Schroeder, "An Appraisal of Soviet Wage and Income Statistics," in Vladimir G. Treml and John P. Hardt, eds., *Soviet Economic Statistics* (Durham: Duke University Press, 1972), pp. 303-312.

8. Per capita consumption in the USSR was estimated at 33 percent of the U.S. level in 1968 and 34 percent in 1972. *Economic Performance and the Military Burden in the Soviet Union*, Joint Economic Committee (Washington: 1970), p. 97; and *Allocation of Resources in the Soviet Union and China*, Joint Economic Committee, Hearings (April 12, 1974), p. 52.

9. Irving B. Kravis et al., *A System of International Comparisons of Gross Product and Purchasing Power* (Baltimore: Johns Hopkins Press, 1972), pp. 169-187.

10. Keith Bush, "Indicators of Living Standards in the USSR and Eastern Europe," in *COMECON: Progress and Prospect*, NATO, Directorate of Economic Affairs (Brussels: 1977), pp. 201-210.

consumption of meat among Socialist countries, consumption in the USSR in 1975 was well below that in all other East European countries except Romania. The USSR had a mere 4 passenger cars per 100 families, a level that was exceeded by all other East European countries except Romania. All in all, the various measures indicate a substantial Soviet lag in levels of living relative to most countries with which Soviet consumers might wish to compare themselves. Although relative gains have been made since 1950 in respect to the U.S. and the U.K., progress in catching up has been slow. Moreover, Soviet consumers have lost ground by comparison with those in Germany, France, Italy and Japan.[11]

EVOLUTION OF POLICIES TOWARD CONSUMERS

While never giving up the absolute priority accorded to investment and defense, post-Stalinist regimes have upgraded the priority given to consumption and have pursued a variety of policies likely to win popular favor. Statistically, the higher priority for consumption is reflected in the fact that on the average it has grown at approximately the same rate as the GNP since the early 1960s, which means that its share of the total has remained about the same. This situation is a far cry from the days of Stalin, when consumption was rising at less than half the rate of GNP. Nonetheless, this share—57 percent in 1975—is low in relation to much of Western Europe and the U.S.

Even more revealing of the relatively higher priority for consumers, perhaps, are the changed policies with respect to agriculture. First of all, the government has set itself the goal of bringing per capita consumption of meat close to levels prevailing in Western (and East European) industrialized countries. This ambitious program, requiring a rapid buildup of livestock herds, has proven exceedingly costly in investment resources and foreign exchange. Second, to further this goal and to raise and stabilize agricultural output in general, the Brezhnev regime has sharply raised the priority given to agriculture in the allocation of investment resources. Thus, its share rose from 15.5 percent of the total in 1961-65 to 20.6 percent in 1976.[12] If investment in rural infra-structure and in manufacturing plants producing inputs for agriculture is included, agriculture's claim on investment amounts to about one third of the total. Third, both Khrushchev and Brezhnev sanctioned the use of large amounts of gold and scarce hard currency to pay for imported grain in

11. Abram Bergson, *Productivity and the Social System—the USSR and the West* (Cambridge: Harvard University Press, 1978), pp. 170-192.
12. *Narodnoe Khoziaistvo SSSR za 60 let*, p. 437.

Prospects for the Consumer 115

periods of bad harvests. Since 1970, the USSR has imported nearly $10 billion in grain and is now doing so on a regular basis, not only in years of harvest failure. Moreover, the USSR has begun to import meat on a substantial scale. Fourth, to provide incentives for farmers, the government has drastically increased the prices it pays them, while simultaneously maintaining stable retail prices for food purchased in state outlets. The result has been a rapidly growing subsidy bill; for meat and milk products alone, it amounted to nearly 19 billion rubles in 1975—almost one tenth of total state budget outlays.[13] Finally, the government has once more sacrificed ideology for pragmatism by encouraging the expansion of private agriculture. If the past is any guide, however, this shift is unlikely to be permanent.

Besides providing more and better food, clothing and durables—and belatedly a modicum of automobiles—Stalin's successors have adopted a number of measures designed to improve the lot of various groups in the population. Above all, the traditional policy of maintaining full employment—a job for everyone whether he wants one or not—has been persistently maintained. Undoubtedly the cost in efficiency has been high, but the Soviet people can boast that their system is not beset with the large-scale unemployment that periodically plagues capitalist countries. Hours of work have been cut from 48 to 41 per week. Money incomes have risen steadily, although at a reduced rate in the past decade, and income differentials have narrowed considerably. In particular, the once huge gap between urban and rural incomes has been so reduced that, unless the trend is reversed, wage incomes of the two groups will have been equalized, although large differences between amenities in urban and rural areas will still persist. Beginning in the mid-1950s, the government adopted a number of programs that have substantially upgraded pensions and other types of welfare benefits. Collective farmers, long treated as second class citizens, have been brought under the social security system applicable to state employees and are now allowed to have internal passports like other workers.

In sum, the post-Stalin leaders have made some progress toward fulfilling the goals of communism. For three decades the people have been reaping increased benefits from the socialized economic system. Gains have been steady, even though at a diminishing rate, and they have been highly visible—more and better housing at very low rents, more household appliances and cars, greater access to higher education. The workweek is short, even by Western standards, and paid vacations are available to all, at subsidized resorts for many. And above all, there are the perennial promises of more gains to come.

13. *Pravda*, February 8, 1977.

ESCALATING PROBLEMS AND POLICY DILEMMAS

Up to now, the discussion has been concerned with improvements for consumers—more goods and services and higher incomes—in a vacuum, so to speak. These substantial quantitative advances, however, have produced a Pandora's box of seemingly intractable problems. As in every country, when minimum needs for food, clothing, shelter, and a few luxuries have been met, people become choosy about what they will buy; by voting with their rubles, Soviet consumers now insist on higher quality and more variety, style, and assortment in the product mix; they are also demanding more and better personal services. The production system has proved to be uniquely unsuited to meeting these new demands, despite numerous official decrees ordering an improvement and despite a great deal of tinkering with economic organization and incentives. The results have been visible waste in the form of production of goods that nobody wants, periodic inventory pileups of one or another product, annual bargain sales at slashed prices, and budget subsidies to defray the costs. At the same time, there are perennial, random shortages of one item or another—toothpaste today, meat grinders tomorrow, eyeglass frames the next day. This obvious malaise is compounded by a clumsy distribution system that often delivers excessive amounts of some product to one area, while another area experiences acute shortages. Standing in queues and spending hours in daily shopping are routine, with the burden falling mainly on women.

Rising money incomes, along with the state's policy of severely restricting consumer credit and its failure to meet increased demand for goods such as meat, have produced rapidly rising deposits in government savings banks. At the end of 1977, deposits totalled 116.7 billion rubles, equal to a half year's volume of retail trade.[14] The average deposit, 972 rubles, was equal to somewhat more than a half year's wages for the average state worker. Although savings rates in the USSR are not high compared with other countries at similar levels of development, the total accumulation represents an excess of liquid purchasing power, which evidently worries Soviet planners. These savings are particularly irritating when, at the same time, the planners observe mounting stocks of goods that nobody wants to buy. A rapidly growing subsidy bill for food, housing and other goods is the price of the government's present policy of keeping retail prices from rising in the face of rising costs and higher prices paid to producers.

The rapid rise in money incomes and savings in the post-Stalin era brings up the question of the government's record in controlling

14. *SSSR v Tsifrakh v 1977 Godu*, p. 198; 205.

inflation. Considerable controversy exists in the West concerning this issue. According to the official Soviet retail price index, prices have remained essentially stable since 1955. However, this index merely reflects prices on official price lists, not actual transaction prices.[15] The USSR has ceased publishing indexes of collective farm market prices, which have been rising steadily. The price index implicit in a comparison of Western measures of real consumption of goods sold at retail and Soviet reported retail sales in current prices yields an average annual price change of 1.3 percent from 1955 to 75;[16] this may be interpreted as a minimum estimate of disguised inflation. Econometric studies suggest that there has been little overall suppressed inflation during this period.[17] In contrast, emigrés invariably declare that the cost of living has been rising steadily, and that queues and random shortages of individual products are a familiar part of the Soviet scene. What can one make of this seemingly contradictory evidence? Certainly, there is strong evidence of a moderate rate of consumer price increase that the faulty official price index fails to reveal. Evidently, there is a palpable rise in the average worker's cost of living, resulting from the disappearance of lower grade and lower priced goods from the market, which leaves him no choice but to buy higher grade and higher priced goods if he wants the product at all. Also, new products (and old ones purportedly of better quality) are put on the market with substantial price markups that are not commensurate with the alleged novelty or quality improvement. Sometimes, as in the case of vodka, the only change to justify the rise in price is a new label on the bottle. Both the Soviet press and emigré reports suggest that these are common phenomena. Bonus and pricing arrangements established for producing enterprises encourage such practices; relative prices are distorted, producing queues and random surplusses and shortages. On balance, however, it would appear that aggregate inflationary pressures have been manageable in recent years, but could become serious if the government fails to limit the growth of money incomes in accord with its reduced ability to provide a flow of goods and services. That the planners are aware of this problem is indicated by the reining in of the growth of wages since 1970.

The failure of the state production and distribution system to supply the goods and services that people want "when and where they want them" has fostered another vexing phenomenon—a flourishing second economy—whose many-faceted activities not only add

15. For a description and critique of Soviet price indexes see Morris Bornstein, "Soviet Price Statistics," in Treml and Hardt, *Soviet Economic Statistics*, pp. 355-376.
16. Schroeder and Severin, "Soviet Consumption," p. 631.
17. Richard Portes, "The Control of Inflation: Lessons from East European Experience," *Economica*, 44:174 (May, 1977), pp. 109-130.

to real stocks of goods and services, but also alter relative prices and incomes in significant ways.[18] This economy, illegally or semi-legally, produces goods and services, e.g., *samogon* (home brew), repair of apartments, and so on. Black markets in all kinds of scarce items, such as secondhand cars, raise prices and thereby help to equilibrate supply and demand. Bribes given to retail clerks to reserve desired items both raise prices and redistribute incomes. Graft and corruption of public officials is ubiquitous. As long as the malfunctions of the official economy remain, the second economy continues to prosper. The government's persistent harassment serves only to keep its activities within tolerable limits.

Stemming at least in part from the general disarray in consumer goods markets is the evident problem of motivating workers to be more productive. According to press testimony, indifference, absenteeism and job-hopping are widespread. Soviet sources estimate that one out of every five industrial workers quits his job voluntarily each year.[19] Alcoholism is reaching alarming proportions, if one may judge from the variety of approaches being taken to reduce it, and drinking on the job seems to be the rule among males. One Soviet source asserts that losses in worktime and productivity due to alcohol abuse equal the annual value of sales; if true, the cost could amount to as much as 30 billion rubles in 1976—about 10 percent of total consumption.[20] With material incentives having lost much of their cutting edge, the supplemental and much touted moral incentives are not apparently very effective either. The evidence of disaffection among workers and farmers, too, poses serious problems for a government that desperately needs to boost productivity in order to maintain economic growth rates while developing resources and industries in inhospitable climatic areas, such as Siberia and the Far East.

WHAT MAY LIE AHEAD?

Two major developments will have a potentially large impact on the welfare of Soviet consumers and workers over the next decade or so.

---

18. For a general description and analysis of the second economy see: Gregory Grossman, "The Second Economy of the USSR," *Problems of Communism* (September/October, 1977), pp. 25-40; Gertrude E. Schroeder and Rush V. Greenslade, "On the Measurement of the Second Economy in the USSR," *Aces Bulletin*, 21:1 (Spring, 1979).

19. Data are cited in Murray Feshbach and Stephen Rapawy, "Soviet Population and Manpower Trends and Policies," in *Soviet Economy*, p. 143.

20. *Ekonomika i organizatsiya promyshlennogo proizvodstva* (4:1974), pp. 49-50.

One is the near-certainty of a continued slowdown in the rate of economic growth; the other is the inevitable change in the top political leadership. Although these developments will no doubt impact on each other, they can be analyzed separately.

Slower economic growth. The rate of economic growth has slowed markedly during the 1970s—to less than 4 percent annually, compared with over 5 percent in the 1960s and nearly 6 percent in the 1950s.[21] Soviet growth has been achieved largely by rapid additions to the labor force and to the capital stock. Less than one-quarter of the growth has resulted from improvements in the productivity with which these resources were used—a pattern of growth in marked contrast to that of Western Europe and the U.S. The growth of inputs has decreased somewhat, capital more than labor, but productivity growth has declined much more; during the 1970s it has actually stagnated.

There is no way that the Soviet Union can avoid a further slowing in the rate of economic growth. As a result of the low birth rates of the 1960s, the growth of the labor force will drop sharply, declining from near 2 percent annually in recent years to a mere 0.5 percent annually during the last half of the 1980s.[22] With labor force participation rates already the highest of any comparable country, little help can come from that source, except perhaps in the form of relatively less productive persons of pension age. Because investment growth has been falling recently, the growth of the capital stock will also continue to drop unless there is a return to much higher investment rates. Only an unprecedented upsurge in productivity could halt the decline in the growth of output. The internal forces that could produce such a development are not evident; indeed, the USSR will do well to maintain even the average rate of the past two decades. Some observers see the USSR's economic salvation in a concerted turning to the West for modern machinery and know-how. However, unless Western governments wished to grant massive aid, the possibilities of greatly expanded trade would be severely limited by the USSR's inability to pay for these imports. Its machinery and other manufactures remain largely unsalable in the West (they made up less than 5 percent of Soviet exports to the West in 1975), and the principal hard currency earner, oil, may soon be needed for domestic consumption. After 50 years of overriding priority for heavy industry, the USSR has a trade pattern like that of underdeveloped

21. Rush V. Greenslade, "The Real Gross National Product of the USSR, 1950-1975," in *Soviet Economy*, p. 279.

22. Stephen Rapawy, *Estimates and Projections of the Labor Force and Civilian Employment in the USSR, 1950 to 1990*, United States Department of Commerce, Bureau of Economic Analysis, Foreign Economic Report, 10 (September, 1976), pp. 12-25.

countries—importing manufactures and exporting raw materials. Massive imports of Western technology and Soviet efforts to develop salable manufactures for export over the past dozen years have not altered this situation. Moreover, the payoff on imported Western technology has not been decisive, since, despite its infusion, productivity growth has deteriorated. The bureaucratic production system has not been conducive to efficient adaptation, diffusion, and use of sophisticated modern technology.

If the USSR experiences severe oil shortages and periodic crop failures, as some analysts have suggested could well occur, advances in productivity might be halted entirely and foreign trade severely restricted.[23] However, if productivity gains continue at least at the average rate attained in recent decades—about 1 percent per year—and investment is not radically accelerated, then GNP will rise at 3 to 3.5 percent in the 1980s, faster in the first half than in the last half. This rate of progress is about the best that realistically can be expected; if the government were to raise investment rates substantially, in order to spur economic growth, the cost to consumption would be severe.[24] On the other hand, if productivity advance is halted by raw materials and energy bottlenecks, then GNP might rise at only 2 to 2.5 percent annually; this could be regarded as a worst case scenario.

What do such rates of economic growth imply for consumers? With an overall growth rate of 3 to 3.5 percent, per capita consumption probably would increase at about 2 to 2.5 percent per year. If the GNP rises at 2 to 2.5 percent annually, per capita consumption would increase at 1 percent or less annually. In both cases, improvement in the level of living would be much slower than in recent decades. Indeed, the worst case scenario implies a return to the minuscule consumption gains of Stalinist years.

How might Soviet consumers and workers react to much slower improvement in their level of living? In order to consider this question, it is essential to translate these abstract annual percentage gains into concrete terms. After all, consumers do not think or react in terms of a construct labeled "annual percentage increase in real per capita consumption." Rather, they think in terms of availability of more and better food, clothing, durables and services, as well as the prices at which goods and services can be acquired. Since the economic system has been able for a quarter century to provide

---

23. *Soviet Economic Problems and Prospects*, Joint Economic Committee, Congress of the United States (Washington: United States Government Printing Office, 1977).

24. Abram Bergson, "Toward a New Growth Model," *Problems of Communism* (March/April, 1973), pp. 1-9; "Soviet Economic Prospects Revisited," in *The USSR in the 1980's*, NATO, Directorate of Economic Affairs, (Brussels: 1978), pp. 231-242.

reasonably steady gains in all these categories at relatively stable prices, Soviet consumers no doubt expect a continuation of these trends. The Soviet press constantly reinforces these expectations. Positive rates of annual growth in per capita consumption, even if only 1 percent, should meet minimum expectations of progress. The key element probably will be the government's ability to provide better food, which makes up nearly half of consumption. With the massive inputs into agriculture of recent years and in prospect, along with imports of feed grain and continued tolerance of the private sector, Soviet farms should be able to raise output appreciably faster than the population is growing. In turn, consumers will be able to perceive progress on the food front. Growing supplies of agricultural raw materials will also permit increased production of clothing and textiles. The problem in this area is quality, rather than quantity. While progress has been at a snail's pace, the unwieldy production apparatus has managed to improve quality and variety to some degree, as anyone who has visited the USSR several times in the past decade can testify. There is no obvious reason why the system cannot continue to eke out small gains in this area. In respect to both food and clothing, then, some progress can continue even under the worst case scenario; it will not be fast, but it should be perceptible.

The most spectacular gains have been made in providing consumer durables. The Soviet Union has now developed the capacity to produce these symbols of modern civilization, including automobiles and color television sets, and can continue to turn out such desirable goods, gradually improving their design and quality. Certainly, the USSR will not produce and allocate passenger cars to the population at the high rates of growth of recent years, for it cannot afford to provide the requisite roads and service facilities. But stocks will continue to increase, nonetheless. The addition of half a million or so new cars each year is a visible sign of progress in a country with a mere stock of 3 million privately owned cars. With respect to shelter, the USSR has been constructing more than 2 million new apartments annually, and some 11 million persons obtain new housing each year. Again, these gains are highly visible; housing projects are being built in cities throughout the country for all to observe. Even with the probable reduction in investment allocations to housing, the government should be more than able to keep up with the slower population growth that is in prospect. Personal services are in grossly inadequate supply but growing rapidly. Provision of these services requires relatively little investment, but much labor; the government might, however grudgingly, permit more scope for private activity in this field. Finally, the expansion of health and education services is bound to slow in the face of reduced economic growth and a tight labor supply. But the USSR is already ahead of other countries at its level of development in respect to such services—at least in a quantitative sense.

Thus far, the analysis has focused on supply, suggesting that increased availabilities of goods and services probably can be wrung from a slowly growing economy. But what of demand? A key factor in consumers' reactions to slower growing supplies will be the growth of money incomes. To avoid serious erosion of incentives and other undesirable phenomena the government will have to limit the growth of money incomes. This task will not be easy, but the government in the past several years has displayed both the willingness and the ability to do so. During 1971-75, wages rose considerably less rapidly then originally planned. In 1977, average money wages of state employees increased by only 2.7 percent, compared with 4 percent annually during 1960-76. A gain of only 2.4 percent is planned for 1978. If the government fails to limit the growth of money incomes to available goods and services, inflationary pressures in the economy will be increased, with a negative impact on incentives and labor productivity. Savings deposits might continue to pile up, leading a worried government to take some action such as currency revaluation, freezing withdrawals or perhaps diverting them to 'voluntary' public use. A recent press article suggests that people ought to give their savings for building schools, clubs and vacation resorts, rather than squandering them on conspicuous consumption.[25] How the populace would react to such measures is uncertain, but the government has taken similar steps in the past without producing serious popular unrest. Judging from both Soviet and East European experience, strikes and riots are more apt to result from sudden and large increases in prices of staple foods or other long-subsidized items that significantly affect an individual's cost of living.

Assuming that the government continues to provide visible gains across the board, consumers should be able to perceive forward motion, more so, if the economy grows at 3 percent than if it grows at 2 percent. Frequently, the question has been asked: will this be enough? In reply, two questions must be posed: enough for what? and what alternatives do Soviet consumers have? If economic growth continues, even at the reduced rates that are likely, Soviet living standards can still improve perceptibly at best and marginally at worst. Barring unpredictable catastrophies, levels of living will not deteriorate or even stagnate. People tend to judge their lot today in comparison with their lot yesterday; according to this criterion, Soviet consumers should be able to sense modest improvement. Soviet consumers will remain poorly off relative to their counterparts in Western Europe and the United States, where rising real incomes

25. *Literaturnaia Gazeta*, December 14, 1977, p. 10.

are likely to continue, even if also at reduced rates. But the fact that their counterparts in capitalist countries are better off materially may well be a matter of indifference to most Russians. In the first place, they cannot migrate to these countries; and second, they can point to offsetting evils there—unemployment, slums, crime and the like. Surely, the Soviet people are not likely to take to the streets because their own material advance has slowed or their capitalist neighbors are much better off.

A more problematic situation arises in the case of comparison with Eastern European socialist countries, where consumers already fare better in many respects than do Soviet consumers and probably will continue to do so, even with the slower economic growth in prospect there. Should the Soviet government appear to aid Eastern Europe to forestall unrest at the cost of reduced welfare for its own populace, consumer resentment might manifest itself openly, posing a political challenge to the regime. The balance of the needs and interests of client states against those of the domestic populace so as to keep both quiescent will be a delicate task for Brezhnev and his successors. No matter what the outcome, Soviet consumers' wants will remain far from satisfied, leading to much grumbling. But that is an aspect of the human condition; people grumble everywhere. Soviet consumers are accustomed to coping with shortages and the malfunctions of the distribution system; in fact, large numbers of them have found ingenious ways to profit from the disarray. Consumers and workers alike now have a considerable stake in the system. Whatever its faults, it has at long last provided them with something to lose.

One might argue that a substantial slowdown in the growth of real incomes would have an adverse affect on workers' morale and productivity, thus exacerbating the forces leading to reduced economic growth. Russian workers have never been noted for devotion to their jobs; lackadaisical work attitudes and behavior seem characteristic, at least to Western observers. The Soviet press, with its perennial fulminations about lack of labor discipline, seems to agree. It is not obvious that the rapid advance in living standards of the past 25 years has called forth significantly greater work effort, however difficult such things are to assess. Nonetheless, matters might get worse, especially if the government fails to keep a tight lid on the growth of money incomes, in the face of reduced growth of consumer goods production. Presumably, controls, campaigns and penalties would keep things under control.

What measures, then, could elicit the substantially greater work effort that the USSR so urgently needs? One is obvious—more scope for private property and private economic activity. A flourishing second economy and the legal private plots provide ample evidence of the efficacy of private enterprise. Whenever in the past the government has eased restrictions on the private plots, as it has done recently to elicit more meat production, the peasants have responded quickly with increased output. Any relaxation of restrictions on private artisans and the provision of private services would yield similar speedy benefits for consumers.

With industrialization and urbanization have come social ills of the kind that plague modern societies everywhere—crime, disaffected youth, population congestion, drugs, alcoholism, divorce and weakening of family influences. For the USSR, perhaps the most serious social problem is alcoholism, with its adverse affects on work performance and health. Modernization, urbanization and industrialization will continue, even with the reduced economic growth rates that are in prospect. Will slower growth aggravate these social problems? This is a difficult question. The state will have fewer resources to invest in amenities that might alleviate some of the pressures and reduce the drabness and boredom of Soviet life which surely contribute to many of the growing social problems. Housing and recreational facilities are in desperately short supply in relation to demand and can be expanded only very slowly. Relatively fewer goods and services can be provided as an alternative to alcohol. In Western societies social ills are worsened in periods of low economic growth by the presence of large-scale unemployment. In the USSR, where unemployment is replaced by pervasive underemployment, it might be argued that social malaise would be worsened by the general attenuation of incentives and fewer material pleasures that a slower rate of economic progress implies.

The conclusion of this analysis is that the Soviet government and its people can cope with the reduced growth of the economy per se without experiencing serious destabilization. Implicit in this assessment is the assumption that conditions will continue more or less normally. Unpredictable crises could occur, of course, perhaps a series of harvest failures, some kind of operational paralysis of the administrative bureaucracy, large scale uprisings in the USSR or Eastern Europe, or a foreign war. Both the events themselves and their consequences are unpredictable.

A New Political Leadership. In the postwar years, Soviet consumers gained initially from changes in political leadership. Following Stalin's death in 1953 his successor, Georgii Malenkov, announced a "New Course" for the economy with higher priority for production of consumer goods as opposed to producer goods. Rejecting that heresy, Nikita Khrushchev nonetheless initiated measures that at first benefitted consumers. His diverse agricultural policies introduced in the 1950s produced a rapid expansion in farm output and thus in the supply of food, and an even more rapid increase in incomes of the long-neglected farmers. For other groups, welfare benefits were raised, work hours cut, and investment in housing substantially boosted. Khrushchev's latter years saw a retreat from these pro-consumer policies. The new team of Brezhnev and Kosygin began by launching a many-sided program designed to stimulate agricultural output, notably in the production of meat. They, too, expanded welfare programs, extending them to collective farmers. They also put the Soviet Union on the road to the age of the automobile by initiating the mammoth Fiat project to make passenger cars for sale to the population. Furthermore, they launched an economic reform that was designed, among other things, to induce the makers of consumer goods to pay attention to satisfying consumer wants.

If past precedent is any guide, Brezhnev's successors can be expected to seek to curry favor with the population by initiating pro-consumer measures of some kind with a quick, visible payoff. What these measures might be is difficult to predict. The options that will be available are much more limited than those available in previous new booms. Short of a radical systemic reform, there is little more that can be done for agriculture. Agriculture's already large claim on investment resources can hardly be raised further. Large increases in imports of Western food and manufactured consumer goods—which would be greatly welcomed by the populace—would compete for increasingly scarce foreign exhange with imports of Western technology needed for the development of industrial efficiency, Siberian energy, and raw material resources. The same imperatives would constrain any sizeable diversion of dwindling investment funds to the consumer sector. Further increases in wages and welfare benefits would be popular, but to be effective they would have to be matched with corresponding increases in goods and services. As already noted, such gains would be harder to wrest from a more slowly growing total product.

The new leadership will inherit an economy in a state of massive disequilibrium, its consumer sector ridden with problems of the kind already described. The options for dealing effectively with these problems are few and involve unpleasant choices. Alleviation of problems, such as the backlog of neglect in housing, personal services and retail trade facilities, would require large-scale investment. But diversion of funds to those ends would conflict with the needs of other sectors and, in any case, would reduce the overall rate of economic growth. Raising prices to eliminate queues and subsidies (e.g., meat, housing, children's clothing, publications) might spark civil unrest, if the increases were sizeable; moreover such a move would conflict with the much touted policy of preserving stable retail price levels and the socialist approach to redistributing incomes through relative prices. Gradual, piecemeal adjustments in relative prices, however, might be both beneficial and feasible. Expansion of food supplies and personal services by permitting extensive private activity, runs counter to a cherished ideology that worships state ownership of the means of production.

The need to gear production and distribution toward satisfying consumer wants is critical, not only to raise welfare but also to avoid gross waste of resources. The piecemeal, so-called reforms of the past decade have demonstrated that little if anything can be accomplished by half-measures. To be effective, a reform must remove the causes of the malaise. These are: central planning of output and bureaucratic monitoring of the results throughout the economy; a system of incentives geared to meeting these plans with a myriad of details; inflexible and irrational relative prices; and government rationing of materials and equipment to producers. Only a thoroughgoing "marketization" of the production and distribution system promises any significant improvement in these areas. To "marketize" the consumer goods sector alone, as some have suggested, would not be enough. The makers of consumer goods must depend on the producers and distributors of raw materials and machinery for the quality, tailored assortment, and timely deliveries required to ensure a speedy and flexible response to changing consumer demands. A demand-oriented production system is an intricate chain of closely intertwined relationships. Nothing can be accomplished, if some links in the chain are expected to respond flexibly to consumers while other links are required to respond to the instructions of bureaucrats. Moreover, market socialism, despite its persistent advocacy by a few economists, has been ideological anathema to all Soviet leaders since Lenin. Only a profound economic crisis could produce a second NEP.

It is possible, though unlikely, that a new regime might seek a quick remedy for the malaise in the consumer sector by dramatic actions of some kind—perhaps by means of a major reallocation of investment or a genuine reform of economic working arrangements. If the regime were to do so, it would find the short-run costs high, the short-run benefits small, and the opposition of entrenched bureaucracies unrelenting. Any leadership foolhardy enough to increase consumer prices sharply in order to eliminate subsidies or reduce demand would surely have to cope with civil disturbances, as Khrushchev did in the early 1960s. Up to now, no mention has been made of the possibility of curtailing the rapid growth of defense expenditures in order to provide a larger margin for investment or consumption. A bold and less paranoid new leadership might opt for such a policy, but the probable trade-offs in terms of faster growth of civilian output would not be large and would be slow to benefit consumers.[26]

26. *Soviet Economic Problems and Prospects*, p. 16.

Realistically speaking, there is little that a new regime of any political persuasion can do about the state of the consumer sector or about the rate of annual gains in consumption. Leaders and the population alike seem locked into a socio-economic system that has persisted without essential institutional change for fifty years. The problems of economic efficiency and consumer satisfaction are largely systemic in origin. Fundamental solutions to these difficulties require fundamental systemic change, i.e., the bureaucratic economy must be replaced with market relationships. But the experience of other countries shows that market economies, too, are beset with problems, different ones it is true but no less painful. Faced with the high political and human costs of radical change, leaders and the population may prefer to continue with existing, familiar arrangements. Both now have high stakes in the system's preservation, and over the years both have found ways to make its inherent malfunctions more tolerable.

Teresa Rakowska-Harmstone

The Nationalities Question

ETHNIC TRENDS

In the aftermath of World War II a new impetus developed towards national and international integration, and it was widely assumed in the West that ethnic nationalism was a spent force. But the events since show a contradictory trend. Not only has ethnic nationalism provided a major impetus for international conflicts, but it has also emerged as a main force for change within existing states, few of which are ethnically homogeneous. Scholars in numerous disciplines have come to a conclusion that

> ... in the welter of contemporary forms of group expression and group conflict there is both something new and something common; there has been a pronounced and sudden increase in tendencies by people in many countries and in many circumstances to insist on the significance of their group distinctiveness and identity and on new rights to derive from this group character.[1]

1. Nathan Glazer and Daniel P. Moynihan, "Introduction," in Nathan Glazer and Daniel P. Moynihan, eds., *Ethnicity: Theory and Experience* (Cambridge, Mass.: Harvard University Press, 1975), pp. 2-3.

Ethnic conflict, to be sure, is not a new phenomenon, but in multi-ethnic societies around the world it has acquired new and increasingly important political dimensions. First, it has been ascertained that, although the origins and causes of ethnic rivalries are not new, their incidence, scale and intensity around the world have increased rapidly. Secondly, there is growing evidence,

> that *interest* is pursued effectively by *ethnic groups* today as well as by *interest*-defined groups; indeed, perhaps it can be pursued even more effectively. As against class-based forms of social identification and conflict—which of course continue to exist—we have been surprised by the persistence and salience of ethnic-based forms of social identification and conflict.[2]

This has been so because, in a society where the apportionment of resources has become a function of the state (in a Western type welfare state as well as in the socialist one-party states), it is now strategically more efficacious to aggregate interests on an ethnic base.

The strategic efficacy of ethnicity as a basis for asserting claims against the government has its counterpart in the seeming ease whereby government employs ethnic categories as a basis for distributing its rewards.[3]

Thirdly, while interests continue to play a key role in group demands, their aggregation based on ethnic affiliations

> has become more salient [than class] because it can combine interest with an affective tie. Ethnicity provides a tangible set of common identifications—in language, food, music, names—when other social roles become more abstract and impersonal. In the competition for the values of the society to be realized politically, ethnicity can become a means of claiming place or advantage.[4]

Western theories of ethnicity, of national and international integration, and of communal conflict management, have been derived largely from the experience of Western democracies and of the developing world; the Soviet Union and the other classic multi-ethnic Communist state, Yugoslavia, enter the discussion only mar-

2. Ibid., p. 7.
3. Glazer and Moynihan, p. 10.
4. Daniel Bell, "Ethnicity and Social Change," in Glazer and Moynihan, p. 169.

ginally, and little if any empirical evidence has been drawn from the study of Communist states. Nevertheless, and despite very different systemic constraints, most of the Western scholars' findings are readily applicable to Soviet experience, and provide valuable insights into future trends there.

The Soviet Union is a multi-ethnic state par excellence. Moreover, the intensity of ethnic rivalries within it is maximized because the Soviet state is also a double anachronism: it is the last surviving 19th century colonial empire (if I may be forgiven for using a cliché), and the legitimacy of its political system rests on a 19th century ideology struggling to maintain its salience under modern conditions. In ethnic relations the meaning of the first anachronism is that major non-Russian ethnic groups have never had the experience of realizing their aspirations for national statehood[5]—as did East-Central Europeans in the interwar period and Asians and Africans after World War II—and thus they combine "old-fashioned" 19th century nationalism with ethnic demands generated by modern conditions. Their drive for national self-assertion is therefore fuelled by what Daniel Bell calls "historical energies driving them forward to seek a place on the stage of history"[6] (as will be seen below, the importance of this factor is recognized also by Soviet scholars), and places them in direct conflict with the then and still imperial Russian nation. The second anachronism imposes an obligatory framework on the direction of ethnic studies and policy. Contrary to empirical evidence—in the Soviet Union as elsewhere—it postulates disappearance of ethnicity and the emergence of class as the basis for integration. This outdated ideological perception conditions Soviet analysis of ethnic relations as well as relevant policy decisions.

As discussed by this author and others elsewhere, the last two decades in the Soviet Union have been marked by a remarkable growth in the manifestations of ethnic self-assertion by major non-Russian ethnic groups, a phenomenon accompanied also by a visible upsurge of Russian nationalism within the official establishment as well as among dissident groups.[7] The existence and growing intensity of ethnic conflict has been recognized by the Soviet leadership— even though the "national problem" is officially said to have been solved—and this recognition has been reflected in a new impetus in the development of Soviet ethnic studies. Historians are generally in charge of interpreting and elucidating the party line, projecting it

5. The three Baltic republics are an exception here.
6. Bell, p. 164.
7. See Alexander Yanov, *The Russian New Right: Right-Wing Ideologies in the Contemporary USSR* (Berkeley: Institute of International Studies, University of California, 1978), Research Series, No. 35; and John Dunlop, *The New Russian Revolutionaries* (Belmont, Mass.: Nordland Press, 1976).

back into the past and forward into the future, but the main burden of the reconciliation of empirical data with ideological postulates rests on the shoulders of ethnographers.

Ideology, and particularly Lenin's postulates on the nature of national relations and their direction of development, impose a straitjacket on Soviet ethnographers; even so, many of their findings parallel those of the Western scholars—another indication that ethnic trends in the Soviet Union are not unique just because they occur at the "socialist stage of historical development" (as the party maintains), but are a part of a world-wide phenomenon. The interpretation of the findings, nevertheless, has to conform to the ruling dogma, and the direction of research is subordinate to political needs of the party. The bias is explicit. Ethnography is a "historical science based on Marxist-Leninist ideology": it "performs not only cognitive but also ideological functions (and) is opposed to objectivism and indifference to politics."[8] Lenin's myth more than ever supplies the regime's legitimacy, and Lenin's dicta are more binding now than when he was alive. Thus his expectations that national loyalties will be replaced by class loyalty as the basis for political integration impose binding interpretations on the study of ethnic phenomena, and his "discovery" that each national culture contains two cultures, a progressive and a reactionary one, "requires a partisan approach to the cultural legacy of each people and an ability to distinguish what is advanced and progressive in this legacy,"[9] to be determined authoritatively by the party.

The party line for the 'sixties and 'seventies has been formulated by the 1961 program of the Communist Party of the Soviet Union (CPSU). It proclaimed that as a result of the implementation of the Leninist nationality policy, a "new historical community, the Soviet people," has emerged in the Soviet Union, with all Soviet nations and nationalities "ever growing closer together," in a process of rapprochement *(sblizhenie)* leading to an eventual merger *(sliianie)* in a dialectical leap that would result in a qualitatively new entity.[10] In the 'seventies, however, the growing realization of the complexity of the problem forced some modifications. The timetable for the merger was extended into an indefinite future, and new emphasis was placed on the need to accelerate research into ethnic phenomena. The study

---

8. Yu. V. Bromley, *Soviet Ethnography: Main Trends* (Moscow: USSR Academy of Sciences, "Social Sciences Today" Editorial Board, 1977), Problems of the Contemporary World (42), p. 72.

9. Ibid., p. 65.

10. Leo Gruliow and Charlotte Saikowski, eds., *Current Soviet Policies IV: The Documentary Record of the 22nd Congress of the Communist Party of the Soviet Union* (New York: Columbia University Press, 1962), p. 26.

of factors functional to Soviet national integration is seen as "particularly urgent."[11]

A leading Soviet ethnographer, Academician Yu. V. Bromley, supplies the current version of the theory of ethnic processes.[12] It starts from a basic Leninist assumption that the development of nations under capitalism is characterized by two tendencies. First, characteristic of early capitalism, is the tendency towards national awakening which develops as a response to national oppression; it leads to the formation of national states. Second, stimulated by "the creation of international unity of capital, of economic life in general, of politics, science, etc.,"[13] is the tendency to develop international contacts which serve to break down national barriers. The latter occurs in the period of mature capitalism and continues into the period following the socialist revolution. But the actual experience after the Bolshevik Revolution led to certain modifications in Lenin's analysis. Both tendencies are acknowledged to have survived, and ethnic characteristics are said to continue to evolve, "in a transformed shape."[14] The two tendencies were accordingly redefined by the 1961 CPSU Program. Under socialism the tendency towards national consolidation took the form of flourishing *(rastsvetanie)* of each nation; the tendency towards integration took the form of rapprochement. Interaction of both can be observed in the socio-economic as well as in the ethnic sphere.

Reality intruding, the continuation and the strength of the tendency to flourish had to be explained even though, with national oppression (by definition) removed, it should have disappeared. The official explanation is that Soviet nations and nationalities were unable to fulfill their national destiny under tsarism (compare Bell's point of "historical energies"), and thus had to undergo "particularly intensive" and "accelerated" processes of "national consolidation" under socialism. In the borderlands, national consolidation took the form of "the amalgamation of linguistically and culturally kindred tribal and territorial groups" (new nations of Central Asia are an example); in the more developed areas, "large peoples became even more closely knit" and in the process absorbed smaller ethnic groups. The effects of the latter type of assimilation can be observed by

    11. Bromley, p. 148.
    12. The discussion of the theory of ethnic processes is based on Bromley, *Soviet Ethnography*, III. 1, "National (Ethnosocial) Processes in the USSR," pp. 142-169, and Bromley, "Ethnic Aspects of Contemporary National Processes," *Istoria SSSR*, 3 (May/June, 1977), pp. 19-28.
    13. Bromley, *Soviet Ethnography*, p. 145.
    14. The tendencies were transformed because of the radical change in all of the characteristics of a nation after the establishment of socialism: economic base, class structure, socio-political aspirations, and spiritual aspects. Ibid., p. 147.

comparing decreasing numbers of enumerated ethnic groups in successive Soviet censuses.[15] On the whole

> Soviet experience shows that the abolition of antagonistic classes in socialist society sharply intensifies the processes of the so-called ethnic consolidation, that is the rapid growth of the ethnic homogeneity of nations.[16]

The rapprochement tendency is defined as "processes of interaction of basic ethnic units substantially differing in terms of their linguistic and cultural parameters, which result in an appearance of some common ethnic features."[17] Based on Leninist "objective laws of economic development," the processes are assumed to be taking place in the Soviet Union because of the "removal of inequalities," because of the "division of labor based on professional, not national identity," on "regional and not ethnic factors," and because of "ethnic intermixture" in urban centers, all caused by economic development. Economic integration thus achieved complements political integration and a new "homogeneous social structure," and is cemented by common ideology, seen as the main integrative value. Rapprochement in all the above spheres is said to be accompanied by rapprochement in the ethnic sphere (defined narrowly as cultural attributes and self-perception).[18] The evidence of lack of progress in the latter has been troublesome, however. It is conceded that ethnic change proceeds "much more slowly" than socio-economic rapprochement, because of the markedly stable and conservative character of ethnic attributes, which have been known to survive (even if "transformed") several changes in socio-economic historical formations.[19]

Interaction between flourishing and rapprochement is said to be a complex one, and for any one group it may proceed "on different tiers or sometimes even in different directions," so that it "finds itself

15. Ibid., pp. 151-152. In 1926 there were 194 groups; in 1959—109; in 1970—104. The process of assimilation of smaller groups, notes Bromley, is now almost completed as seen in insignificant variation in numbers between 1959 and 1970. It continues for individuals who move away from their ethnic territory and for dispersed groups. In the discussion of assimilation Lenin is always carefully quoted to the effect that while forced assimilation is "bad," "natural assimilation" is "progressive," and is proceeding happily in the Soviet Union as seen in the statistics of linguistic assimilation (see Table 2), and mixed marriages (see below).

16. Ibid., p. 16.
17. Ibid., p. 46.
18. Ibid., pp. 154-156.
19. Ibid., pp. 47-49. The Armenian culture, for example, survived the changes from slave to feudal to bourgeois capitalist to socialist, historical stages in the development of socio-economic systems.

involved both in the 'internal' development of the ethnos toward consolidation as an independent system, and simultaneously in the process toward uniting this ethnos with other ethnic formations."[20] Thus the interaction "still bears a dialectically contradictory though not antagonistic character."[21] Obviously, serious Soviet students of the ethnic problem do not find it as easily solved as one might expect from official pronouncements, and they experience increasing difficulties in trying to reconcile contradictory trends involved with the deterministic expectations of Lenin, whose observations were based on experience that is no longer relevant.

The following sections of the paper are devoted to an analysis of the direction of ethnic trends as they relate to key features of the Soviet system and society. These will be assessed in the light of available empirical evidence and scholarly findings. The key question directing this inquiry is whether the trends are indicative of further ethnic/national differentiation, as is the case in other multi-ethnic societies, or whether the trends indeed point to an inevitable integration as claimed by the official Soviet doctrine. The answer to this question will determine available policy alternatives; these then will be assessed in the light of the likelihood of their adoption and their probable future impact on centrifugal ethnic forces.

NUMBERS AND CULTURE

There is a consensus among students of ethnicity that a balance in the weight of ethnic communities and their relatively equal status in multi-ethnic societies, as well as a high degree of shared culture values, are important prerequisites for a successful integration. Both these factors facilitate adjustments and compromise in negotiating ethnic conflicts. Neither of these conditions is present in the Soviet Union. The Soviet ethnic mix is unbalanced, and cultural differentiation of major ethnic groups remains and grows despite 60 years of intensive political socialization.

In 1970, the date of the last population census, ethnic Russians constituted 53 percent of the total Soviet population of 242 million. The remainder was divided among over one hundred other ethnic groups. Of these, 21 groups numbered over 1 million people each (see Table 1). It is major nations that have experienced the flourishing phenomenon, in contrast to most of the smaller groups that appear to be assimilating either into the dominant Russian or into surrounding larger and culturally more cohesive ethnic communities. The 14

20. Ibid., p. 47.
21. Ibid., p. 163.

(Russians are the 15th) union republic nations are among the 21 with a population over 1 million, and it is their growing national self-assertion that poses a threat to Russian hegemony and places in doubt the hopes for a successful integration of the Soviet state. Four among the 21 have lower level autonomous republics[22] (border location is a prerequisite for union republic status). These also show signs of flourishing, but at much lower intensity. The remaining three (the Jews, the Poles and the Germans), are geographically dispersed and under strong assimilatory pressures.[23]

The Russians' leading role is assured not only by their quantitative weight but also by their qualitative standing. Their traditional ruling status survived intact the transition from the Russian Empire to the Soviet socialist state and has been a key factor in the consolidation of the Soviet political system. Only the Latvians and Estonians top the Russians in co-efficients of socio-economic development. The perception of the Russians' ruling status by other groups is further enhanced by the memory of imperial conquests. As is well known, Soviet historiography has run the whole gamut in their interpretation, from condemning Russian imperialism in the 'twenties, through a theory of the lesser evil, to the current recognition of the conquests as progressive because they enabled conquered peoples to experience the Revolution and thus to enter the socialist stage of development. The hegemonial role of any one national group in an internationalist society is ideologically indefensible but the Russian leading role is, in fact, officially recognized in the concept of the most advanced nation (better known as the "Big Brother" syndrome). The Russian hegemonial role fuels social dynamics of inequality, one of the key sources of conflict in multi-ethnic societies, and gives the lie to Soviet assertion that the national oppression of the minorities no longer exists.

> In a situation of mixed ethnic groups where one group is dominant, which is to say that its norms are seen as normal not just for it but for others also, there follows an almost automatic consignment of other groups to inferior status.[24]

22. The Tatar group includes Volga Tatars with an autonomous republic, and the Crimean Tatars who were deprived of their autonomous republic during the war for alleged collaboration with the invading Germans. They were deported to Central Asia. The saga of the Crimean Tatars' efforts to regain their national home, despite dispersal, is well known. The Tatar group is the most highly urbanized group among Soviet Moslems. (See Table 2.)

23. The Volga Germans, who had an autonomous republic, were also deprived of their national status for alleged collaboration with the enemy and were also deported to Central Asia. They continue to petition the authorities for the restoration of their national area.

24. Glazer and Moynihan, p. 14.

In the opinion of this author, the "Russian fact" has been the catalytic agent in the growth of national self-assertion of major non-Russian groups and has generated ethnic conflict, triggering the demands for the redistribution of power and resources and for the "redefinition of equality as a major value."[25]

A compact settlement pattern of large ethnic communities has been another related factor that has contributed to the strength of their national self-assertion; geographic dispersal favors assimilation. The major interregional population shifts that have taken place since the Revolution primarily reflect movements by ethnic Russians; among other groups, only Ukrainians and Byelorussians have migrated out of their ethnic-regional areas in statistically significant numbers. Migration trends of the non-Russians generally have been rural to urban rather than interregional, and consequently their areas of settlement and concentration have remained largely unchanged through the years of Soviet power (see Table 1). The geographic compactness of ethnic settlement has preserved and nourished national cultures, has assured continuous socialization by traditional agents (family and religion), and has facilitated the prevalent endogamy.[26] In general, it has provided major ethnic communities with a basis for what Soviet ethnographers call "national consolidation." At present there are no signs of impending changes in ethnic settlement, but change could be effected if, following official encouragement and economic incentives, spontaneous migration between regions picks up, or if there are any new large-scale deportations or directed resettlement.

The pattern of migration stimulated by industrialization and economic development has resulted in rapid urbanization, but the rate of urbanization for all the non-Russian ethnic groups (except the Armenians and the dispersed and urbanized Jews) has been lower than the USSR average; for the Russians it has been significantly higher (see Table 2). Following economic opportunity, favorable conditions, and political, administrative, and managerial needs, the Russians flocked into urban and industrial centers throughout the Union. This means that cities in national republics and national areas are predominantly Russian in ethnic composition. As the rural to urban migration of the non-Russians is stimulated by modernization, the resulting competition for jobs and a "place in the sun" contributes to ethnic antagonism.

The impact of modernization has also affected fertility rates which, predictably, have declined for most developed groups. The

25. Bell, p. 146.
26. Bromley considers endogamy a "unique stabilizer" of ethnic identity. See I.2, "Ethnos and Endogamy," pp. 24-39, and supplement, in Bromley, *Soviet Ethnography*, "Discussion of Yu. V. Bromley's Article 'Ethnos and Endogamy'," pp. 247-301.

Russians now have a reproduction coefficient lower than 1, while the less developed groups have continued to maintain high birth rates reinforced, in the case of Soviet Moslems in particular, by cultural factors. This has resulted in the population explosion in Central Asia, a subject of much concern to Soviet decision makers with regard to its political as well as economic consequences. As a result, the Russian share in the Soviet population has declined between the last two censuses (1959 to 1970) as did its predominance in the populations of the Caucasian and Central Asian republics (see Table 1), trends that are projected to continue, even if at reduced rates, for the next two decades. The aging of the European population contrasts with the growing cohorts of young people in the southeastern regions. This will affect the manpower situation (with future labor available only in Central Asia and consisting of unskilled, culturally alienated Moslem youths, most of whom do not speak Russian) as well as the military draft. It may require political decisions that would either strengthen ethnic aspirations (if long-range investments are authorized for economic development and equalization of Central Asia) or might lead to possible uprisings (if unwilling Central Asians are subjected to forced labor draft or resettlement).[27]

Cultural differentiation characteristic of the peoples of the Russian Empire at the time of the Revolution ranged from traditional Moslem communities in Central Asia and Azerbaidzhan, and ancient Orthodox cultures of Georgia and Armenia, to culturally western Baltic regions, differences being reinforced by linguistic and religious factors. Under the impact of the policy of national form (to be discussed below) this differentiation in the case of major ethnic groups is not only undiminished but is accelerating. Soviet sources acknowledge that, despite the diffusion of "internationalist ideology" the development of national ethnic culture "was of an ethnically differentiating rather than integrating type," emphasizing "such elements of traditional culture and . . . national art as are primarily linked with satisfying the spiritual needs of the members of the respective ethnic communities."[28] Neither the ethnic intermixture in the cities, nor the widely heralded increase in ethnic intermarriage (which at any rate does not exceed 10 percent of the total, USSR-wide), nor the spread of the knowledge of Russian as the universal language

---

27. For the discussion of the impact of demographic trends see Murray Feshbach and Stephen Rapawy, "Soviet Population and Manpower Trends and Policies," in *Soviet Economy in a New Perspective,* Joint Economic Committee, Congress of the United States (Washington: United States Government Printing Office, 1976), pp. 113-154; and this author's forthcoming "Ethnicity and Demographic Change in the Soviet Union; Problems and Prospects," *Ethnicity.*

28. Bromley, *Soviet Ethnography,* p. 157; 163.

as seen in the statistics on bilingualism,[29] has had any impact on a veritable national cultural renaissance among major non-Russian ethnic groups; nor has it influenced their refusal to integrate into the largely Russian-in-content internationalist culture. This is dysfunctional to integration: broad consensus exists among Western scholars on the disintegrative effects of cultural diversity in multi-ethnic societies.

In almost all theories of integration, a high degree of cultural homogeneity, and especially a homogeneous political culture, is considered a prerequisite for political integration.[30]

Such a cultural homogeneity should include community of thoughts and feelings, common attachment to symbols, and mutual compatibility of main values. In the Soviet Union, ethnic elites have been socialized into the Marxist-Leninist political culture, but its integrative value is negated by their resentment of the "Big Brother." Consequently, the ethnic elites are in the forefront of national self-assertion and thus have an affective tie with the masses and a strategically efficacious base for the assertion of particular demands.

STRUCTURAL FEATURES

The Soviet Union is a federal state, run on the principle of democratic centralism by a unitary Communist party that exercises total

---

29. Ibid. According to Bromley, there were 102 mixed families for every 1,000 in the USSR in 1970, but the ratio was higher for the urbanites in Byelorussia (237), in the Ukraine (263), and in Moldavia (269). The ratio was less than 10 percent, however, in the cities of the Baltic republics (4.6 percent in Tallin, 7.4 percent in Riga), and over 50 percent of the children of mixed families opted for the titular nationality (52 percent in Vilnius, 52 percent in Riga, 62 percent in Tallin). See L.N. Terentieva, "The Determination of National Identity by Youths in Nationally-mixed Families," *Sovetskaia Etnografia*, 3 (1969), pp. 20-30. At the same time it is acknowledged that "if no more than 10 to 15 percent marry outside the group, it is still comparatively 'safe' as far as the integrity of the ethnos is concerned." See, I. M. Zolotareva, in Bromley, *Soviet Ethnography*, supplement, p. 281. For the statistics on bilingualism, see Table 1.

30. Arend Lijphart, "Cultural Diversity and Theories of Political Integration," *Canadian Journal of Political Science*, 4:1, p. 4. Compare Deutsch's emphasis on integration as the "attainment of a sense of community" in "Political Community and the North Atlantic Area," in Karl Deutsch et al., eds., *International Political Communities: An Anthology* (New York: Anchor Books, 1966), pp. 1-91; also L. Binder, "National Integration and Political Development," *American Political Science Review*, 58:3 (September, 1964); and J. S. Coleman and C. G. Rosberg, *Political Parties and National Integration in Tropical Africa* (Berkeley: University of California, 1964).

monopoly of political power. The structure of the system is based on the formula, "national in form—socialist in content," devised by Lenin as a compromise (and perhaps as a transitional device only) between the contending claims of the autonomists and assimilationists in the early 'twenties. Both aspects of the formula have had far-reaching effects on the development of ethnic relations. The "socialist content" aspect was the vehicle for integration, but also for Russian hegemony. The "national form" aspect resulted in the implementation of a cultural policy that allowed for the use and development of national languages (in education, mass media and cultural offerings) and culture forms, the better to transmit the socialist message. Now these have been turned into the vehicle for national self-assertion. Even more important, the national form resulted in a federal arrangement whereby main units of territorial administration (the republics) were carved out along the lines of ethnic settlement. This gave major ethnic groups an economic and a bureaucratic base (both within the state and party organization) for interest aggregation. Soviet ethnographers readily recognize the importance of Soviet state structure for national consolidation processes:

> The rise of national state forms (republics, regions, districts) not only fixed the results of such (national) amalgamation but created favourable conditions for the development of the peoples that had come into being, of their culture, language, etc.[31]

The ethnic base for interest aggregation thus created has been enhanced by other features of the system. By definition, the Soviet Union is a conflict-free society of non-antagonistic classes. Thus Western style interest groups of the associational type cannot be formed as autonomous subsystems and there are no institutionalized mechanisms for conflict resolution. This, in effect, leaves the ethnic based territorial administrative units—the republics—as the only legitimate subsystems for interest aggregation for the non-Russians. Institutional interest groups and "tendencies of articulation" that do exist and significantly influence political process[32] are of little value to ethnic elites. Under the operational principle of democratic centralism ethnic leaders have no hope to influence decision making at the federal level, where they are an under-represented and fragmented minority, except by aggregating interests vertically

31. Bromley, *Soviet Ethnography*, p. 152.
32. See H. Gordon Skilling and Franklyn Griffiths, eds., *Interest Groups in Soviet Politics* (Princeton: Princeton University Press, 1971) and other literature on Soviet pressure groups.

along the ethnic axis. Overlapping group memberships (which provide a balance to ethnic aggregation) are considered essential for the purposes of successful integration.[33] In the absence of associational groups in the Soviet Union, two structural subdivisions cut across republican boundaries: economic regions and military districts. It is the federal prerogative to manage both. There are few, if any, inputs from the ethnic elites and, thus, such management has no value as a balancing factor to ethnic based cleavages.

With its de facto centralization the Soviet federal system has contributed to ethnic disintegration. It divides the country along the lines of basic cultural cleavages, ethnic, religious and linguistic (as in the case of India and Canada, where such division is felt to reinforce ethnic conflict[34]), and at the same time channels ethnic interest aggregation along vertical lines.

IDEOLOGICAL MATRIX

> Marxist-Leninist ideology, which is internationalist and rejects all elements of ethno-religious and nationalist ideology, is a most important element of interethnic integration.[35]

Is it really? The claim that Marxist-Leninist ideology has "everywhere ousted the elements of ethno-religious and nationalist ideology" in the perception of Soviet ethnic groups (including the Russians) appears to be no more than wishful thinking. Marxism-Leninism is so much at variance with Soviet reality that its impact, along with continuous and repetitive efforts at political socialization, appears to be counterproductive. At the same time it provides an ideological matrix that lends legitimacy to ethnic claims. Lenin recognized the principle of national self determination as a valid one in the transition period before a common class-based sense of political identity is established. Assuming that each national group concentrates on the development of the progressive aspects of its national culture, its right to flourish is not only legitimate but is officially encouraged. At the same time, the ideology precludes legitimization of the hegemonial position of the Russians in the Soviet system despite the recognition of their "leading role." This proscription appears to be a source of growing frustration to some elements in the Russian dominated leadership. Any changes, however, in this

---

33. Lijphart, p. 5; also, S. M. Lipset, *Political Man; The Social Bases of Politics* (Garden City: Doubleday, 1963), p. 77; and D. B. Truman, *The Governmental Process: Political Interests and Public Opinion* (New York: 1951), pp. 508-516.
34. Lipset, pp. 91-92.
35. Bromley, *Soviet Ethnography*, p. 113.

crucial internationalist aspect of ideology might affect not only the system's domestic legitimacy but also the global goals of Soviet foreign policy. Internationalist unity is the base for Soviet-East European relations in the newly emergent World Socialist system: the relations between its members are said to be based on the same "national in form—socialist in content" principle, and involve the same rapprochement process as do the relations between members of the Soviet "family of nations."[36] The internationalist claim (combined with the CPSU's senior role as the most experienced partner), also supplies the first line of defense against Eurocommunists' emphasis on their own road to socialism and against Chinese accusations of hegemonism. It also plays an important role in Soviet aspirations to the leadership of Third World's progressive forces. All of these foreign policy ventures have had an impact on the ethnic demands of Soviet national elites. Examples of relative sovereignty of East European states, the independence from Soviet dictates of China and Yugoslavia and of most non-ruling parties, and the success of national self-assertion in Asia and Africa are observed and translated into demands for greater autonomy and for real participation in decision making.

A point has been made that, except for anti-imperialism, there has been a marked decline in the appeal of old ideologies worldwide, and as civil theology is breaking down, centrifugal forces gain.[37] Marxism-Leninism seems to be a case in point. Moreover, in the domestic context, the Soviet Union appears to be particularly vulnerable to anti-imperialist appeals despite the fact that, or possibly because, it has set itself up as the champion of anti-imperialism outside its own borders.

IMPACT OF MODERNIZATION

It is an article of faith in the Soviet Union that economic development serves to break down ethnic barriers and to undermine specific national loyalties (as posited by Lenin). Thus economic integration, which has now been largely achieved, contributes to national integration, a point of view not far removed from classical Western theory of modernization as formulated by Karl Deutsch. Western theories have been significantly modified in line with empirical findings in Western Europe and elsewhere, but a recogni-

36. See this author's "'Socialist Internationalism' and Eastern Europe—A New Stage," *Survey*, 22:1, 98 (Winter, 1976); and "'Socialist Internationalism'—Part II," *Survey*, 22:2, 99 (Spring, 1976).
37. Bell, pp. 149-151.

tion in the Soviet Union that the "objective laws of economic development" do not work would be tantamount to an admission of bankruptcy of the system's major ideological premise.

The Soviet Union is undergoing rapid urbanization against a background of universal literacy and broad access ... to the achievements of modern culture made possible by an extensive and efficient system of public education and modern technical means of communications. As national cultures develop (and this is accompanied by corresponding changes in the traditional forms of people's everyday life), they are at the same time drawing closer together in all spheres of material and intellectual life; social distinctions and barriers are disappearing owing to increasing social mobility.... All these processes point to the fact that a new historical community—the Soviet people—is being formed. ...[38]

In fact, while economic development and modernization have broadly affected all of the Soviet nations and nationalities, the results have served to maximize rather than to minimize the old ethnic rivalries. All of the national areas have achieved high rates of economic growth and benefitted from expanded educational, social service, and communications networks, with rates of growth highest in the areas which initially had been least developed. But, given differentials in the initial take-off base, growth rates have done little to change relative economic and social status of ethnic groups or to fulfill the avowed commitment to equalization. Economic and social development co-efficients are still highest in the northwest and lowest in the southeast (see Table 2). Asian parts of the country are still the raw materials base of the Soviet economy, with manufacturing and processing centered west of the Urals. Social benefits per capita for the Asians are still one-third to one-half of those available to the Europeans.[39] The discrepancies appear even greater when

38. Bromley, *Soviet Ethnography*, pp. 102-103.

39. A Kazakh economist who argues for a massive increase in long range investments in Central Asia reveals that industrial production per capita in Central Asia equals approximately one half of the USSR average, machine-building production is three times less, and petroleum production almost two times less. Eastern and southeastern regions lag behind European regions in distribution of consumer goods, communal services (health, education and culture), in the infrastructure (energy, transport, communications), and in real wages. A. A. Koshanov, "Socio-economic Aspects of Regional Development in the Period of Mature Socialism," *Izvestiia Akademii Nauk Kazakhskoi SSR*, Seriia Obshchestvennykh Nauk, 3 (May/June, 1975), pp. 20-29.

considered in the light of rural-urban differentials. On the whole, major national groups underwent social mobilization at differential rates, with the resulting juxtaposition of rising expectations and a sense of relative deprivation articulated in ethnic terms by their newly evolved modernized elites. Because of the nature of the Soviet political system the sense of relative deprivation applies not only to the socio-economic sphere (where Baltic nations, for example, would have little to complain about), but also to political life. Ethnic elites participate in the power structures of their republics, and occasionally emerge at the federal level, but always as junior partners to the Russians.

The impact of economic integration and modernization on ethnic relations in the Soviet Union, in fact, differs little from the impact observed elsewhere. Experience with integration in Western Europe indicates that a functional economic approach is not sufficient for purposes of political integration if there is no parallel political commitment and that success in economic integration leads to the growth of political disagreements, triggered by conflicting national interests.[40] Deutsch observes also that an increase in the volume and range of mutual transactions—inherent in modernization as well as in an international integration effort—tends to create greater opportunities for conflict;[41] yet an increase in the range and volume of inter-ethnic transactions has been deliberately pursued by Soviet policy makers as a part of the rapprochement process. Experience of modernization in the Third World also indicates that it tends to exacerbate ethnic conflict, to intensify hostile beliefs and feelings, and to heighten competition for access to educational opportunities and to jobs.[42] Moreover, as seen in Africa, expectations that modernization will foster universalism—reminiscent of Soviet expectations of assimilation into a common Marxist-Leninist value system—have not been realized.[43] As modernization and economic development policies continue in the Soviet Union, for reasons of integration as well as the country's economic needs, such expecta-

40. Lijphart, pp. 11-12.
41. Karl Deutsch, *Political Community at the International Level: Problems of Definition and Measurement* (Garden City: Doubleday, 1954), pp. 39-40.
42. Bell, pp. 149-151.
43. As Pierre van den Berghe observes: "A polity of universalism based on merit is represented by the 'backward' groups as a cloak to maintain the head start by the 'advanced' groups. . . . Given this restricted opportunity structure, and the existence of ethnic cleavages, it can be expected that competition within the privileged classes would be along ethnic lines . . . ," "Ethnicity; The African Experience," *International Social Science Journal*, 23:4 (1971), p. 515.

tions may contribute even further to aggravation of inter-ethnic rivalries.

ROLE OF THE ELITES

The crucial role of national elites in the articulation and regulation of ethnic conflict is generally recognized in the literature on ethnicity. The elites' contribution toward maximization or moderation of conflict is seen variously as the function of political culture, commitment (or lack thereof) to system maintenance, the nature of issues involved and their bargainability, prospects of power and/or economic gain, legitimacy and a degree of mass support, structural leeway and incentives available, and so on.[44] In the Soviet Union, the articulation of national demands by ethnic elites within the system (those outside are either liquidated or have no access to the power structure), dates to the "autonomists" among the Bolsheviks, of whom the Ukrainian communists were the most prominent. It was continued, by the new elites which evolved under the *korenizatsiia* (building of national roots) policy of the 'twenties (both groups were purged in the 'thirties), and in the last two decades by the increasingly numerous national cadres which began to ascend party and state apparati after World War II. Their participation in the power structure has been growing, but, as pointed out above, their power has always been circumscribed by the ubiquitous Russians. The Russians tend to dominate the federal level of both bureaucracies, and federal representatives at the republic level—whose major function has been to maintain central control—have generally been of Russian ethnic origin or Russified, injecting an element of ethnic rivalry into federal-republican relations. In the republics the ratio of local functionaries in key party and government bodies has grown since the 'fifties, although pivotal positions (such as that of Second Secretary of the republican parties' Central Committee who controls personnel appointments), continue to be staffed by emissaries from the center. Greater access to politically important posts at the republic level has resulted in more clearly articulated ethnic demands.

An espousal of local interests serves purposes of legitimization at home. It generates support by local bureaucracies and good will of a

---

44. See Arend Lijphart, "Consociational Democracy," *World Politics* (January, 1969); Eric A. Nordlinger, *Conflict Regulation in Divided Societies*, Occasional Papers in International Affairs (Center for International Affairs: Harvard University, 1972); Richard Rose, *Governing Without Consensus: An Irish Perspective* (Boston: Beacon Press, 1971), and others.

broader mass constituency, the latter particularly when cultural matters are involved. In the political sphere, ethnic demands generated by national leaders center on the promotion of ethnic cadres locally (at the expense of the Russian element), and on greater access to decision making, locally and in Moscow. In the economic sphere, republican interests are more and more clearly and insistently articulated. Demands are directed primarily at securing a greater share of the federal pie (especially as resources are getting scarce) and minimizing contributions, as well as trying to protect the republics from unwelcome ventures or innovations. In cultural matters, where leeway is broadest because of the "national form" policy, local leaders openly and vigorously promote the development of national cultures at the expense of internationalism and Russian models, and frequently in violation of official policies. Local leaders, the most outspoken of whom risk being purged, nevertheless seek to operate strictly within systemic constraints. They seek legitimacy in Lenin's views on national relations, interpreted in favor of genuine equality, as well as in formal constitutional provisions. They play power politics in Moscow, seeking powerful patrons and bargaining away the support of their regional power base in factional struggles. Participation in All-Union power politics has for obvious reasons been more rewarding to ethnic elites during the periods of collective leadership than in times of one man's ascendancy.

Because of the centralized nature of the system, there can be no question of real autonomy for the republics. In Moscow the influence exercised by republican elites is generally minimal, even though the republics' formal representation in central state and party bodies has increased since the 'fifties. Ethnic elites have little collective input into All-Union decision making processes, except in cases of individual pull. In the economic sphere in particular, the command planning system assures central supremacy and there is almost no recognition of republican demands. This generates a growing and steadily more visible conflict over resource allocation and jurisdictional matters. Cultural independence exhibited by the republics' political leaders and intellectual elites has been the subject of constant criticism from Moscow. Conflicts over language purification, over the use of national languages in higher professional and technical education, over the use of contemporary internationalist vs. traditional and historical themes in literature and fine arts and, last but not least, the battle of historiography, have been the source of constant aggravation to both sides and a reason for the downfall of many an ethnic leader.

In their political roles, ethnic elites exhibit ambiguity and divided loyalties. Those who succeed in ascending to the federal level tend to assume the prevalent Russian coloration and to pursue centrist interests, except when they are in charge of their republics (as in the case of the republican First Secretaries who are all members of the CPSU Central Committee, some of whom have a seat on the politbureau). When at home they promote local interests, but it is by no means clear whether they do so from national loyalty or because it is required by their political roles; Shelest and Mzhavanadze, recently purged First Secretaries of the Ukrainian and Georgian party organizations, are cases in point. Mikoyan, for many years a member of the CPSU leadership, is said to have been very "Armenian" when at home. Members of ethnic elites are committed to system maintenance because they are a part of its power structure and share many of the common political values although, in some cases, the pull of national culture may be very strong. Nevertheless, the issues in conflict appear to be increasingly abrasive and, when symbolic or cultural values are at stake, decreasingly bargainable. As ethnic elites grow in number and in importance in the power structure, and as their contacts develop with counterparts in other republics, with functionaries of other socialist states, and with the world outside, their resentment of the double yoke they have to bear, that of central control and of Russian hegemony, grows apace.

WHITHER THE NATIONAL PROBLEM?

In answer to the question, "Whither the Soviet national problem?" there is little doubt that the tendency to flourish—to paraphrase Lenin—is fast outpacing the tendency towards rapprochement; the resulting synthesis may well come out on the wrong side of the dialectical leap, with flourishing having been an antithesis rather than a thesis all along. The thrust of the revival of national self-determination, moreover, not only exhibits most of the characteristics of ethnic differentiation currently observable in other multi-ethnic societies, but also carries the mark of old-fashioned nationalism of a type that wrought havoc with the political map of Europe in 1918. Most of the minority ethnic communities in the Soviet Union display unmistakable signs of accelerating ethnic antagonism generated on a 'We vs. They (the Russians)' dichotomy. This is most visible in cultural matters but begins to appear also in economic and political spheres. The conclusion seems inescapable that the national conflict in the Soviet Union has reached proportions more serious than its surface visibility would indicate. This invites the proverbial tip of an iceberg metaphor, the applicability of which in Sovietology is recognized by all serious observers of Soviet reality. All the major criteria employed by students of ethnicity worldwide indicate that conditions are favorable for the growth of ethnic conflict and trends that will strengthen centrifugal forces.[45]

This is not to say that integration has not taken place in the 60 years of Soviet rule, or that the political system is incapable of controlling centrifugal forces. Despite its propensity to stimulate ethnic antagonisms, social mobilization has left its mark both in an integrated socio-economic base (as hopefully pointed out by Soviet scholars) and in the impact of political socialization, if not on the masses, then on the elites who have to share the dominant political values even as they press for the greatest amount of autonomy compatible with systemic constraints. Despite the decrease in the irrational uses of terror, the political system has retained formidable powers of coercion (and has a tradition of success in their implementation), and the sheer weight of Russian hegemony makes any efforts at emancipation by smaller groups puny in comparison. For pur-

---

45. Elsewhere I examined criteria relevant for Soviet national integration, derived from international experience (Deutsch et al., *International Political Communities*, pp. 37-44) with similar conclusions:

"Not many of the 12 conditions for a successful 'amalgamated security community' . . . are met in the Soviet Union today. A 'mutual compatibility of main values' and a common 'distinctive way of life' exist as surface phenomena, but are undermined by . . . cultural cleavages. Expectations of 'stronger economic ties and gains' exist, but the pattern is asymmetrical; a 'marked increase in political and administrative capabilities' and a 'superior economic growth' have accrued for all partners . . . but only one . . . has reaped disproportionately high benefits on both counts. . . . 'links of social communication' are also characterized by asymmetry. 'The broadening of political elites' as well as an increase in political mobility have again benefited all partners, but in a setting when one partner continues to maintain a dominant position; and a 'multiplicity of ranges of communications and transactions has developed, but on a pattern that again is one-sided. . . .' There are no 'compensations in the flows of communications and transactions' and there is no 'interchange of group roles.' 'Considerable mutual predictability of behavior' undoubtedly exists, but . . . has failed to generate an attitude of confidence and trust as is assumed by the integration model.

"At the same time, the conditions conducive to disintegration can be readily ascertained. Soviet ethnic communities are indeed subjected to what may be considered an 'excessive military commitment without compensating gains in prestige and privilege. . . .' On the other hand, there has been a 'substantial increase in political participation on the part of populations, regions or social strata which previously had been politically passive' and politically and economically underprivileged, and this participation is now beginning to generate 'disappointments and frustrations of the new hopes, claims and expectations.' There has also been a significant increase in 'ethnic and linguistic, as well as in cultural, differentiation.'" See, C. A. Linden and D. K. Simes, eds., "Integration and Ethnic Nationalism in the Soviet Union; Aspects, Trends and Problems," in *Nationalities and Nationalism in the* USSR: *A Soviet Dilemma* (Washington: Center for Strategic and International Studies, Georgetown University, 1977), pp. 36-37.

poses of Soviet unity, therefore, the coercive powers of the system and ethnic elites' identification with it may be listed on the credit side. Few ethnic elites are willing to court martyrdom by trying to organize outside the system: clandestine separatist groups have appeared briefly, mostly in the Western regions, but their life span has been short. Nationalists, along with dissidents, are ruthlessly suppressed; sporadic violence, even of mass character, has been easy to control. Furthermore, there is no united front of non-Russian republics. Not only are they competitive in pursuit of their interests, but the intensity of national assertion varies. The Ukraine and the Baltic republics are the leading offenders; their demands are most clearly voiced and separatist sentiments have been articulated there, if covertly. Georgia and Armenia follow closely, but there national pressures center on demands for greater autonomy. The central Asian republics and Azerbaidzhan are culturally alienated; self-assertion there is expressed primarily through cultural issues, although economic and political demands begin to appear also. Because of their uniform Islamic culture, their developmental potential, their population explosion, and their importance in Soviet foreign policy, they may well move into the forefront of nationalist demands in the near future. Byelorussia and Moldavia exhibit least manifestations of nationalism, and assimilationist pressures there appear strongest. Assimilation also seems strong in most of the non-union republic national groups. It is difficult to pinpoint exactly what marks the watershed that makes a national group slide into an assimilational pattern or ascend the curve of nationalism. No single criterion appears decisive; rather, a number of key attributes have to combine in order to trigger a drive for national self-assertion: size, cultural cohesion, strength of historical national traditions, adherence to national language and religion, compact area of settlement, degree of modernization, and, last but not least, a perception of being unique.

Given the contradictory forces of ethnic nationalism and integration, the first, as indicated above, develops at a faster rate than the second. What, if anything, can be done to reverse or control the trend? What are the policy alternatives available to Soviet leadership and which are most likely to be adopted? It should be pointed out that the choices will be made by the governing Russian elite with some input, presumably, by a few non-Russians. Among the choices is the current immobilism, which can be maintained in the hope that the flourishing may yet dialectically leap into integration with the continuation of present policies. These have been characterized by a dialectic of partial concessions punctuated by retreats, the balance of which serve to intensify ethnic tensions. There is the past experience of Stalinist suppression and forced assimilation. There is decentralized federalism within constraints of a Communist political system of a kind adopted in Yugoslavia. As indicated by experience elsewhere, there is democratization based on a pluralistic pattern characterized by voluntary negotiations, compromise, and a redistribution of jurisdiction and resources. And finally there is secession.

Formal constitutional provisions to the contrary, secession is obviously excluded as a viable alternative. Given the nature of the system, a democratic type of solution also has to be rejected out of hand, because it would require systemic change of a kind for which there is no precedent in Russian political culture and little, if any, precedent in the political cultures of non-Russian groups, with the exception of the numerically negligible Balts. This type of change was attempted in Czechoslovakia in 1968 (inclusive of real equalization for the Slovaks within the Czechoslovak federation) which was stopped by Soviet-led Warsaw Pact invasion.

The current policy is likely to continue as long as the Brezhnev leadership remains in power, largely because a radical move in any direction is fraught with potential for a snowball effect. If so, ethnic tensions will continue to accelerate. The adoption in 1977 of the new USSR constitution reflected immobilism, because it did not introduce change in the Soviet federation either in the direction of its abolition (as advocated by some), or in the direction of greater autonomy (as desired by national elites). A new leadership may decide to move on the nationality front after a period of relative relaxation such as usually accompanies a struggle for succession. The perception of the magnitude of the problem has increased gradually at the policy making level as has the perception that small concessions seem only to fuel further demands. There is a growing realization that a change of policy is needed, and pressures mount in both directions to do something about it. As correctly noted by Academician Bromley, the path towards the merger predicted by Lenin

> is long and involved, and not all the sections of this path are plainly visible . . . [but] it is perfectly clear that on the way ahead a struggle is still in prospect both against national nihilism, against attempts to hasten artificially the process of the drawing together and merging of nations, and against manifestations of nationalism that impede this process. . . ."[46]

Given the paramount need for system maintenance, the temptation to return to coercive Russian hegemonial role may be inescapable. A policy of greater concessions would lead towards a Yugoslav-

---

46. Bromley, *Soviet Ethnography*, p. 165. In the text this passage is heavily reinforced by preceding and following quotations from L. I. Brezhnev, to the effect that the problem is indeed complex and troublesome.

type model that would provide conflict-resolution mechanisms and trade-offs for contending national groups while preserving the systemic imperative of party control. But in the Soviet Union there are no preconditions of the kind that made this model attractive to the Yugoslavs. The imbalance in favor of the Russians is overwhelming; national elites are not masters in their own homes; and, unlike the Serbs in Yugoslavia, the Russians are neither prepared to make concessions nor do they see a need to do so.

A new emphasis on repression and assimilation would preserve the leading position of the Russian elite and would—in the short run at least—drive the ethnic conflict under the surface of political life. Such a policy would, most likely, stop short of the abolition of the federation, substituting loyalty to "Mother Russia" as a base for integration, because of the weight of key republican bureaucracies imbedded in the power structure, and because of the requirements of foreign policy's global outreach. Instead, an attempt is likely to draw the "Soviet family of nations" closer to the "Socialist Commonwealth," offering a broader international arena to ethnic elites as a quid pro quo for their willingness to integrate—comparable to the Third World role East Europeans now play under the Soviet umbrella. But domestic repressions of nationalist "deviations" would intensify, inclusive of mass purges, resettlement, and so on. Spontaneous mass resistance to such measures is possible but unlikely. The terror apparatus exists and can be applied effectively and selectively; national leaders can be liquidated or manipulated by the classic "divide and rule" tactics. New and selective application of terror combined with forceful policy measures on the cultural, social and economic fronts, would go a long way to lower the visibility of the ethnic problem and to push it under the surface. It would not disappear, however, and the compression might accelerate a momentum toward spontaneous combustion that is now slowly building up. An explosion may occur, also, if there is a domestic crisis of major proportions or if external factors intervene. International conflict would inevitably trigger separatist tendencies, if the experience of World War I and II is indicative, the more so since Soviet ethnic groups have reached a level of national viability they did not have earlier. Intervention by an outside power on behalf of an oppressed group is also a possibility, notably in the case of China, if favorable conditions occur. The discussion of alternatives above is speculative. On the whole, the ethnic conflict in the Soviet Union is not tractable by any of the alternatives discussed short of the country's dissolution, and it will remain the main—and growing—fissure in the Soviet body politic for a long time to come. I am reminded of Professor Seton-Watson's simile: the Soviet Union is like a splendid and powerful ship; if an explosion occurs it will sink without a trace. Western democracies are like leaking rafts; water sloshes all over, but they float.

TABLE 1. USSR NATIONAL GROUPS; POPULATION INDICATORS

NATIONAL GROUPS	Abs. figures (thousands) NUMBERS—1970	% of total population	% Point change in total population 1959-1970	% Point change in group weight in republics' pop. 1959-1970 Tit. Group	% Point change in group weight in republics' pop. 1959-1970 Russians	Settlement distribution in % of group members resident in own national unit[a]
Union Rep. Nations:						
Slavs						
Russians	129,015	53.37	-1.28	-1.1	-1.1	83
Ukrainians	40,753	16.86	-.98	-1.9	+2.5	86
Byelorussians	9,052	3.74	-.05	0	+2.2	80
Central Asians						
Uzbeks	9,195	3.80	+.92	+3.6	-1.0	84
Kazakhs	5,299	2.19	+.46	+2.6	-.4	80
Tadzhiks	2,136	.88	+.21	+3.1	-1.4	76
Turkmen	1,525	.63	+.15	+5.3	-2.8	93
Kirgiz	1,452	.60	+.14	+3.3	-1.0	89
Caucasians						
Azerbaidzhani	4,380	1.81	+.40	+6.3	-3.6	86
Armenians	3,559	1.47	+.14	+.6	-.5	60
Georgians	3,245	1.34	+.05	+2.5	-1.6	97
Moldavians	2,698	1.12	+.06	-.8	+1.4	85
Balts						
Lithuanians	2,665	1.10	-.01	+.8	+.1	94
Latvians	1,430	.59	-.08	-5.2	+3.2	94
Estonians	1,007	.42	-.05	-6.4	+4.6	92
Aut. Rep. Nations:						
Tatars	5,931	2.45	+.07			26
Chuvashi	1,694	.70	0			n.a.
Mordvinians	1,263	.52	-.10			n.a.
Bashkirs	1,240	.51	+.04			n.a.
Dispersed:						
Jews	2,151	.89	-.20			
Germans	1,846	.76	-.02			no unit
Poles	1,167	.48	-.18			
USSR Total	241,720					

SOURCES: Ts.S.U.SSSR, *Narodnoe Khoziaistvo SSSR v 1975 g.* (Moscow: Statistika, 1976) pp. 32, 33, and *Itogi Vsesoiuznoi Perepisi Naseleniia 1970 g.*, 4 (Moscow: Statistika, 1973).

[a] Except for the Slavs, members of titular nationality nonresident in their republics are settled primarily in neighboring areas.

TABLE 2. USSR NATIONAL GROUPS; SOCIO-ECONOMIC INDICATORS

NATIONAL GROUPS	URBANIZATION—1970 % of total by group	URBANIZATION—1970 % of total by rep.	LANGUAGE—1970 % by group, of speakers of nat'l lang. as first lang.	LANGUAGE—1970 % by group, of speakers of Russian as first lang.	Russian as second lang.	COEFFICIENT of development by republic (1965)
Union Rep. Nations:						
Slavs						
Russians	68	62	99.8	99.8	.1	1.05
Ukrainians	49	55	85.7	14.2	36.6	1.04
Byelorussians	44	43	80.6	19.0	49.0	1.01
Central Asians						
Uzbeks	25	36	98.6	.5	14.5	.71
Kazakhs	27	51	98.0	1.6	41.8	.88
Tadzhiks	26	37	98.5	.6	15.4	.69
Turkmen	31	48	98.9	.8	15.4	.77
Kirgiz	15	37	98.8	.3	19.1	.76
Caucasians						
Azerbaidzhani	40	50	98.2	1.3	16.6	.71
Armenians	65	59	91.4	7.6	30.1	.84
Georgians	44	48	98.4	1.4	21.3	.87
Moldavians	20	32	95.0	4.2	36.1	.97
Balts						
Lithuanians	47	50	97.9	1.5	35.9	1.02
Latvians	53	62	95.2	4.6	45.2	1.17
Estonians	55	65	95.5	4.4	29.0	1.14
Aut. Rep. Nations:						
Tatars	55	52	89.2	10.2	62.5	n.a.
Chuvashi	23	36	86.9	13.0	58.4	n.a.
Mordvinians	36	36	77.8	22.1	65.7	n.a.
Bashkirs	27	48	66.2	4.5	53.3	n.a.
Dispersed:						
Jews	98	no unit	17.7	78.2	16.3	no unit
Germans	46	no unit	66.8	32.7	59.6	no unit
Poles	45	no unit	32.5	20.7	37.0	no unit
USSR average		56				

SOURCES: Ts.S.U.SSSR, *Narodnoe Khoziaistvo SSSR v 1969 g.* (Moscow: Statistika, 1970) pp. 13, 15, 16-18; *Narodnoe Khoziaistvo SSSR, 1922-1972, Jubileinyi Statisticheskii Ezhegodnik,* (Moscow: Statistika, 1972), pp. 32, 33; *Itogi Vsesoiuznoi Perepisi Naseleniia 1970 g.,* 4 (Moscow: Statistika, 1973), pp. 20, 27, 28. Coefficient of development calculated by Soviet economist, K. Vermishev, as the ratio of the given republic's share of total USSR gross domestic product in 1965 to the share of the given republic's population in total Soviet population in the same year. K. Vermishev, "On the Level of Economic Development of the Union Republics", *Voprosy Ekonomiki,* 4, (1970), p. 128.

Frederick C. Barghoorn

Political Dissent

One of the central threads of Soviet political history has been the bitter struggle between dissidents and authorities dating from the seizure of power by Lenin's Bolsheviks in 1917 and still continuing today. For various reasons—among which Soviet censorship perhaps looms largest—this struggle has not in my opinion received as much attention as it merits. Such attention as has been paid by scholars to opposition, dissent, and related phenomena has been notably retrospective. We have tended to accept too nearly at face value the claims of Soviet rulers that unity has prevailed in their realm. One reason for widespread skepticism among scholars regarding the possibility of significant and enduring dissent in the Soviet Union and other socialist countries was the influence of the concept of totalitarianism which, as usually interpreted, seemed by definition to deny that dissent could exist in a totalitarian system. In my own case, perception of "dissent or fear of dissent"[1] even in Stalin's Russia, to which I referred in an article I published in 1948, did not lead, until recent years, to further vigorous investigation of what I should have seen as an anomaly worthy of the most serious attention.

1. See Frederick C. Barghoorn, "Notes on Life and Travel in Russia," *Yale Review* (Summer, 1948), pp. 596-617, at p. 597.

The ferment of post-Stalin protest on which this study focuses has been, for many Western observers and perhaps for the Soviet rulers too, one of the most surprising features of the contemporary Soviet scene. However, Western analysts are increasingly aware that they had tended earlier to seriously underestimate both the depths of frustration, resentment and moral indignation generated in the minds of many Soviet citizens by the repressive and unresponsive character of the Soviet system, and also the propensity of disaffected citizens to avail themselves of any opportunities afforded by occasional relaxations of controls for articulation of dissent. One conclusion that emerges from a survey of the total span of Soviet history is that whenever controls over freedom of expression are relaxed, dissent proliferates. Much of the dissent articulated, largely in the least orthodox official channels, during periods of liberalization might be termed authorized or tolerated; but some of it strains the limits of orthodoxy and arouses official displeasure, even repression. Thus far, periods of relative permissiveness have been succeeded by times of tightened controls during which some opinions previously tolerated were regarded as objectionable. Some individuals then face harsh choices between suppressing their convictions or running the risks of violating new or newly interpreted official norms.

A minority of those who during a liberal period had engaged in authorized or within-system dissent have continued to do so in the more conservative period that followed. The historial record indicates that the size of such a minority is determined largely by the degree of coercion employed by the regime against dissidents, which in turn is related to other variables, domestic and foreign.

The New Economic Policy (NEP) of the 1921-28 period, which saw the greatest degree of freedom thus far enjoyed by Soviet citizens, was followed by ever harsher controls, indeed by almost total suppression of dissent. This reached a crescendo in the great purges of 1936-1938, which were followed by years of routine terror. The slight relaxation that ensued during World War II was succeeded by a new phase of severe repression. Finally, Khrushchev's flawed but significant liberalization gave way to a new period of ideological-political retrenchment in the sphere of literature, the arts and the "spiritual" realm generally. It is, of course, important to recognize that the post-Khrushchev regression stopped far short of a return to arbitrary and massive terror. Indeed, it is perhaps this fact as much as anything else that explains the persistence of dissent on a considerable scale despite the tightening of controls after the ouster of Khrushchev. The hopes generated by the Soviet Union's wartime alliance with Britain and the United States and those inspired by Khrushchev's de-Stalinization campaign were not fulfilled. In both cases some Soviet citizens experienced anger born of frustration;

many withdrew into apathy and despair. However, the differences between the two periods are enormous, sufficient to justify forecasting a far greater role for dissent after Brezhnev than it played in the last eight years of Joseph Stalin's rule. No Soviet leader since 1953 has commanded authority remotely comparable to that of the dread *vozhd*. Criminal though Stalin's regime was, it inspired awe, pride generated by the greatest military victory in Russian history, and a vast increase in Soviet world influence. Today the Soviet Union is much more powerful militarily than it was in Stalin's time, but it faces, at home and abroad, problems more worrisome and intractable than those of the 1940s. In particular, the complex requirements of the scientific-technological revolution as well as the continued inability of Soviet agriculture to assure an adequate diet for the Soviet people without imports of foreign grain, would seem to require a far higher level of technical, scientific, commercial and intellectual interactions with the West than Stalin permitted. It would be difficult to envisage in the Soviet future anything approaching the economic and intellectual isolation from the world effected by Stalin.

The most important difference between the two situations, however, and the most significant for the future of dissent, is the vast reduction in the role of terror since Stalin's death. This makes it necessary, it seems, for the regime to rely much more heavily than did Stalin on persuasion, socialization, and material rewards as instruments of rule. The balance of power between the regime and dissidents is hence not as overwhelmingly tilted in the regime's favor as it was under Stalin. It seems safe to predict at least that dissent cannot be totally eliminated and that over the long run it may well increase in scope, range, intensity, and effect.

CHARACTERIZATION OF DISSENT

It is assumed in this paper that the better we understand the sources of past dissent, the more light we may cast on its future. Accordingly, the next section of the paper—following some further characterization of the nature of dissent in the contemporary period—will be devoted to an attempt to explain why dissent burgeoned after Stalin's death, particularly after Khrushchev's dismissal.

The term 'political dissent' in this essay refers to statements, judgments, proposals, demands and other utterances in conflict with or incompatible with the Soviet regime's policies, practices and doctrines. In regime-dissenter relations, it takes only one to quarrel. The content of the statements produced by dissenters, often referred to in the official press as "people who think differently" (*in-*

akomyslyashchie) or as "renegades" *(otshchepentsi)* is important; but it often appears that from the regime's point of view the real sin of the dissidents is that they speak out without official authorization and thus violate the authorities' claim to monopoly control of communication.

As far as the authorities are concerned, dissent is whatever they choose to label as such. For the strongest personalities among the dissidents, however, it is an assertion of individuality and personal integrity. By dissenting, they establish and maintain their identity. Activities that to citizens of Western democracies seem entirely legitimate, such as Alexander Ginzburg's compilation of a factual record of the trial of the writers Andrei Sinyavski and Yuli Daniel (for producing objectionable works of fiction!) in February 1966, are often categorized as "anti-Soviet agitation," or as the "circulation of false fabrications defaming the Soviet state and social system." Those who have been legally prosecuted for these "crimes" have invariably been found guilty and have often been punished with startling severity. After their release from forced labor camps they have been kept under police surveillance and in many cases again prosecuted or forced to emigrate.

The relationship between dissidents and authorities in political systems of the Soviet type is characterized by exceptional asymmetry and, in particular, by the authorities' exercise of arbitrary power. The dissidents are harassed before arrest, dismissed from their jobs, flayed in the courtroom and the press, and treated much worse than the most hardened non-political prisoners in prisons, labor camps and mental hospitals. It is not surprising that both those Soviet citizens who in greater or lesser degree share the ethical, legal and political values basic to democracy, and also many citizens of the world's democracies, find much cause for moral outrage in the Soviet government's treatment of dissidents. In the Soviet Union, expression of moral outrage, except in response to official command, is dangerous. Nevertheless, since the mid-1960s, many thousands of Soviet citizens have exposed themselves, not only participants in the democratic or human rights movement, but also citizens who demanded that the authorities respect rights claimed by representatives of various ethnic and religious groups, such as Jews, Germans, Crimean Tatars, Orthodox Christians, Evangelical Christian Baptists, Pentecostalists and others. Many more have engaged in such activities as composing or signing protest petitions and distributing *samizdat* (self-published, uncensored) documents, such as the famous *Chronicle of Current Events*. Large numbers have taken part in street demonstrations, of which the most important in recent years occurred in Tbilisi, the capital of the Georgian Soviet socialist republic, in April 1978. This demonstration—against the omission in the draft of the new constitution of the Georgian Soviet republic, of the clause contained in the previous constitution explicitly naming Georgian as the state language of the Georgian republic—uniquely attained its objective.

Denunciations of what their authors regarded as violations by Soviet officials of individual or group rights provided in the constitutions and other legal instruments of the USSR and its republics have, over the years, bulked far larger than any other category of *samizdat*.[2] This literature of accusation and exposure has pressured and irked the Soviet authorities. It has also become one of the most important sources of data concerning the realities of Soviet life available outside the USSR. The careful gathering by dissidents of information about violations of legal rights and the dissemination of this information by means of *samizdat* within the USSR, and on a far larger scale in Western mass media, is one of the most significant developments in post-Stalin Russia. The conduct of this dangerous operation has required deep moral commitment, great skill, determination and tenacity, and above all civic courage. To a large extent, this activity has become the meaning and mission of the lives of some of the best Soviet people.

However, it is important to realize that exposure of abuses of power is not the only function of dissent in the USSR. Dissidents, particularly those associated with what is often referred to as the democratic movement, have also offered a positive alternative to established political and legal practices. This paper cannot discuss in detail the widely varied proposals for change offered by democratically oriented Soviet dissidents. Two points, however, should be made. First, despite the extreme diversity which has characterized *samizdat*, most of its producers, including the most distinguished, such as the physicist, Academician Andrei Sakharov, have advocated "democratization" of Soviet political, economic and cultural life. Even authors widely regarded both in the USSR and in the West as nationalist or authoritarian thinkers—for example Alexander Solzhenitsyn or Vladimir Osipov—in many of their statements and actions supported some of the central demands of the Soviet democrats, particularly the softening or abolition of censorship.[3] Many Soviet dissenters, including not only liberals like Sakharov but Marxists like the historian Roy Medvedev and members of other

2. This remains as true today as when it was pointed out by Ferdinand Feldbrugge in his *Samizdat and Political Dissent in the Soviet Union* (Leyden: Sijthoff, 1975), p. 7.

3. On the similarities, and the deep and significant differences, between Solzhenitsyn's political views and those of Sakharov and other Soviet advocates of democratization see my *Détente and the Democratic Movement in the USSR* (New York: Free Press, 1976), pp. 20-21; 47-52; 55-72.

dissident currents, use the concept of democratization in the meaning attributed to it by Robert A. Dahl. Dahl, in his major work, *Polyarchy*, identifies the movement toward polyarchy, or the "development of a political system that allows for opposition, rivalry, or competition between a government and its opponents," as an important aspect of democratization.[4]

As Soviet dissidents and exiled former dissidents have often emphasized, there is nothing on the Russian horizon like political opposition as it is understood in the West.[5] Nevertheless, some of the most important dissident documents such as the long letter-essay addressed by Sakharov, Roy Medvedev, and computer scientist Valentine Turchin to the Soviet leaders in 1970, or Roy Medvedev's impressive book, *On Socialist Democracy* (published in Russian in Amsterdam in 1972 and in English in New York in 1975), contain proposals which, if implemented, might inaugurate a transformation of the Soviet political system in the direction of polyarchy. A reluctant but striking admission that aspirations toward political freedom and even a "multiparty system" characterized the views of most Soviet citizens who "rejected the official mode of thought" was made by Alexander Solzhenitsyn, whom I would categorize as a moderate authoritarian thinker, in a major statement written in 1969 and published in 1974.[6]

Two other closely related characteristics of contemporary Soviet dissent are perhaps even more significant than its aspiration toward democratization. I refer to the rejection of violence by most dissenters and dissenting groups and their equally firm conviction that, as Shragin has put it, law "is not a means but an end, for it is only on a basis of respect for the law, and for human beings as its subject, that further objectives can be set."[7]

ACCOUNTING FOR POST-STALIN DISSENT

Of conceptual tools that might help us to account for the attitudes underlying dissent in the USSR, the most useful seems to me to be the relative deprivation theory developed by Gurr. Gurr defines relative deprivation as "a perceived discrepancy between men's value expectations and their value capabilities." Value expectations are the things to which people believe they are rightfully entitled. Conditions that

4. Robert A. Dahl, *Polyarchy* (New Haven: Yale University Press, 1971), p. 1; 14.
5. See, for example, Boris Shragin, *The Challenge of the Spirit* (New York: Knopf, 1978), especially chapter V, "The Dissidents."
6. See Barghoorn, *Détente and the Democratic Movement*, pp. 20-21; 188.
7. Shragin, p. 211.

increase intensity of expectations without increasing satisfactions increase discontent. Also, "societal conditions that decrease men's average value position without decreasing their value expectations similarly increase deprivation, hence the intensity of discontent."[8] Of course, as Gurr points out, the history, structure, culture and other attributes of regimes and their opponents must be taken into account in applying relative deprivation theory. No attempt will be made here to apply it systematically to dissent in Soviet Russia, a task that would require a longer study. Rather, reference is made to it to provide a broad conceptual framework for our effort to account for the attitudes and behavior of Soviet dissidents. There was, I believe, a discrepancy perceived with varying degrees of clarity in the USSR during the Stalin era between value expectations and capabilities. In fact, such a discrepancy was probably perceived by millions, in view of the harsh fate of tens of millions of people resulting from Stalin's policies of forced collectivization of agriculture and coercive industrialization, and the deaths of millions in forced labor camps. Not many citizens or their relatives, friends, or colleagues escaped the direct or indirect impact of Stalin's terror. To be sure, there were important countervailing forces, especially the pride and sense of efficacy resulting from the industrial progress achieved during Stalin's Five Year Plans.[9]

Certainly there was a great deal and a wide range of pent up discontent in the USSR when Stalin died. However, there were enormous obstacles to the expression of dissent, let alone organized opposition. The habit of fear, of a degree of caution almost unimaginable to people who have not lived under a regime of terror, and of "doublethink" (to borrow from George Orwell's *1984*) tended to paralyze even unspoken resistance to authority.

Khrushchev's de-Stalinization campaign, limited and inconsistent though it was, doubtless raised the value expectations of many Soviet citizens. It appeared to legitimize petitions by citizens whose loved ones had perished in Stalin's camps, demanding that at least symbolic amends be made for past injustices. It even emboldened some to articulate liberal values such as freedom of information and expression, at least in literature and the arts. It also kindled hopes that

8. Tedd Robert Gurr, *Why Men Rebel* (Princeton: Princeton University Press, 1970), p. 13.

9. See Alex Inkeles and David H. Smith, *Becoming Modern* (Cambridge, Mass.: Harvard University Press, 1974). Gabriel Almond and G. Bingham Powell have captured much of the essence of the Inkeles-Smith study in their statement regarding the clear relationships between "modernizing experiences" such as industrialization and the "secular, efficacious and participant attitudes" described by Inkeles and Smith. See Almond and Powell, *Comparative Politics Today* (Boston: Little, Brown, 1978), pp. 46-47.

impartial justice and social equality, still believed by some despite the immensely disillusioning experiences of the Stalin era to be basic ingredients of socialism, would begin to be realized in practice, instead of remaining on paper. Khrushchev emptied the labor camps of most of their inmates. Among the survivors who emerged were Alexander Solzhenitsyn, Evgenia Ginzburg, and the historian Peter Yakir, all of whom were to pen powerful descriptions of the horrors of the Gulag system. Thus knowledge of past wrongs, and the indignation generated thereby, grew. For several years, especially while Khrushchev remained at the helm of the Soviet state, official channels, such as the literary journal *Novy Mir*, served as outlets for what in retrospect seems a surprisingly broad and deep articulation of dissent.[10] Perhaps the most dramatic and significant single episode in *Novy Mir's* battle against the cultural and political conservatives, against whom its liberal (in the Soviet context) editor, Alexander Tvardovski, and Khrushchev himself were forced to struggle, was its publication of Solzhenitsyn's novella, *One Day in the Life of Ivan Denisovich*.

If Khrushchev carried liberalization so far that conservatives in the Soviet elite became convinced that he was gravely damaging the political system built by Stalin, he did not carry it nearly far enough to satisfy some idealistic intellectuals such as Alexander Ginzburg, Vladimir Bukovskii, Vladimir Osipov, General Peter Grigorenko and others. These individuals were among many, including thousands of students, who protested Soviet suppression by military force of the 1956 Hungarian uprising and who experienced repression during the Khrushchev era. It must also be kept in mind that Khrushchev pursued highly repressive policies with regard to religious groups, especially dissident Baptists. As far as critically minded intellectuals were concerned, one of the worst blots on Khrushchev's record was his role in the hounding of Boris Pasternak for publication abroad of his novel, *Doctor Zhivago*, which led to the great writer's involuntary refusal of the Nobel Prize for literature in 1960. Yet it would probably be fair to say that for a substantial segment of the Soviet intelligentsia—many of whom were enabled to publish works for which they would have perished under Stalin's regime—expectations and capabilities were in reasonable balance as long as Khrushchev's leadership lasted.

Khrushchev's successors soon signaled their intention to narrow the limits of permissible critical opinion, especially in the moral, esthetic, historical, and philosophical realms, although they encouraged discreet discussion (largely in specialist journals) of proposals

10. See, for example, Dina Spechler, "Permitted Dissent in the Decade after Stalin," in Paul Cocks et al., eds., *The Dynamics of Soviet Politics* (Cambridge, Mass.: Harvard University Press, 1976), pp. 28-50; and Nancy Whittier Heer, "Political Leadership in Soviet Historiography," in Cocks et al., pp. 11-27.

considered likely to promote economic, scientific and technical development. The Brezhnev leadership ended de-Stalinization and partially restored Stalin's name to a place of honor. Instead of the revelations of Stalin's misdeeds that had poured fitfully from Khrushchev's lips, his successors suggested that it was time to stop washing dirty linen in public—the cult of personality of J. V. Stalin having been criticized sufficiently—and to get on with the urgent task of assuring economic growth by efficient administration. In 1965 the new leadership arrested scores of Ukrainian intellectuals, put some of them on trial in the Ukraine, and staged the much better known Sinyavski-Daniel trial in Moscow. The frustration sparked by these policies was indicated by protest petitions and other expressions of disapproval. The wave of non-violent protest generated by the Sinyavski-Daniel trial and on a considerably larger scale by the trials of Vladimir Bukovski, Alexander Ginzburg and Yuri Galanskov in 1968 (more than 700 persons signed protests on behalf of Ginzburg and Galanskov) was, as its participants perceived it, a legitimate, morally obligatory response to the Soviet regime's unlawful effort to suppress criticism of suppression of criticism. There is general agreement among knowledgeable Soviet participants and observers as well as Western analysts that the movement reached its highest point in terms of numbers of participants in 1968, after the trial of Alexander Ginzburg and Yuri Galanskov for compiling a *samizdat* record of the trial of Sinyavski and Daniel. This action was denounced as subversion on behalf of Western "reactionaries" by the press, judges, and prosecutor of Ginzburg and Galanskov. About a thousand persons signed individual and collective petitions protesting the rigged Ginzburg-Galanskov proceedings.

Pavel Litvinov, one of the most prominent participants in the civil rights movement of 1967-68, after several years of prison and Siberian exile followed by further protest activity, was forced to emigrate in 1974 to the United States. He has written an authoritative account of what he calls the human rights movement in the USSR. According to Litvinov the "probable causes" of this development were: (1) the effort of the new Soviet leadership to nullify "even the timid moves toward liberalization, which had taken place under Khrushchev and had given rise to many hopes"; (2) concurrent events such as the "Czechoslovak spring" and Polish student unrest; (3) the continuity of the Ginzburg-Galanskov with the Sinyavski-Daniel case, which had already evoked a "massive negative reaction in the intelligentsia to the revival of Stalinist methods of suppressing freedom of thought."[11] The aspects of the movement especially

11. Pavel Litvinov, "O dvishenii za prava cheloveka v SSSR" [On the human rights movement in the USSR], in *Samosoznanie* [Insights] (New York: Khronika Press, 1976), pp. 63-88, at pp. 80-81. The above mentioned figure regarding protest petitions in 1968 is also based on Litvinov, p. 80.

stressed by Litvinov were its demand for openness and public information about court trials and its participants' public disclosure of their own identities. As he notes, since the Soviet authorities did not see fit to allow protest statements in the official press, the concept of openness *(glasnost)* came logically to entail their distribution in *samizdat* and publication in the foreign press. He emphasized that the regime did not succeed in suppressing the protest movement. Instead, it became a "constant phenomenon, which has persisted to the present." The formation in May 1976 by the physicist Yuri Orlov and others of the Public Group to Promote the Fulfillment of the Helsinki Accords *(Obshchestvennaya Gruppa Sodeistviya po Vypolneniyu Khelsinkskikh Soglashenii)* and the subsequent activity of Orlov's Moscow group and parallel groups in Kiev, Tbilisi, Vilnius and Erevan confirmed the validity of Litvinov's belief in the movement's staying powers.

The list of "problems" that, as Litvinov said, held the close attention of the human rights movement sheds light not only on its scope but on its sources. His list included:

(1) the situation and rules of confinement of political prisoners in camps, prisons and psychiatric hospitals;
(2) the movement of the peoples of the USSR for a free national, cultural and religious life;
(3) the struggle of peoples, forcibly exiled from their lands in the Stalin era to return to their homelands;
(4) the possibility for a free choice of place of residence within the country;
(5) the problem of departure from the country, particularly of Jews to Israel;
(6) persecution of the Orthodox Church and of various religious minorities;
(7) the problem of press censorship of uncensored manuscript literature, and persecution of its authors and distributors and of independent culture as such;
(8) various socio-economic problems.

Litvinov adds that the above and many other problems, ignored for years by official agencies and the press, flowed into *samizdat*.[12] Readers familiar with the writings of Academician Sakharov, Andrei Amalrik, Peter Grigorenko, Roy and Zhores Medvedev, and other liberal, and liberal-Marxist dissidents, exponents of the Jewish emigration movement, and representatives of other ethnic and also religious groups will, I think, agree that Litvinov's list mirrors well

12. For the above list, see Litvinov, p. 82.

the foci of democratic dissent in the USSR from 1965 to the present.[13] The major omission in Litvinov's list is Russian nationalist dissent, an important body of opinion, but one that really advocates—insofar as its exponents extol authoritarian rather than democratic values—turning the clock back to Stalin or to the tsar. Hence it can perhaps be said to be of interest to those who seek democratization of the Soviet political system only as one of many obstacles. I believe that an ideology and program giving priority to Russian nationalist interests and sentiments would, in the multinational Soviet society, be extremely destructive to political integration and cohesion. I refer not to relatively moderate nationalists of the type of Solzhenitsyn and Osipov but to those, such as the publicists Victor Chalmaev and Sergei Semanov, or the artist Ilya Glazunov, who have enjoyed the support of powerful elements in the Soviet elite and have, unlike Solzhenitsyn and Osipov, never been subjected to persecution.

The foci of this essay are explanatory and predictive rather than historical and descriptive. Therefore, I shall not attempt to trace in detail the line of argument already set forth in this section. However, a few words should be said about the most recent phase in the saga of the struggle for democratization in Russia, namely, the activities of the already mentioned Public Group to Promote the Fulfillment of the Helsinki Accords, better known in the West as the Helsinki Watch or often simply as the Helsinki group.

Beginning in February 1977 with the arrest of one of the founding members of the Moscow Helsinki group, Alexander Ginzburg, Helsinki Watch activists in all five republics where the new movement was active were subjected to perhaps the fiercest harassment and repression that has befallen dissenters in the period since Stalin's death. The KGB warned the physicist Yuri Orlov, the leader of the Moscow group, even before the movement began its activities, that it considered it to be an illegal organization.[14] The Politburo's anger and concern were indicated by the treason charge on which the young computer scientist Anatoli Shcharansky was tried in July 1978—one of a very small number of invocations of the treason article (Article 64 of the Russian Republic Criminal Code) against a dissident in the post-Stalin era. Very severe sentences were meted out to Ukrainian writer Michael Rudenko and other members

13. See works contained or analyzed in Peter B. Reddaway, *Uncensored Russia* (New York: McGraw Hill, 1972); Michael Meerson-Aksenov and Boris Shragin, eds., *The Political, Social and Religious Thought of Russian 'Samizdat'—An Anthology* (Belmont, Mass.: Nordland Press, 1977); Ferdinand Feldbrugge, *Samizdat;* and Rudolf Tokes, ed., *Dissent in the USSR* (Baltimore: Johns Hopkins, 1975).

14. See Ludmilla Alexeeva, "Moskovskaya Gruppa Sodeistviya," *Novoe Russkoe Slovo,* March 15, 1977. This was the first of a series of informative articles by Alexeeva on the history of the "Helsinki" movement.

of the Kiev Helsinki group. Zviad Gamsakhurdia, a distinguished Georgian writer, and two other members of the Tbilisi group had gone to labor camps by the fall of 1978. The head of the Lithuanian group, Thomas Venclova, poet, translator and son of one of the founders of the Lithuanian Communist Party, was forced to leave the USSR shortly after the Vilnius group began its activities. In the summer of 1978 other members of the Lithuanian group were sentenced to long terms in camps. General Peter Grigorenko, famous for his defense of the rights of the exiled Crimean Tatar people and twice victim of forced treatment in KGB special psychiatric hospitals, who had for a time acted as liaison between the Moscow and Ukrainian groups, was deprived of Soviet citizenship while in the United States for medical treatment. Forced emigration befell the editor and historian Ludmila Alexeeva, chronicler in exile of the Helsinki movement and also, in 1976, 1977, and 1978, other prominent dissidents, some of them members of the Helsinki group. As of late 1978, a substantial majority of the sixty-odd participants in the Helsinki movement had been subjected to more or less severe repression at home or to enforced exile abroad.

Before pointing to aspects of the Helsinki group's output—for such a small number of participants it was vast—which appear to have aroused the Politburo's alarm, it will be appropriate to indicate briefly the movement's relationship to previous manifestations of dissent. Some, but by no means all, of the Helsinki Watch activists had played prominent roles in earlier dissident organizations. For example, Alexeeva was a member of the Action Group for the Defense of Civil Rights in the USSR, formed after Grigorenko's arrest in 1969. Although, unlike many members of the Action Group, she had not suffered arrest, imprisonment or forced exile, Alexeeva had been expelled from the Communist party and fired from her job. Through Elena Bonner, a Moscow Helsinki group member and Academician Sakharov's wife, the Helsinki Movement had a close link with the by now honored tradition that Sakharov had created by his tireless humanitarian activity in the face of enormous regime pressures. According to Alexeeva, the Moscow Helsinki group for a time held its foreign press conferences in the Sakharovs' apartment. Alexander Ginzburg, of course, had begun his dissident activity in the early 1960s, well before the petitions and letters protesting the Sinyavski-Daniel affair. Yuri Orlov had lost his job as a physicist in Moscow in 1956 because of statements indicating that his interpretation of Khrushchev's "secret speech" was far too radical for the authorities (including Khrushchev) and had found employment in Armenia, where he even became a corresponding member of the Academy of Sciences of Armenia. Resuming dissident activity in the 1970s, he had been subjected to harassment and the deprivation of employment, the usual lot of persistent dissidents, before he organized the Moscow Helsinki group, which he headed from May 1976 until his arrest in February 1977.

In addition to these and other veteran dissidents (including Anatoli Marchenko, author of the famous and horrifying account of Soviet concentration camp life, *My Testimony*), there were a few very young participants in the Helsinki movement, such as the paramedical worker Alexander Podrabinek, whose subgroup of the Helsinki Watch specialized in combatting the abuse of psychiatry for political purposes, and Shcharansky, whose role in the Moscow group was primarily that of liaison between the group and the Jewish emigration movement.

Why did the regime react so angrily to the activities of the Helsinki groups? Why did it seek so energetically to cut the communications links between those groups and the outside world, in the process employing tactics certain to blacken the Soviet image in the West, such as the 1977 police interrogation of a *Los Angeles Times* correspondent and the charge in 1978 that a *New York Times* correspondent, as well as one representing the *Baltimore Sun*, had "slandered" Soviet television by reporting that relatives of Gamsakhurdia had cast doubt on the genuineness of Gamsakhurdhia's "confession" broadcast by Soviet television?

For answers to these questions and light on the sources and motivation of the activities of the Helsinki movement, we turn to some of the statements issued by the Moscow group. These statements reflected their authors' intense commitment to correct what they regarded as intolerable defects and evils in Soviet domestic policies, as well as to the belief that stable world peace depended on democratization of the Soviet domestic political regime. Moreover, they indicated their authors' opinions that if anything could be done to remedy the evils they attacked, the chief means available was to bring information about them to the attention of world public opinion. The members of the Helsinki groups considered it appropriate to exert pressure on the Soviet government to fulfill the obligations it had, in their opinion, assumed by signing the Final Act of the Conference on Security and Cooperation in Europe at Helsinki in 1975. Knowing that under Soviet conditions they could not form organizational coalitions with other groups inside their own country they appealed, as had the Action Group and other dissident elements in the 1960s and 1970s, to "external publics."[15]

15. For a discussion of this strategy, see Howard L. Biddulph, "Protest Strategies of the Soviet Intellectual Opposition," in Rudolph L. Tökés, *Dissent in the USSR*, pp. 96-115. According to Biddulph, this strategy failed in 1967-71, because it violated the mores of Soviet political culture, and for other reasons. However, Boris Shragin, in *The Challenge of the Spirit*, argues vigorously that Biddulph is wrong and that "the appeal of the 'dissidents' to Western public opinion was no more a 'tactic' than a drowning man's cry for help; it is the only course open to them." Shragin, p. 203.

In its first public statement, the Moscow Helsinki group said that it considered its primary task to be "informing all heads of governments that signed the Helsinki Final Act, and informing public opinion regarding cases of direct violations" of the principles listed in Point VII of the Final Act. With this end in view, asserted the ten signers of the statement, they would accept written complaints regarding violations. With respect to "especially inhumane actions," such as separation by Soviet authorities of children from parents who wished to bring up their children in their religious faith, or forced psychiatric treatment for purposes of control of beliefs, conscience, and so on, the group envisaged requesting "heads of government and public opinion" to form commissions to verify the facts, as the group itself would not always be in a position to conduct on the spot investigations. The group expressed the hope that its information would be taken into account in the Belgrade meetings of representatives of the CSCE participating governments envisaged in the Final Act. The group also stated that it assumed that "problems of humanitarianism and disclosure of information" were directly related to assuring international peace.[16] Almost a year later the Moscow group issued another statement, thirteen pages in length, entitled "Evaluation of the Influence of the CSCE on Human Rights in the USSR." This important document drew attention to the close relationship between "the struggle for human rights and the effort to establish stable peace" in the world. Analysis shows, it asserted, that the Soviet authorities did not intend to fulfill their obligations in the field of human rights. It hailed "timid but unprecedented" efforts of Western governments to insist on the fulfillment by the USSR of its obligations. It also expressed the opinion that information reaching the outside world about Soviet violations of human rights and about "the true character of the Soviet democracy" was even beginning to influence the tactics of some foreign Communist parties. The Soviet government had been forced to make a few concessions in the human rights area, and if the movement could be expanded and received "operative support" from Western public opinion, the Soviet authorities would have to moderate their repressive policies. This, in turn, would foster the realization of democratic rights in the USSR.

But, the document emphasized, the Soviet government had basically persisted in its harsh, repressive policies since the Helsinki conference. Hundreds of political prisoners were still in prisons and camps, in some cases in even worse conditions than before. Since

---

16. *Arkhiv Samizdata 2605*, Radio-Liberty—Radio Free Europe (Munich, 1976). Subsequent references to documents in this series will be referred to by AS, followed by the document number.

Helsinki, well known human rights advocates such as Vladimir Osipov, the biologist Sergei Kovalev, and the physicist Andrei Tverdokhlebov, had been sentenced. A long list of persecuted dissenters was appended to the document. The authorities were, as before, putting all manner of obstacles in the way of Jews who desired to emigrate. All forms of "independent information" continued to be suppressed. All attempts to form organizations not dependent on the leadership of the CPSU were still forbidden.

However, the activity of the group was productive, said the nine signers of this document. More and more people were getting in touch with the group, supplying it with first hand information about violations of human rights. Further exposure of such violations would produce positive results.[17]

There is evidence that the determined exposure campaign conducted by the Helsinki groups was beginning to mobilize segments of the Soviet public hitherto unreached by dissenters' messages—several smaller organizations, such as the Christian Committee for the Defense of the Rights of Believers, led by Orthodox priest Gleb Yakunin, the Jewish Movement for Emigration, and others affiliated with the basic Moscow group led by Orlov.[18] Perhaps particularly important was the fact that in 1977, links began to develop between the mainstream dissidents and a number of Soviet workers who sought to form a labor organization independent of the Soviet official organization, the All-Union Council of Trade Unions, which these workers, led by Vladimir Klebanov, regarded as totally unresponsive to the rights and legitimate demands of labor.[19] In this connection Alexeeva's account of a growing number of letters, and of visitors "from all parts of the country," reaching Orlov and other members of the group in Moscow is significant. Alexeeva states that "we were especially pleased that among those who appealed to the group there were not only intellectuals but workers and peasants."[20] There can be no doubt that, as Orlov himself pointed out shortly before his arrest, the exposure campaign enraged the authorities.[21]

As of May 1978 nearly 200 documents had been produced by the five Helsinki groups, as Valery Chalidze, editor of the New York

17. AS2605.

18. Ten groups are listed in a *Samizdat* item published in *Novoe Russkoe Slovo*, May 12, 1977.

19. See, for example, AS2755 and 3215, written, respectively, by Valentine Turchin for the Moscow group shortly before his emigration to America and by Elena Bonner, Sakharov's wife.

20. *Novoe Russkoe Slovo*, March 27, 1977.

21. AS2858.

based Khronika Press, has noted.[22] While what has been presented above only faintly suggests the volume, force and pathos of this material, it perhaps enables the reader to better understand the moral commitment and intellectual perspectives underlying the activities of the Helsinki movement. This understanding is essential to the effort, made in the following section of this study, to forecast the future of Soviet dissent, in particular the struggle for human rights and democratization.

PREDICTION

In conclusion, I predict that unless the Soviet regime alters the conditions that generate discontent and alienation, it will be permanently unable to prevent some courageous men and women from openly articulating attitudes held by the far greater number who fear to speak out openly. It seems safe to predict that as long as the Soviet political system remains as unresponsive and coercive as it is at present, both dissent and harsh repression, as well as the revulsion elicited by the latter in the freer societies of the West, will persist. In this connection it is appropriate to recall words written in 1865 by the famous Russian liberal thinker, Alexander Herzen.

> Was there ever a country with a censorship and an arbitrary government where secret presses and the underground distribution of manuscripts did not exist—once intellectual movements and the desire for liberty existed? This is just as natural a state of affairs as the publication of material abroad and emigration.[23]

It is true that in the Fall of 1978, after the hammer blows struck by the KGB, democratic dissent was at a low ebb. Most of the leaders and activists of the Helsinki groups were either in exile in the West or behind bars. Moscow had expressed defiance of Washington and contempt for Western public opinion by staging the trials of Ginzburg and Shcharansky at a time when American Secretary of State Vance was about to meet with Soviet Minister of Foreign Affairs Gromyko for important arms control talks. However, as the

22. "On the Activity of the Helsinki Watch Group in the USSR," in *Documents of Helsinki Dissent from the Soviet Union and Eastern Europe*, compiled and edited by the staff of the Commission on Security and Cooperation in Europe (Washington: 1978). Some of the Soviet Helsinki Group's documents are available in English in this volume.

23. Quoted by Peter B. Reddaway in *Uncensored Russia*, p. 15.

London *Economist* indicated, Soviet terror against dissidents reflected not only the arrogance of material power but a confession of moral debility:

> The [Soviet] government claims to have overwhelming support among its own people: dissent, it says, is confined to a handful of malcontents, madmen and corrupt elements manipulated by hostile foreigners. But there is only one rational explanation for the steam hammer-nutcracking treatment which it has felt obliged to give to Mr. Ginzburg, Mr. Shcharansky and other human rights campaigners. The Soviet regime is so doubtful of the underlying loyalty of its own people that it does not dare to tolerate the raising of even a few voices in non-violent, legal, factual criticism.[24]

The steadfastness and coolness displayed by Orlov—reminiscent of Bukovski's demeanor at his 1967 and 1971 trials, and of Amalrik at his trial in 1970—were typical of the behavior of Soviet dissidents in similar circumstances. So were the open hostility of the spectators at the trial (undoubtedly mainly party activists and KGB operatives) and the obstructive conduct of the prosecutor and the judge. Orlov argued that he was being tried not for criminal offenses but for ideological ones, not for attempting to undermine the Soviet system but for advocating gradual democratic reforms. He insisted that the criticisms he had made of official Soviet policy, such as abuses of psychiatry for political purposes, were true. He asserted that "ideological intolerance" was incompatible with peaceful coexistence and harmful to Soviet culture and science. Perhaps Orlov's most significant statement, which the members of the court disdained to hear out, was as follows:

> You can sentence me to seven years in prison, or five years, or you can shoot me, but I am convinced that trials like this one do not help to remove the misfortunes and deficiencies of which the documents of the Helsinki group are testimony, and of which I tried to speak here. . . . [25]

In fact, Orlov received a sentence of seven years in a strict regime labor camp and five years internal exile. The sentences imposed on Orlov, and the even more severe one meted out to Alexander Ginzburg, may well, in view of the two men's poor health be equivalent to death.

24. *The Economist*, July 15, 1978, p. 15.
25. See "Scenes from a Soviet Courtroom," *The Economist*, July 15, 1978, pp. 41-42. The report was made from memory by Orlov's wife, Irina, whose notes, written in the courtroom, were taken from her.

It seems unlikely that the spirit of Orlov or of Sakharov, the central figure of Soviet democratic dissent for some ten years now, can be broken, or that the voices of Sakharov and his small band of supporters still left at large can be stilled by anything short of incarceration or commitment to a mental hospital. Fear that the latter fate might be in store for Sakharov unless world opinion strongly supported him and his group was expressed by General Grigorenko in a communication addressed to "progressive mankind," published in a New York Russian language daily.[26] To be sure, some civil rights activists such as Peter Yakir and Victor Krasin, victims of the first post-Stalin Soviet show trial in 1973, Ivan Dzyuba, author of an important book criticizing Russification in the Ukraine, and, in connection with the 1978 police drive against the Helsinki groups, Zviad Gamsakhurdia, have yielded to KGB pressures and blandishments and have reportedly "repented," at least outwardly. It is surprising that there have been so few such cases. More typical was the heroically defiant behavior of the teacher Valentine Moroz and of the psychiatrist Semen Gluzman in the Ukraine, or of Amalrik, Bukovski, Orlov and many others in the Russian republic. It appears from the record to date that once a Soviet dissenter, impelled by conscience and conviction, embarks on the path of open resistance, he usually remains true to his commitment, although some who have served terms in prisons, camps or exile have kept silent after their release. It is also true that a considerable number of individuals who signed protest petitions in the 1960s, such as the composer Dmitri Shostakovich, for example, quickly ceased to protest and do not appear to have suffered any serious deprivation subsequently, presumably because the KGB was satisfied that in future they would conform to official norms and would be more useful to the regime at work than in enforced idleness or in confinement.

A much more serious weakness of the Soviet dissent movement than backsliding by participants, is the unwillingness of more than a tiny minority, even of intellectuals, to speak out openly against official policy, especially once the KGB has inaugurated a hunting campaign against such mild forms of dissent as circulation of *samizdat*.[27] Bloch and Reddaway in their definitive study of the abuse of psychiatry in the USSR reported that they knew of only two Soviet psychiatrists who "publicly displayed their opposition" to abuses, although there were "many who acted toward dissenter-

26. See *Novoe Russkoe Slovo*, June 21, 1978.
27. See Theodore Friedgut, "The Democratic Movement: Dimensions and Perspectives," in R. Tőkés, *Dissent in the USSR*, pp. 116-138, at p. 124. There are numerous vivid illustrations of the authorities' ability to scare and silence incipient or potential dissenters and their sympathizers in such works as Valentine Turchin's *Inertsiya strakha* [Inertia of fear] (New York: Khronika Press, 1977).

Political Dissent 173

patients with implicit benevolence" and a few who expressed criticism anonymously.[28] Bloch and Reddaway's finding seems not untypical of the attitude of Soviet professionals generally. However, some scholars, including Reddaway, perceive a slowly accelerating process in Soviet society that might be described as disidentification with official values. This, as it gathers momentum, might be expected to produce a growth of open, public dissent.[29] Perhaps Reddaway exaggerates the regime's weaknesses.[30] But his findings at least point to tensions and frustrations in Soviet society that seem likely to generate increasing alienation and dissent, some of which might erupt in violence if peaceful protest continues to elicit only scorn and repression.

One speculates that the leadership may have considered it inexpedient to unleash the KGB against the earlier mentioned Christian Committee for the Defense of the Rights of Believers. Although this committee reportedly was formed in 1976 at the suggestion of Yuri Orlov and cooperated closely with Orlov's Moscow Helsinki group, as of October 1978 none of its members had been arrested. The KGB's caution in respect to this group—which contrasts sharply with its heavy use of coercion against all of the other organizations involved in Orlov's campaign to promote fulfillment of the Helsinki Final Act, cries out for explanation. It has been suggested that it may have reflected the Soviet leadership's potential difficulties of confrontation with the fifty million member Russian Orthodox Church, of which apparently the Christian Committee, rather than the party-controlled official Orthodox church leaders, is increasingly regarded as representative. Also significant in connection with any attempt to evaluate the role of the Christian Committee and, one might add, of religion in the USSR generally is increasing church attendance and other signs of the growing vitality of a number of denominations, particularly the Russian Orthodox. There is evidence of ever closer

28. Sidney Bloch and Peter B. Reddaway, *Russia's Political Hospitals* (London: Gallancz, 1977).
29. L. G. Churchward, *The Soviet Intelligentsia* (London: 1973), pp. 136-139. Peter B. Reddaway, in his important article "Notes from Undergound," in the *Times Literary Supplement*, June 16, 1978, asserts that dissent "is endemic and spreading," that "authority is gradually ebbing away from the regime." "What legitimacy it possesses," says he, "comes from the inertia of most of its subjects (now slowly declining) and from a lightly disguised appeal to Russian nationalism."
30. The stability and cohesiveness of the present Soviet system are rated high by some competent scholars, such as Jerome Gilison and Stephen White. See Gilison's *British and Soviet Politics* (Baltimore: Johns Hopkins, 1972) and White's chapter in Archie Brown and Jack Gray, eds., *Political Culture and Political Change in Communist States* (New York: Holmes and Meier, 1977).

links between the Christian Committee and the active remnants of the "democratic movement."[31]

In addition to such evidence of counter-mobilization as is provided by the activities of some organizations—the Christian Committee is particularly significant because of the vastness of its actual and potential constituency—other trends, such as the "growing evidence of nonconformity" among Soviet youth, recently noted by a German authority on Soviet education, have to be taken into account in evaluating prospects for the persistence and growth of dissent in the USSR.[32]

One of the most encouraging results of regime-dissenter conflict since Stalin is that a tenacious tradition of non-violent struggle for liberty under law has put down roots in the Soviet Union, at least since a group of demonstrators on Pushkin Square in 1965 requested the authorities to "respect your own constitution." At times it has seemed as though the secret police had finally suppressed the advocates of legality and democratization, but somehow new people have come forward to continue the struggle. Some of them have been individuals like Andrei Amalrik, who has written that he had from childhood been repelled by a system that had destroyed several members of his family. Others, like young Anatoli Shcharansky, or Vladimir Bukovski before him, came from orthodox Communist homes. Since the late 1960s, a growing role in the movement has been played by highly qualified, in some cases very distinguished scientists, such as Sakharov, Andrei Tverdokhlebov, Yuri Orlov, and most recently, the nuclear physicist Sergei Polikanov. The recent action of Polikanov is perhaps portentous. A corresponding member of the USSR Academy of Sciences and director of a laboratory at the important Dubna international science center, Polikanov was angered by the refusal of the Soviet authorities to trust him sufficiently to allow him to take his wife and daughter with him to Switzerland, whither he had been invited to do research. He refused to go, held a press conference with foreign newsmen, and was expelled from the Communist party. Almost immediately after the Ginzburg and Shcharansky trials, Polikanov announced that he was formally joining the Moscow Helsinki organization.

Participants in the Helsinki groups, in the Christian Committee, in the Soviet chapter of Amnesty International, in the Moscow Human Rights Committee, in the Action Group for the Defense of

31. My remarks concerning the Christian Committee are based largely on a paper presented by Dr. John B. Dunlop in Spring, 1978, at the Kennan Institute, of which Dr. Dunlop kindly provided me a copy.

32. Oskar Anweiler, reviewing Abraham A. Kreuzter, *Contemporary Education and Moral Upbringing in the Soviet Union. Slavic Review* (June, 1978), p. 315.

Human Rights, and in the painstaking, often dangerous compilation and distribution of the *Chronicle of Current Events* have acted—and, I am confident, will continue to act—in the belief that world peace and the struggle for human rights throughout the world are indivisible. They have contended with difficulties that would have deterred lesser spirits. Unable to elicit any response at home, save threats and repression, they have sought support from Western democratic governments and public opinion, in the conviction that only thus could they follow the guidance of reason and the promptings of conscience. For such people and for many in the West, "the conception of active international defense of human rights . . . has acquired the significance of an international ideology."[33]

33. Andrei Sakharov, *Trevoga i Nadezhda* [Alarm & hope] (New York: Khronika Press, 1978), p. 17.

Myron Rush

The Problem of Succession

Soviet political institutions have won a measure of legitimacy because of their durability and accomplishments—in economic development, in defeating Germany's war machine, in effectively waging cold war against the U.S., in providing broad social services and a rising standard of living for the Soviet people, and, in recent decades, in avoiding political turbulence. A rough assessment of the prospects for Soviet political institutions would be obliged to project this impressive performance forward at least one decade.

A more refined assessment is needed, however, taking account of: 1) the forthcoming Brezhnev succession; 2) certain vulnerabilities that have been revealed in particular institutions in recent years; and 3) the challenges stemming from developments in Soviet society and in the international environment. Such an assessment suggests that

NOTE: This paper was prepared while the author was Scholar in Residence at the National Foreign Assessment Center of the Central Intelligence Agency. The conclusions and judgments presented, however, are those of the author and do not necessarily represent the views of NFAC or CIA.

Soviet political institutions will be seriously tested in the Brezhnev succession and that crises lie ahead.[1]

Such crises are likely to involve turning points in the further development of Soviet institutions, not necessarily dangers sufficient to destroy them. But the difficulties confronting the Soviet regime in the years ahead should not be discounted merely because the politics of the post-Khrushchev period have been relatively quiescent. It should be recalled, in this connection, that in the People's Republic of China a decade of seemingly tranquil politics ended abruptly in 1965, when the fissures that had been concealed from observers suddenly became apparent in the "Great Proletarian Cultural Revolution," and the resulting divisions in the leadership led to more than a decade of purges and counter-purges.[2]

VULNERABILITIES IN SOVIET POLITICAL INSTITUTIONS

Vulnerable points are to be found in institutions engaged in decision-making as well as in institutions engaged in implementing decisions. In the first place, the ordering of the highest organs and offices of leadership has not been fixed but has varied according to circumstances. As a result, the relative authority of the highest party and government organs has repeatedly been a subject of contention, as has the relative authority of the highest bodies within the party. The Politburo is the decisive legislative and executive organ (its policies being formally confirmed by the Central Committee), but the Politburo has found it difficult to operate as a collegial body and to maintain even a rough equality in the powers of its members. In particular, the great potentialities of the office of the General Secretary have enabled incumbents to arrogate much of the Politburo's powers. The result has been a considerable fluctuation in the relative power of the Politburo and the General Secretary and substantial tension between them.

Since the powers of the General Secretary are neither specified in a statute nor fixed by precedent, no reliable means for the orderly transfer of these powers has yet been devised. More than this: there are no established political means of removing an unsatisfactory

---

1. I have kept footnotes to a minimum in this essay since most of the facts are readily accessible and its judgments and arguments have in good part been elaborated in other writings of mine, particularly *Political Succession in the USSR*, 2nd edition (New York: Columbia University Press, 1968) and *How Communist States Change Their Rulers* (Ithaca: Cornell University Press, 1974).

2. Thomas Robinson, ed., *The Cultural Revolution in China* (Los Angeles: University of California Press, 1971).

General Secretary (though conspiracy may be a poor substitute); there are no established rules for choosing the successor; there is no way of ensuring that a new incumbent will inherit his predecessor's powers. Typically, there has been a double crisis of succession: the first occurs when the incumbent is replaced, and a second arises from the new General Secretary's attempts to assume the powers of his predecessors; powers that he believes are necessary—and may be so in fact—to provide stable and effective leadership. In such crises, the political police and the armed forces have played significant roles at several critical junctures (e.g., in 1953, 1957, and 1964) and may do so again, possibly with disruptive consequences.[3]

THE PRESENT SITUATION IN THE LEADING GOVERNMENT AND PARTY ORGANS

In assessing the stability of Soviet institutions, the initial focus must be on the leading organs, for if the leadership is not seriously weakened the odds are that it will be able to cope with the political and social challenges that it will face. The stability of the leadership is uncertain, however, for the reason noted above: institutionalization of supreme authority has not progressed enough to establish a stable balance between the personal power of the General Secretary and the collective authority of the top organs: the Secretariat, the Politburo, and the Central Committee. The present distribution of power appears to have arisen largely as a result of Brezhnev's effort during the post-Khrushchev period to establish his personal ascendency.

What is the present balance of institutions within the top leadership and how is it likely to be affected by Brezhnev's continuation in office in the near future and by the subsequent struggle for his succession? Brezhnev initially relied heavily on the Secretariat to enhance the powers of his office of General Secretary. He used the General Department of the Central Committee, headed by his close ally, Chernenko, to control the internal administration of the Politburo.[4] He was unable, however, to secure the strong personal control

---

3. Interpretations of Soviet succession that differ from the one presented here are found in Jerome Gilison, "New Factors of Stability in Soviet Collective Leadership," *World Politics*, 19:4 (1976); T. H. Rigby, "The Soviet Leadership: Towards a Self-Stabilizing Oligarchy?" *Soviet Studies*, 22:2 (1970); and Grey Hodnett, "Succession Contingencies in the Soviet Union," *Problems of Communism* (March/April, 1975).

4. Leonard Schapiro, "The General Departments of the CC of the CPSU," *Survey*, 21:3 (1975).

of the Secretariat and its staff that enabled Stalin (in the 1920s) and Khrushchev to decide the composition of the Central Committee and thereby to determine the membership of the Politburo. In the 1970s Brezhnev became more deeply preoccupied with foreign affairs and economic administration. He acquired a second office inside the Kremlin and his involvement in the Secretariat presumably declined; his dependence on Kirilenko, his deputy in the Secretariat, correspondingly increased and with it, perhaps, Kirilenko's scope for independent action.

The Central Committee is too unwieldy to serve as a truly deliberative body, and for many years it has not done much more than confer status on its members and provide important channels of information to them. Because of its size, it is subject to manipulation by the Senior Secretary. In recent years it has assembled twice a year for plenary sessions lasting a day or two, usually to hear Brezhnev report on his foreign policy activities or criticize the economy. The Central Committee is not as important a sounding board to Brezhnev as it was to Khrushchev, however; and it seems questionable, in view of Brezhnev's apparent failure to achieve strong control over appointments to the Central Committee, whether he could confidently rely on that body in a political crisis to protect his position.

Brezhnev's limited ability to choose the members of the Central Committee has lessened his capacity to achieve mastery over the Politburo. Within a half dozen years of their succession, Stalin and Khrushchev (along with Mikoyan) were the lone survivors of their predecessor's Politburo; in contrast, three veterans of Khrushchev's Politburo (Kosygin, Suslov, and Kirilenko) sit with Brezhnev today. Nevertheless, Brezhnev has strongly influenced the composition of the Politburo by adding followers (Kunayev and Shcherbitskiy) and allies of varying dependability (Gromyko, Andropov, Ustinov, and Romanov) and, since 1973, by purging potential rivals and others with independent views (Shelest, Voronov, Shelepin, Polyanskiy, and Podgorny).

THE ROLE OF THE POLITBURO

The Politburo remains central to the working of the system. There the key institutions and information channels come together so that major problems can be dealt with and national policies established. According to the Soviet leaders, the Politburo meets regularly and is consulted on all important questions. The Politburo's integrity as a deliberative body is questionable, however, for several reasons. First, it is big and unwieldy. There are thirteen full members, as against the customary ten or eleven at times when the Politburo has been most decisive, and several members are not in a position to participate effectively in its work. Three of the thirteen have posts outside Moscow (in the Ukraine, Leningrad, and Kazakhstan) and are not in a position to bring informed and independent judgment to bear on disputed issues of policy. Several others, including Gromyko, Pelshe, and Ustinov (and Grechko when he was Minister of Defense), have had specialized careers which probably limit their capacity to judge the full range of issues coming before the Politburo. Of the eight alternate members of the Politburo, three work outside Moscow and are not regularly available for its meetings. For members and candidates who work outside Moscow, Politburo rank may be more important in conferring prestige, which makes them more effective in their assigned posts, than in providing them influence in Politburo deliberations.

Despite these deficiencies in the Politburo's capacity to act as a deliberative body, there can be no question that the Politburo as it currently functions restricts Brezhnev's ability to act independently. To this very limited degree, then, Brezhnev has furthered the institutionalization of the Politburo.

In his 14 years tenure as General Secretary, Brezhnev has acquired powers that have given him the predominant position in the Secretariat and provided him with substantial, if not infallible, means to manipulate the Politburo. In addition, Brezhnev seems to have won substantial, though diffuse, support in the Central Committee, based on his respect for the tenure of officials and the elevation of many of them to membership in the Central Committee.[5] Consequently, Brezhnev's departure from office or a significant decline in his physical capacities is likely to upset the present balance of leadership, giving rise to struggle between individuals and conflict among the leading political organs and institutions.

SOURCES OF SHORT-TERM INSTABILITY

While Brezhnev's health is not likely to force his retirement, the combination of slow physical deterioration and political challenges to his authority, perhaps acting reciprocally, could deprive him of office in the near future; his history of cardio-vascular disease makes

---

5. These accretions of power were not the result of accident, nor were they the inadvertent outcome of defensive maneuvers to protect himself against rivals. There is every indication that Brezhnev actively sought these increased powers and, to achieve them, had to overcome the resistance of some of his colleagues. One revealing sign that Brezhnev has willfully arrogated power is his reticence in recent years about the principle of collectivity of leadership, a reticence that was similarly characteristic of Khrushchev.

him vulnerable to a heart attack or stroke. However, even if Brezhnev remains in office for serveral years, the present balance between personal and collective authority may not persist.

The following are important sources of instability:

1. The balance between collective and personal authority, despite some setbacks suffered by Brezhnev, has shifted markedly in his favor and may reach a point where the Politburo will feel the need to reassert itself as a collegial body.

2. Brezhnev has used his power cautiously in making policy, but he may become the target of strong criticism for a number of decisions the Politburo has taken, such as to reduce sharply the growth rate of investment and to maintain a high priority for agriculture despite lagging production in heavy industry.

3. Although Brezhnev does not appear to be strongly committed to major economic or social reforms which would require him to possess overriding authority, he has reason to try to make his position more secure in the event that his policies suffer severe setbacks.

4. Because of the advanced age and poor health of the Politburo members, vacancies probably will occur in the next two years. They need not be filled, in view of the inflated size of the present Politburo; but the effect, nonetheless, would be to change the balance in the leadership. Moreover, Brezhnev might try to take advantage of vacancies to bring his protégés into the Politburo.

THE FORTHCOMING SUCCESSION

Changes among the leaders during Brezhnev's remaining tenure in office could affect both the institutional balance between the party and the government, and the likelihood that attempts might be made to order the succession in advance. If Brezhnev's position were weakened, a struggle for the succession might occur even before the position of General Secretary was vacated. On the other hand, a moderate increase in his power would not necessarily end his preoccupation with the preservation of his power nor lessen unwillingness to share his authority in an attempt to order the succession.

If he were to consolidate his position so that he had secure control of the Politburo, thereby facilitating efforts to arrange the succession, Brezhnev, in view of his record of caution in using his power, might still choose not to make the attempt. Although the outcomes of previous succession arrangements have often diverged sharply from what their authors had in view, these arrangements have facilitated the transfer of power. Thus, if Brezhnev failed to make preliminary arrangements for the succession, the chances of an orderly succession would be reduced.

To date, Brezhnev has not only failed to groom promising candidates for the succession, but he has taken pains to oppose those who seemed to come forward. He played a crucial role in the weakening or ouster of such credible candidates as Shelepin and Kulakov. Consequently, observers have been reduced to speculation about the prospects of such unpromising figures as: Andropov, the head of the political police, who lacks experience as chief of a major territorial division; Shcherbitskiy, an ethnic Ukrainian, who has never occupied a post outside the Ukraine: Romanov, whose experience till now has been limited to Leningrad; and Ustinov, a 70 year old who has spent his entire career in the military-industrial complex. With such dubious rivals, it is no wonder that Andrei Kirilenko, a 72 year old *apparatchik*, is widely expected to succeed Brezhnev. Kirilenko is the only senior figure who is a member of both the Politburo and the Secretariat, and he also is ambitious and relatively vigorous.[6]

Although Kirilenko deputizes for Brezhnev, he is not formally the presumptive heir. According to Brezhnev's rank-order listing of the newly elected Secretariat following the 25th Party Congress, Suslov is senior to Kirilenko, and this circumstance might enable a younger rival of Kirilenko—though presumably not the superannuated Suslov himself—to contest Kirilenko's claim to the succession, particularly if such an alternative figure were supported by senior members of the Politburo, Moreover, Kirilenko's advanced age and certain limitations of experience, particularly in the realms of foreign and defense policy, would probably result in a substantial weakening of the office of General Secretary. The Secretariat might then become an arena of active conflict once more, as in the mid-60s, and the government might become as strong and assertive as it was in the early post-Stalin period. Were these things to occur, the leadership's capacity to make urgent decisions or to initiate basic reforms would be reduced, perhaps seriously, until such time as a younger, more vigorous man might assume the office and expand its powers.

From this analysis it follows that the prospect in the next several years is for a weakening of the leadership's capacity to act decisively owing to the slow deterioration in Brezhnev's physical powers and to the likelihood that Kirilenko, his probable heir in the event of an early succession, would find it difficult to assert strong personal leadership.

A weakening of the leadership, were it to accompany the Brezhnev succession, would have major political consequences of

---

6. It seems unlikely that Kirilenko would simultaneously obtain Brezhnev's office of Chairman of the Supreme Soviet Presidium although, if he strengthened his position as General Secretary, he probably would emulate Brezhnev in seeking that post as well.

two kinds: it would probably reduce the leadership's capacity to reform institutions and resolve serious political and social problems that have already been too long deferred; in addition, it could lead to a widening of the political arena by activating institutional interest groups in the economic bureaucracy, the scientific establishment, and the creative intelligentsia. The latter development, while it cannot be discounted, may be the lesser danger to the leadership. Despite the expectations of many observers,[7] interest groups in the USSR, other than the military, have displayed neither a strong inclination to engage in higher Soviet politics nor great effectiveness when they have attempted to do so. This was true even when circumstances seemed propitious, as during the succession to Khrushchev. Unless the divisions in the leadership become considerably deeper than they were in the Khrushchev succession (which, as discussed below, is a real possibility), the party apparatus will probably be able to maintain its control over the other institutions and to limit their participation in higher Soviet politics.

PROBLEMS OF RULE THAT MUST SOON BE FACED

In the next few years the leadership will have to deal with institutional defects and adverse social developments that have emerged prominently during the past decade. Many of them were not addressed seriously by the leadership that followed Khrushchev and was repelled by his activism. That group concentrated for the most part on urgent questions of policy rather than on underlying problems that are difficult to resolve, the effects of which might not be felt for some time. In the next few years these problems, which will grow more acute, will have to be dealt with, or their seriously adverse consequences accepted, by a leadership that (as argued above) will be somewhat weakened and perhaps seriously divided.

The overriding problem, in view of the regime's long-established priorities, is the progressive reduction in the rate of growth of the economy. This has been caused in large part by factors that will continue to operate: a decline in the growth rate of investment; a long-term decline in the output obtained from given increments of capital; increased costs of raw materials; and a declining rate of growth in the size of the labor force. The problem of the labor force will worsen over the next few years until a point is reached where increases in production must come entirely from increases in labor

---

7. Gordon Skilling and Franklyn Griffiths, eds., *Interest Groups in Soviet Politics* (Princeton: Princeton University Press, 1971).

productivity. (In the past, these increases have tended to lag behind planned rates of growth.) A partial solution might be sought in institutional reform, by improving the administrative apparatus that directs the country's economic enterprises, which has long been a source of serious dissatisfaction to the leadership. But unsuccessful attempts during the past third of a century to amalgamate the numerous economic ministries (in 1953), to modify them (in 1965, when they were reconstituted), and to create an alternative mechanism (in 1957) suggest that no administrative solution to the problem of reduced economic growth is readily available.

If economic growth continues to decline in the next decade, as expected, the Soviet leaders may confront difficult choices such as further reducing the growth rate of investment, which could accelerate the decline; reducing the rate of increase in consumption, which might adversely affect labor productivity; or sharply reducing the rate of increase in defense spending, which could slow to some extent the decline in economic growth at the possible cost of antagonizing the military establishment and thereby aggravating the leadership's political problems.[8] The basic choice, between accepting a reduced rate of economic growth or a reduced rate of growth in defense spending, has long-term implications for Soviet foreign policy. The first might lessen the USSR's capacity to deal with world problems a decade or more hence; the second choice might require the USSR to moderate its foreign policy in the years immediately ahead so as not to provoke the U.S. into a new and costly round in the arms race.

Major inefficiencies in the regime's bureaucracies have been a serious problem from the beginning, but the disease and its consequences appear to have worsened substantially in the past decade. To remedy the disaffection and uncertainty caused by Khrushchev's numerous disruptive reorganizations, the post-Khrushchev leadership gave officials virtually ensured tenure, except in cases of gross incompetence or serious misfeasance. Thus, inclusion in the *nomenklatura* (pool of officials) at the higher levels has tended to confer a vested right to occupy positions that entail high salaries as well as numerous perquisites and privileges. As a result, opportunities for the rapid advancement of able and ambitious young officials have declined, and discipline, previously a key strength of the regime's institutions, has suffered. Disturbing signs of a weakening of discipline have appeared not only in the work force, in local administration, and in the economic ministries, but also in the army and in the party *apparat* itself. Stalin's means of dealing with this problem,

8. *Soviet Economy in a New Perspective*, Joint Economic Committee, Congress of the United States (Washington: United States Government Printing Office, 1976).

which were effective though costly, are not available to the present leadership.

The party apparatus, the key institution of the regime as it is currently constituted, appears to be suffering from substantial ills. Brezhnev, from the rostrum of the 25th Party Congress in 1976, warned against the Leninist sin of liberalism (i.e., toleration of incompetence and wrongdoing) in party work and revealed that the *apparat's* lack of responsiveness to commands was receiving concentrated attention from the party's leading bodies. In discussing the problem of party discipline in his report to the 25th Congress, Brezhnev spoke at some length and used uncharacteristically sharp language:

> Along with questions of criticism and self-criticism (on which "a liberal attitude" could not be allowed), the Central Committee has also examined another problem, that of the control and verification of fulfillment of adopted decisions. This has often been a subject of discussion at meetings of the Politburo and the Central Committee Secretariat. (The Secretariat, "which held 205 meetings in this period . . . paid much more attention than previously" to this question.) A special letter was devoted to this, which the Politburo circulated to all party organizations, as well as a series of Central Committee decisions. . . . Now and again, after it turns out that some decision has not been carried out, a second is adopted on the very same question, and sometimes even a third. In substance, it might appear, they are not bad. But we are speaking of something that should already have been done. Thus the question inevitably arises: does not the new decision on an old theme appear at a discount, as a manifestation of liberalism? Is not exactingness consequently reduced? It is necessary to put an end to this practice![9]

Frequent reports reach the West from emigrants and journalists that party officials are becoming more openly cynical and increasingly less committed to the official ideology. The *apparat* clearly needs to be rejuvenated, a process that presents opportunities as well as dangers. It may facilitate an improvement in the technical and personal qualifications of its members; but, carried too far, this could undermine the *apparat's* coherence and party spirit, thereby jeopardizing its capacity to give coherence to the Soviet political system as a whole.

The major ethnic minorities and the republics they inhabit will

---

9. *Pravda*, February 25, 1976.

continue to be a source of concern to the leadership. The acute nationalities problem that existed at the time of Stalin's death, however, was ameliorated by Khrushchev who brought ethnic Ukrainians into the central leadership. As long as the Slavic peoples of the USSR are not in conflict, the nationality question is likely to be manageable since the Slavic leaders, if united, probably can cope with the remaining quarter of the Soviet population. There is, however, a residual danger over the next decade that manifestations of nationalist feeling among Ukrainian members of the leadership (like that shown by Shelest in the early 70s, for example) may encounter strong currents of Russian national sentiment (as seen in Polyanskiy) inside the Politburo. In any case, institutional adjustments may eventually be required to accommodate the national and religious sentiments of the republics of the Caucasus, the Baltic area, and, especially, Central Asia where the rapid growth of population in the next quarter century may pose serious social and political problems for the regime.

The problem of dissidence, particularly of demands that the regime respect its nominal guarantees of civil rights, may be intensified if the scientific and creative intelligentsia become more assertive during the Brezhnev succession. Even so, political dissidence is not likely to become unmanageable, since the desire for political and civil rights does not appear to be a serious concern of the working class or the peasantry and is unlikely to become so in the decade ahead.

On the other hand, relations with Eastern Europe, which strongly affect Soviet domestic politics, will almost certainly pose serious problems for the leadership, especially if crises arise in that area, as is likely.[10] In particular, the issue of whether to engage in military repression would seriously strain a Soviet leadership as divided and weak as the one in 1968 that had to deal with the Prague Spring.

ALTERNATIVE CONTINGENCIES FOR SOVIET INSTITUTIONS

The problems of institutional development and policy resolution enumerated here clearly pose a serious challenge to the leadership in the next few years. If the challenge is not effectively met, the resources available to the Soviet leadership for the pursuit of its goals may be seriously reduced. Is it likely, however, to threaten the stability of the regime or of its established institutions?

10. *East European Economies Post-Helsinki*, Joint Economic Committee, Congress of the United States (Washington: United States Government Printing Office, 1977).

The regime's institutions will probably persist without substantial modification for the next several years, possibly for the next decade. In view of their record of solid, if inefficient and wasteful, performance, the odds are that they will neither fail, on the one hand, nor, on the other be reformed to become markedly more efficient and responsive to the leadership's commands.

There are, however, two distinct ways in which basic changes might come about: inadvertently, as the result of a weakening of the top leadership, leading to a widening of the political arena and increased participation by various groups in the making of high policy; or deliberately, if a strong personal leader were to emerge with a broad program for reform and the will to carry it through. The Brezhnev succession could have either outcome.

The first contingency, a serious weakening of the top leadership's cohesion and a reciprocal enhancement of the regime's key vulnerabilities, might occur if arrangements for the succession to Brezhnev are not made in advance. Any successor leadership will have to confront the falling rates of economic growth and an emerging energy crisis, an entrenched bureaucratic machine whose internal discipline may be failing, some domestic agitation for greater ethnic, religious, and personal freedom, and most likely, disturbances in Eastern Europe. A weakened and divided leadership would find it difficult to deal with these refractory problems yet unable to ignore them, and might be further weakened as a result. A crisis of such proportions might call into question the sovereignty of the party apparatus over other interest groups, which has not been seriously challenged since Khrushchev's victory over the Anti-Party Group in 1957. The leaders of institutional interest groups might then take courage and form alliances aimed at weakening the party *apparat's* control over them and assert joint claims to an institutional autonomy and to participation in higher Soviet politics. An incipient movement in this direction did, in fact, occur after Stalin's death; but it was aborted by Khrushchev's victory in 1957.

If the Brezhnev succession brought about such a weakening of control by the party apparatus, the oligarchical elements in the present system would probably become stronger. Leaders of the chief institutions who sit on the Politburo (and perhaps their supporters and allies in the Central Committee as well) would be able to contribute more actively to the formation of national policy. This would probably lead to a reduction in the leadership's capacity to pursue a unified grand strategy embracing foreign and defense policy. The stability of such a modified institutional order is hard to predict. If it proved ineffective in pursuing the regime's ends it could lead, in turn, to the restoration of strong personal rule.

An alternative, but perhaps less likely, method of institutional reform might become feasible if a strong leader were to emerge, as Khrushchev did, to capitalize on the manifest need to purge incompetent officials and to rejuvenate both the supreme leadership and its middle levels. This might enable a successful candidate for the succession to create a strong personal machine which could be employed to strengthen discipline and perhaps also to impose institutional reforms from above. As a result, institutional interest groups would have to submit to direction from the ruling center and the prospects for a liberalization of the regime would be limited.

THE PROBABILITIES

While weaknesses in the present system could lead during the succession to its transformation in the direction of either oligarchy or strong personal rule (perhaps in sequence), the regime that emerges from the Brezhnev succession is likely to have the following features:

1. Continued hegemony of the party apparatus over other institutions.

2. Persistence of the present mode of leadership, with authority concentrated in a Politburo whose members have markedly unequal powers and which is subject to manipulation by the General Secretary of the Central Committee.

3. Inability of the successor leadership to deal effectively with the regime's fundamental problems.

4. A reduced growth rate of the economy, although one that might still provide the resources needed to compete with the West, especially if the West is weakened by a failure to resolve its own economic problems.

George W. Breslauer

Images of the Future and Lessons of the Past

Meaningful scholarly discussion of the Soviet future must be based upon complex foundations. We must not attempt to predict the unpredictable; yet we must not shy away from elaborating the conditions under which certain changes might take place. Moreover, we must become conscious of our assumptions and make them explicit. That is one of the purposes of this chapter. I will lay out a series of alternative scenarios for future evolution of the Soviet system, and highlight the assumptions or premises that underlie contentions that evolution in a given direction is probable.[1] I will then give indirect empirical grounding to the paper by presenting a series of propositions about the nature of the Soviet political process and Soviet regime perspectives. These propositions, which emerge from the evidence I have collected in comparing the evolution of the Khrushchev and Brezhnev administrations, will then be applied to the alternative scenarios as a first step toward the union of theory and practice.

1. This chapter builds upon a conceptual framework first elaborated in George Breslauer, *Five Images of the Soviet Future* (Berkeley: University of California, Institute of International Studies, 1978).

ON THE NATURE OF THE SOVIET SYSTEM

Our conceptions of the direction in which the Soviet Union is heading are frequently a function of the way in which we characterize the contemporary Soviet system. The totalitarian model, for example, focused our attention so exclusively on the political control network that prospects for change eluded our imagination. The term that I find most useful as a summary characterization of the regime-type that has emerged under Brezhnev is welfare-state authoritarianism.

I think of the present regime as authoritarian rather than totalitarian for several reasons. First, it has been characterized by a form of corporate pluralism within the political elite as well as by committee rule within the Politburo. Second, it has broadened and regularized specialist input into decision making processes. Third, it has de-politicized many realms of private life, allowed a good deal of physical security for the political conformist, and put an end to mass terror as an instrument of policy. Although Soviet authoritarianism retains its bureaucratic and mobilizational character, the demise of despotism and mass terror mean that the current regime-type is no longer characterized by totalitarian methods of policy-making and mass mobilization.

I label the regime a welfare-state because its policies have included a commitment to minimal, but rising, levels of material and social security, public health, and education for broad masses of the population. Moreover, this commitment to welfare has included a commitment to job security, subsidized prices for basic commodities, and a relatively egalitarian wage structure. These commitments have been met at the cost of considerable economic inefficiency, lack of worker initiative, and failure to elicit entrepreneurial risk-taking. But these economic drags have been consciously accepted by Soviet leaders in the name of equity.

The distinctive characters of Soviet authoritarianism, and of the Soviet welfare-state, make the Soviet order tension ridden. Conflicts between elitism and egalitarianism abound. The ways in which these tensions might express themselves in the future are hardly self-evident. Those scholars who view them as conflicts among irreconcilable premises, however, tend to believe that some form of systemic change is likely.

FOUR IMAGES OF SYSTEMIC CHANGE

Let us imagine four more or less realistic alternatives to welfare-state authoritarianism. One such alternative would be a profound systemic crisis: varying types or degrees of sustained public disorder (instability) resulting from economic shocks, centrifugal ethnic pressures, or a breakdown in the instruments of political control. A second alternative would be a Soviet form of Dubčekism: political and industrial democracy, or the version of "socialist democracy" propounded by Roy Medvedev.[2] A third alternative would be a form of elitist liberalism, entailing the constitutionalization of political relationships among the corporate groups comprising the political elite (but without mass democratization), coupled with a social policy that would sacrifice social security, welfare, and egalitarian values to the search for economic efficiency. A fourth alternative would entail a return to some form of Stalinism, based upon a fundamentalist reaction to the compromise, secularization, and lack of discipline that characterize the present regime in the eyes of some officials and members of the intelligentsia. Any of these alternatives, then, would constitute systemic change, if system is defined as the social and political policies of welfare-state authoritarianism.

A prediction of systemic change would be based on a view of welfare-state authoritarianism as non-viable and non-durable, either because of perceptions of elite and mass opinion in the USSR, or because of assumptions about structural or historical trends, or because of a combination of these perceptions and perspectives. Thus, in the realm of public opinion, one might buttress such a prediction with a view of the Soviet masses and intelligentsia as highly dissatisfied, impatient, and increasingly willing to act on their feelings—or one might predict that this will become the case as structural tendencies lead to a worsening of the objective situation. One might view policy changes under Brezhnev as a sign that the political elite is split, deadlocked, polarized over critical issues, and increasingly dominated by an extremist psychology of either the left or the right; or one might predict that such polarization will result from prolongation of current structural trends.

Given these perceptions, one would discount the probability of reformist, anticipatory leadership capable of alleviating tensions. Quite the contrary. One would be inclined to argue that welfare-state authoritarianism lacks a crucial ingredient for long-term durability, credible mobilizational fervor, and that the various systemic alternatives would result from a search for new mobilizing values: anti-authoritarianism; technological advance; democracy; Russite-fundamentalism; anti-elitism; or attainment of the utopian vision of a homogeneous social structure. Such a view would also lead one to

2. For full citation of the Western and Soviet dissident literature that foresees these alternative futures, see Breslauer, *Five Images*. Medvedev's scenario can be found in his *On Socialist Democracy* (New York: Alfred A. Knopf, 1975).

envisage crises as major turning points that would spur the rapid demise of welfare-state authoritarianism. In the face of possible public disorder, one would not foresee increased elite cohesion, but opportunistic attempts to mobilize different social constituencies.

Such assessments of elite and mass moods might well be common to any prediction of systemic change, for they are all characterized by profound dissatisfaction with the premises underlying the contemporary regime-type. However, one's assessment of the kind of systemic change likely to take place will depend upon several things: 1) one's estimate of the relative weight of different tendencies within the official and non-official sectors; 2) one's conception of the nature of structural constraints on change, and of the likely impact of these constraints on the weight of different tendencies within the official and non-official sectors; and 3) one's theory of Russian history, or of historical evolution in general.

ON THE PROSPECTS FOR WITHIN-SYSTEM CHANGE

In contrast to a vision of the demise of welfare-state authoritarianism, one might argue that policy changes in the next decade or two are likely to remain within the parameters defined by welfare-state authoritarianism. Such a prediction would be based upon perceptions and perspectives that view the current regime-type as capable of accommodating a variety of combinations of approaches to tensions between elitist and egalitarian premises.

A prognosis of within-system change would be based on a view of the masses and the intelligentsia which acknowledges dissatisfactions, discontents, and grumbling, but which sees these classes as relatively patient and quiescent, having contained their expectations, without new sources of mobilizational fervor, and having more to lose than to gain (in their own eyes) from challenging the authorities. Moreover, from this reformist perspective elite polarization is relatively low, and the official class is increasingly populated by individuals who lack an extremist psychology and are tolerant of ambiguity. A need for some reforms within the context of welfare-state authoritarianism may be acknowledged. However, a reformist perspective would see a relatively high probability that the regime will exercise anticipatory leadership during or after the coming succession. It sees the cleavages in society and within the elite as cross-cutting rather than cumulative, and therefore assumes a reasonable capacity within the regime for conflict-management. The reformist would assume that disorder, should it occur, would be relatively localized, short-lived, or containable, and that the inclination of the elite would be to pull together in the face of the disorder and to accommodate to the social forces. The reformist would view containable crises as catalysts for creative leadership within the context of welfare-state authoritarianism.

TWO VERSIONS OF WITHIN-SYSTEM CHANGE

One can imagine any number of alternative mixes of policies that would be consistent with welfare-state authoritarianism. For purposes of discussion, however, let me distinguish between two extreme versions of this regime-type: a conservative and a liberal version. A conservative version would constitute a retrenchment. It would allocate resources so as to upgrade the priority of military/ heavy industrial investments and Siberian development. Its incentive policy would entail a simultaneous augmentation of material incentives and pressure. Administrative policies would call for a combination of computerization, reconcentration, and pressure. Political participation would combine rational-administrative premises with a tightening of controls against deviant public expression. This would in all likelihood assume a hostile foreign environment, and the regime would be less receptive to foreign economic or cultural penetration. The authority-building strategy of the General Secretary would be likely to combine a commitment to corporatism with an attempt to augment his personal power and generate popular appeals through a Great Russian, anti-Semitic, or anti-intellectual tilt, or mobilizational fervor associated with the industrialization of Siberia.

The losers under such a regime would be the dissidents, the technocrats, the elitist liberals, ethnic minorities alienated by the Great Russian tilt, and all those hoping for a significant improvement in the living standard. The winners would be those for whom the highest values are social and physical security, mobilizational fervor derived from tapping the "inexhaustible resources" of the East, Russian nationalism, isolation from foreign influence, military/heavy industrial values, a strong boss, and administrative stability. Although this version of welfare-state authoritarianism would entail a retrenchment, it is important to bear in mind that it would not entail a fundamentalist restoration: i.e., a return to mass austerity, aggressive Russification of the ethnic minorities, the use of terror against entire categories of the population, foreign policy isolationism, or arbitrary, personalistic rule.

At the other extreme, we can imagine a liberal version of welfare-state authoritarianism. This would allocate resources so as to increase investment in consumer durables, while selectively reducing the military budget. It would opt for administrative reforms and selectively introduce such innovations as the link system in rural areas where the payoff would be high and the trauma with respect to mass layoffs relatively low (e.g., in areas already suffering from a labor shortage). In the industrial sector, it would introduce the Shchekino experiment (permitting discharge of redundant workers) in areas and by means that would maximize economic benefits and minimize social costs. It might allow selected forms of autonomy in the service sector, as in the case of repair shops and catering services, or in the private sector of Soviet agriculture. The terms of political participation would remain strictly exclusionary vis-a-vis the masses, but would upgrade the relative political status and access of politically conformist specialists willing to search for means to reconcile the above combinations of deconcentration and decentralization, financial and organizational approaches to economic problems, and egalitarian and technocratic values. The authority-building strategy of the General Secretary would remain corporatist, but would be based upon a coalitional strategy of division, playing off segments within the Party and state apparatuses against each other (e.g., urban versus rural). Finally, the foreign environment for such a strategy might have to be benign in order to foster the kinds of agreements that would relieve the Soviet budgetary strain.

The losers under such an arrangement would be the dissenters, elitist liberals, Russite fundamentalists, isolationists, those for whom political or economic egalitarianism is an absolute value, and those who would consider a strategy of division an intolerable intrusion on the corporate solidarity of the party. The winners would be all those who currently yearn for ways to avoid extremist solutions to the search for a combination of security (national, physical, social, and job) and material betterment. For the essence of this version of welfare-state authoritarianism would be its selectivity; it would not even have to include all the measures listed above, perhaps trading off certain budgetary reallocations for efficiency-oriented reforms. Thus, it would entail selective budgetary reallocations, administrative decentralization, inegalitarian rationalization of production, and openings to the West, but would not involve systemic change in the form of an end to censorship, a move toward market socialism, the rejection of *nomenklatura,* constitutionalization of political relationships, or a confrontational authority-building strategy on the part of the General Secretary.

If we think of the conservative and liberal versions, not as dichotomized alternatives, but rather as the end points on a series of policy continua which would allow for a large number of centrist variations of welfare-state authoritarianism, we see that the Brezhnev regime of 1978 is located relatively far to the right on most—but not all—of the continua. A conservative retrenchment has been under way in the Soviet leadership for at least five years and, in some policy realms, for eight to ten years.[3] The key questions for the short-term Soviet future, therefore, relate to the probability that this retrenchment will continue after Brezhnev. And if it does not continue, what is the probability of reformist leadership in the direction of the liberal version of welfare-state authoritarianism?

If one looked solely at the evolution of Soviet policy since 1957, one might be inclined to conclude that the recent conservative retrenchment represents the survival of the fittest in a process of policy evolution. Extending this trend into the future, one would be inclined to predict continuity. At a minimum, one would expect no challenges to the military and/or heavy industrial budgets, no change in the terms of political participation, and rejection of decentralist or technocratic proposals for administrative efficiency.

On the other hand, if one looks at the evolution of policy initiatives taken by Khrushchev and Brezhnev (regardless of whether or not those initiatives succeeded), one arrives at somewhat different conclusions about the direction of future policies emanating from the political elite. In a recent study of the evolution of the Khrushchev and Brezhnev administrations, I have gathered evidence which would challenge the premises underlying predictions of immobilism after Brezhnev. Without laying out the evidence per se (a practical impossibility in a short article), let me summarize the salient findings of that study with respect to the questions at hand. Those findings may be condensed into twelve propositions about the Soviet political process and Soviet elite perspectives. The propositions need to be tested further, from different angles, in a constant process of discovery and verification. But they emerge from a large body of evidence covering twenty-five years of Soviet history, and therefore cannot be ignored. They will be of greatest interest to those who embrace reformist assumptions about the present state of elite and mass opinion in the USSR, and who therefore entertain the possibility that anticipatory leadership within the context of welfare-state authoritarianism may be adequate for dealing with emergent social and political tensions.

LESSONS OF POST-STALIN CHANGE: A PROPOSITIONAL INVENTORY

The first seven propositions relate to the political environment within which the General Secretary guides the formulation of policy. They

3. For documentation of this retrenchment, see George Breslauer, "On the Adaptability of Soviet Welfare-State Authoritarianism," in *Soviet Society and the Communist Party*, Karl Ryavec, ed. (Amherst, Mass.: The University of Massachusetts Press, 1979).

bear upon the structure of expectations to which he is subjected, the sources of his legitimacy other than patronage, and the consequent probability that he will feel compelled to offer innovative programs for change.

Proposition #1: Policy immobilism is the exception rather than the rule in Soviet politics. Bold policy initiatives, within the context of the policy parameters considered realistic or viable at a given time, are the rule. Thus, both the Khrushchev and Brezhnev administrations began with periods of relatively balanced collective leadership (1953-1956; 1965-1968) during which programmatic innovations in many realms of policy were proposed by the national leadership. During the subsequent four year period (1957-1960; 1969-1972), the party leader expanded his role into other policy realms, and came to the fore with his own synthetic and expanded program for change. In the following four year period (1961-1964; 1973-1976), in the face of a sudden frustration of his program, the party leader retreated from advocacy of certain components of his program, but pushed harder still for the remaining components. What this pattern suggests is that there exists within the Soviet political elite an expectation that the General Secretary will provide dynamic leadership. Conversely, it would appear that the General Secretary operates within a structural context in which the image of an immobilist would be a politically costly one.

This pattern of change has long been obscured by several tendencies in Soviet studies: the tendency to overstate the idiosyncratic component of Khrushchev's dynamism; scholarly neglect of Brezhnev's innovative program of 1969-1972; the tendency to characterize the Khrushchev and Brezhnev administrations according to global comparisons of their approaches to socio-political transformation; and the absence to date of historical studies which incorporate a long view of both administrations.

Proposition #2: The General Secretary is not only expected to offer innovative programs. He is expected to exercise effective leadership as well, with improvements in consumer satisfaction or quiescence ranking high on the list of criteria by which such effectiveness is judged. Khrushchev felt the need to propose consumer-oriented programs or to identify himself with the promise of consumer satisfaction. When his program faltered in 1960-1961, the First Secretary was clearly on the defensive politically, and made every effort to dissociate his personal authority from the economic slowdown. Similarly, Brezhnev felt the need to offer a consumer-oriented program during 1969-1972. When this program faltered after the droughts of 1972 and 1975, the General Secretary showed signs of being on the defensive politically. Like Khrushchev, Brezhnev responded by trying to blame others for the slowdown, to expand his personality cult, and to further consolidate his power base through patronage and a strategy of falling back on the military/heavy industrial complex for support. Yet this was a fall-back position. The fact that it was accompanied by an increase in defensive political rhetoric supports the conclusion that the ability to devise programs that will upgrade the prospects for consumer satisfaction is an important component of leadership effectiveness within the Soviet political elite.

Proposition #3: If my first two propositions are correct, it would follow that General Secretaries have an institutional interest in policy innovations geared toward upgrading consumer satisfaction. Such innovations would require acts of leadership toward selective budgetary redistributions or efficiency-oriented reforms, any one of which would generate controversy. Hence, one could argue that the General Secretary has an institutional interest in challenging (though not necessarily confronting or radically depriving) some major interests within the political elite. Brezhnev's behavior during the period from 1969 to 1972 is a prime example of such a challenge.

Proposition #4: If selective technocratic reforms are to take hold in the bureaucratic context of Soviet politics, they should be sponsored by the General Secretary of the CPSU, rather than by the Chairman of the Council of Ministers. The initial periods of collective leadership after Stalin and Khrushchev were both marked by power competitions that increased the weight of opportunistic political behavior against technocratic approaches. Thus, Khrushchev undercut the technocratic thrust of Malenkov's and Bulganin's proposals by appealing to the forces of party activism and mobilization in the political elite. Brezhnev undercut further elaboration of the Kosygin reforms of 1965 in similar fashion, by appealing to the forces of mobilization, whose predilections, social values, or political status were closely linked to using pressure as the primary means of stimulating worker and managerial initiative.[4] Were the General Secretary to sponsor such reforms to begin with, they would be less tainted by technocratic political associations and would enjoy the additional advantage of being reinforced by the party leader's greater control over the levers of patronage.

Proposition #5: The General Secretary is faced by sets of crosscut-

---

4. This point is worth underscoring. Administrative reform in the USSR is not simply a matter of "power versus efficiency." It is also (and in some cases primarily) a matter of economic efficiency versus egalitarian social values.

ting expectations that tempt him to play a liaison role within the political elite, offering innovative programs that attempt to synthesize contradictory yearnings within the political elite. Khrushchev's program of 1957-1960 was far-reaching but synthetic, a response in part to deep yearnings for a combination of physical security and a sense of policy dynamism with both economic and ideological appeal. Brezhnev's program of 1969-1972 was not as far-reaching as Khrushchev's, but it was synthetic, reincorporating advocacy of many of the technocratic premises the General Secretary had sought to undercut during polemics with Kosygin in 1968. A program of selective reform akin to that suggested by my liberal version of welfare-state authoritarianism would allow the General Secretary to play such a liaison role, simultaneously appealing to technological zealots or technocratic proclivities within both the Party and state bureaucracies, without assaulting within unaffected bailiwicks those who believe in pressure and political intervention as the most desirable means of getting things done. Moreover, such a program would appeal to the desire for job security by promising no widespread purge of the administrative or political elite. At the same time, it would appeal to yearnings for a sense of dynamism in policy.

Proposition #6: A powerful lever available to the General Secretary to legitimize challenges to major interests is an apparent fear of the masses within the political elite. Khrushchev and Malenkov sensed this fear and played upon it; once Khrushchev had outflanked Malenkov, he then played this card to the hilt, warning the political elite constantly of the dangers inherent in frustrating consumer expectations (even as the First Secretary worked to raise these expectations for other purposes). Brezhnev initially played down this theme, which reinforced the Western view that much of Khrushchev's behavior sprang from within the man, rather than being a product of his perception of moods within the political elite. But in 1970, when Brezhnev was pushing hard for his expanded program of investment in agriculture, and before the Polish riots of December 1970, the General Secretary suddenly reincorporated "Khrushchevian" allusions to the threatening mass mood into his speeches. This suggests that a General Secretary seeking to advance an innovative program may have an institutional interest in tacitly or selectively allying with the masses against intransigent bureaucratic interests— or in furthering his intra-bureaucratic coalition-building strategy by threatening possible mass retribution for policy immobilism. The systemic temptations are there.

Proposition #7: In order to foster official responsiveness to his program, the General Secretary also has an institutional interest in manipulating the relative political or ideological status of groups in the official and non-official sectors. Khrushchev took this to the point of advocating political status equalization and a populist, confrontational relationship between members of the *aktiv* and intransigent bureaucrats. Brezhnev sponsored (or went along with) a conservative reaction against such populism. However, in seeking to promote official responsiveness to specialist input throughout his administration, Brezhnev sponsored redefinitions of the political status of science, scientists, and empirically-oriented specialists in the social sciences that would increase the political leverage of those specialists whose input was required to realize the program that Brezhnev was offering.

The next five propositions relate to the cognitive environment of Soviet policy-making—the character of the ideology and the nature of contemporary regime perspectives. Predictions of immobilism either ignore changes in the character of regime perspectives, or ignore those aspects of the ideology which would legitimize policy innovation.

Proposition #8: The Soviet ideological tradition (what I prefer to call the regime political culture) is both dualistic and progressive. Many of the changes in Soviet policy since Stalin have been legitimized with reference to socio-economic and political values or beliefs contained in the egalitarian strands of Marxist-Leninist doctrine, early Stalinist practice (1928-1931), and even late Stalinist rhetoric. Moreover, the necessity for policy innovation per se has been constantly legitimized by the Leninist conception of the "building of communism" as a stage by stage process, and by the Leninist notion that the Communist party has a moral obligation to history and to "the people" to provide the leadership required to bring closer the eventual communist society.

Yet other strands of the Leninist and Stalinist traditions point in very different directions, and provide justification for maintenance of much of the institutional and ideological legacy of Stalinism— once the extremes of Stalinism have been rejected. As a result, much of the drama of post-Stalin change has revolved around the tension between efforts to legitimize and expand the more egalitarian policy commitments embraced after Stalin, and efforts to sustain and reinforce attitudes, beliefs, and values legitimized by the elitist strands of the regime political culture. The existence of these dualisms, and of the ideological imperative to avoid immobilism, would strengthen the hand of any General Secretary seeking to legitimize a synthetic program of selective reform. The specific policies that might emerge from another effort to synthesize elitist and egalitarian premises would not be self-evident, but that is not at issue here. What is at issue is the importance of avoiding the frequent tendency to view ideology as synonymous with dogma, and the tendency to ignore the facilitating function of the regime political culture in identifying and legitimizing policy innovations. (At the same time, there are limits: neither the elitist nor the egalitarian strand condones the emergence of markets as primary coordinating mechanisms.)

Proposition #9: Within the context of this dualistic regime political culture, a learning process has taken place over time, incorporating perspectives that would support movement in the direction of selective reform. These new concepts and understandings would be difficult to ignore or repudiate in formulating or justifying a new program. Thus, the Brezhnev regime has operated with a much more realistic and sympathetic appreciation of the dilemmas of the local official in a command economy. It has also come to acknowledge the limits on the capacity of the economic system for innovation and efficiency within the context of a command economy that relies on pressure. It has re-evaluated the role of pressure as an effective means of getting things done. It has incorporated into elite discourse a more differentiated appreciation of the environments it is seeking to manipulate. And it has come regularly to acknowledge the need for further reforms to make material incentives effective. (Thus, at the 25th Party Congress, Brezhnev and Kosygin agreed that one of the main problems in Soviet public administration is that the structure of indicators does not relate intermediate efforts to final results, a crucial practical justification for such experiments as the Shchekino experiment and link system, and an intellectual acknowledgment that had contributed to Khrushchev's embracing the link system in 1963-1964.) The conclusions to be drawn about specific policies are not self-evident, but the important point is that elite terminology which focuses on complexity and differentiation is suited to legitimizing a strategy of selective reform.

Proposition #10: The Soviet leadership is not satisfied with present rates of growth in economic capacity and consumer goods availability. Indeed, the level of apparent elite conflict over these issues appears to have risen sharply at the 25th Party Congress, as compared with the 24th Party Congress. In 1971, Alexei Kosygin's speech at the Party Congress echoed almost all the important themes and formulae articulated in Brezhnev's main report. In 1976, quite the reverse was the case, with the Prime Minister embracing anti-egalitarian and selectively decentralist causes that Brezhnev had abandoned, and with the Prime Minister also challenging Brezhnev's financial approach to the agricultural problem.

Proposition #11: Leonid Brezhnev (or those for whom he speaks) does not view the importation of foreign technology as a substitute for administrative reform per se. Brezhnev's advocacy of intermediate forms of administrative change (project planning, Shchekino, Zlobin) actually increased at the time of his programmatic redefinition of 1973, when his reliance upon détente and Western credits for the success of his program also increased. Brezhnev's rhetoric at the 25th Party Congress suggests his belief in the need for significant, though intermediate, administrative reform as a precondition for progress.

Proposition #12: Leonid Brezhnev (or those for whom he speaks) has come to view the low incentive effect of material rewards at their current levels and structure as a serious drag on growth and productivity in military and heavy industrial sectors. Kosygin expressed this belief at the 23rd Party Congress, and Brezhnev embraced it at the 24th and 25th Party Congresses, which suggests that representatives of the military/heavy industrial complex may acknowledge this as well. If this is the case, this circumstance would facilitate the political coalition-building task of a General Secretary seeking selective budgetary redistributions, inegalitarian administrative reforms, or arms control agreements geared toward upgrading consumer satisfaction and the incentive effect of material rewards.

CONCLUSION

Let me begin this conclusion by restating the primary methodological caveat of this paper. I am not predicting that programmatic innovation in the direction of a liberal version of welfare-state authoritarianism will take place during the next ten years. Too many intervening factors could alter the course of events. The international situation (both West and East), for example, could take any number of turns. A liberal version would appear to require an international environment that was at least benign, if not benevolent. A hostile international environment would probably strengthen the forces of retrenchment, who might place greater emphasis on nationalist or chauvinist sources of mobilizational fervor. Similarly, an unexpected crisis or the vagaries of personality could have a very real impact on political coalition-building in the fluid situation that is likely to obtain in the Soviet Union after Brezhnev.

However, it is also important to bear in mind that, while the task of the social scientist is not prediction of specific events, a legitimate task for our profession is the construction of alternative scenarios based upon the manipulation of critical unknowns. This can then be the first step toward exploring and testing assumptions about the nature of the Soviet political process and the Soviet political elite. Those assumptions will be persuasive to the extent that they are based upon documented patterns in post-Stalin Soviet politics. The result of such an exercise in the second half of this paper has been the contention that, assuming a benign or benevolent international environment, ignoring the role of accidents, and embracing reformist rather than radical assumptions about the nature of elite and mass opinion in the USSR, movement in the direction of a centrist or liberal version of welfare-state authoritarianism after Brezhnev seems a good deal more probable than further retrenchment or immobilism.

On the other hand, if the assumptions underlying predictions of systemic change are correct, then the reader will have to draw upon his or her own theories of history and perceptions of the relative weight of different interests in Soviet politics to guess what kind of systemic change is likely to take place.

Donald R. Kelley

The Soviet Image of the Future

Concern with the nature of the future has been an integral part of Marxist-Leninist thinking since Marx first articulated the theory of dialectical materialism over a century ago. In a very real sense, Marxism is about the future; and as in any millennial ideology, the image of the future which it presents has evolved into a complex amalgam of predictions, promises, and scenarios which serves the present.

Any assessment of the present Soviet concept of the future must begin with the 1961 party program.[1] While the optimistic timetable predicting the initial transition to communism by 1980 has quietly dropped from view and the pace of the transformation slowed, the substantive provisions of the program remain essentially intact, modified only by recent attention to the "scientific and technological revolution" and the creation of a "developed socialist society." Thus

---

1. The text of the 1961 program is printed as an appendix to Leonard Shapiro, ed., *The USSR and the Future* (New York: Praeger, 1963), pp. xi-xix; see also Jerome M. Gilison, *The Soviet Image of Utopia* (Baltimore: Johns Hopkins, 1975); Daniel Tarschys, *Beyond the State: The Future Polity in Classical and Soviet Marxism* (Stockholm: Swedish Institute of International Affairs, 1971); and Theodore Denno, *The Communist Millennium: The Soviet View* (The Hague: Martinus Nijhoff, 1964).

the contemporary view of the future is best understood as a modernized and scientized version of the 1961 program, with the principal changes occurring in (1) the nature of the forces contributing to the further development of society, (2) the nature of the current stage of developed socialism, and (3) the pace of future change.

The cautious nature of the Brezhnev regime must be taken into account in assessing the altered tone of Soviet thinking about the future. Gone are the frenetic élan of the Khrushchev years and incautious promises of an early transition to communism. Born of the political realities facing the party, the policies of elite stability and "respect for cadres" militate against emphasis on a disruptively rapid transition. Perhaps as importantly, Soviet leaders have come to realize the true complexity of managing an advanced industrial society and have countered with attempts to rationalize and fine-tune administrative and economic mechanisms. Political and intellectual caution have bred a sense of pragmatic, incremental reformism devoid of the tone of quick-paced, voluntarist activism which marked the Khrushchev years. Expressed both in the concept of developed socialism, which is viewed as a long-term intermediary stage preceding the transition to communism, and in the new Soviet constitution, which stresses institutional continuity and, as Brezhnev put it to some overly zealous comrades, the need "not to put the cart before the horse," this cautious approach to the nature of the future signals a considerable scaling down of expectations for meaningful transformations in the near future.[2]

THE SCIENTIFIC AND TECHNOLOGICAL REVOLUTION

An examination of the transformation of the Soviet image of the future must begin with the scientific and technological revolution, which is seen as a complex amalgam of scientific, technological, and social changes associated with the emergence of a mature industrial society.[3] Viewed as a series of ongoing transformations of the material and social basis of society, it is held to be both an important

2. *Pravda*, October 5, 1977, pp. 2-3.
3. *Nauchno-tekhnicheskaia revoliutsiia i sotsial'nyi progress* (Moscow: Nauka, 1977); *Soedinenie dostizhenii NTR s preimushchestvami sotsializma* (Moscow: Mysl', 1977); P. M. Fedoseev, "Sotsial'noe znachenie nauchno-tekhnicheskoi revoliutsii," *Voprosy filosofii*, 7 (1974), pp. 3-17; II. Artobolevskii et al., *Partiia i sovremenniia nauchno-tekhnicheskaia revoliutsiia v SSSR* (Moscow: Politizdat, 1974); "Nauchno-tekhnicheskaia revoliutsiia i formirovanie novogo cheloveka," *Voprosy filosofii*, 8 (1975), pp. 26-44; *Chelovek-nauka-tekhnika* (Moscow: Politizdat, 1973); *The Scientific*

prerequisite for the emergence of developed socialism and a "main link" in building the material-technical and socio-political base of communism. Commenting on its complexity, V. V. Kosolapov offers a sweeping definition of its essence and consequences:

> From the standpoint of systems analysis, the current scientific and technological revolution is a complex of dialectically inter-related changes occurring within the system "science-engineering-production." These affect two aspects of the system: a) the material [aspect]—objects of labor (qualitative changes brought about by mechanization, partial or complete automation of production), sources of energy, and a technological upheaval signifying a radical change in the character of action on materials involved in the production process; and b) the subjective, human [aspect]—the changed pattern of industrial and occupational structure of manpower, and the rising level of qualifications and educational standards. The scientific and technological revolution is affecting every aspect of productive forces. The secondary effects of its impact are qualitative changes occurring in the political, social, and cultural spheres of society.[4]

No less important are its immediate political and policy ramifications. Theorists and political leaders alike admit that the further modernization of industry and management are critically important in overcoming backwardness and inefficiency. Soviet society is seen as standing on the threshold of a second industrial revolution and facing the difficult task of absorbing wide-ranging and potentially disruptive technological and social changes within an inflexible and inherently conservative institutional framework. The opportunities for further development and rationalization of the economy and society are enormous, providing that scientific and technological advances can be translated into economic gains; but great also are the problems and risks. In calling for "a combination of the scientific and technological revolution with the advantages of socialism," Soviet leaders offer a vision of the further technical and social transformation of the USSR within the framework of a de-

---

and Technological Revolution: Social Effects and Prospects (Moscow: Progress, 1972); and Julian M. Cooper, "The Scientific and Technological Revolution in Soviet Theory," in Frederick J. Fleron, ed., *Technology and Communist Culture: The Socio-Cultural Impact of Technology under Socialism* (New York: Praeger, 1977), pp. 146-180.

4. V. V. Kosolapov, *Chelovechestvo na rubezhe XXI veka* (Moscow: Molodaia gvardiia, 1973) [*Mankind in the year 2000* (Moscow: Progress, 1976), p. 18].

veloped socialist society, that is, a modernized and technologically sophisticated economic and social order somewhere in transition between the first phase of socialist construction and the full development of communist social relationships.

The emphasis placed on the scientific and technological revolution is intended in large measure to overcome resistance to innovation and modernization. Whether in the realm of managerial reforms, where Soviet leaders have experimented with new concepts of systems management and integrated industrial associations, or in the area of technological innovation in industry, bureaucratic and political realities have produced a pattern of half-hearted interest and frequent non-compliance with the directives of higher leaders. While the reasons for this reluctance are easily understood—time-honored organizational prerogatives and work styles are under fire, and the system of incentives and rewards penalizes rather than rewards innovative managers—their impact in slowing further modernization and rationalization has been a source of continuing frustration.[5]

DEVELOPED SOCIALISM AS AN IMAGE OF THE FUTURE

In defining the Soviet image of the next several decades, one must deal both with the nature of developed socialism as a long-term intermediary period and with the trends setting the stage for the eventual transition to communism. Timetables are exasperatingly absent from recent Soviet writings; rather one encounters only vague assertions that developed socialism will extend over the next several decades as the material and social prerequisites for full communism are created.[6] But aside from denials that major qualitative transfor-

5. Gail Warshofsky Lapidus, "The Brezhnev Regime and Directed Social Change: Depoliticization as a Political Strategy," in Alexander Dallin, ed., *The Twenty-fifth Congress of the CPSU: Assessment and Context* (Stanford: Hoover Institution Press, 1977), pp. 27-38; Paul Cocks, "Science Policy and Soviet Developmental Strategy," in Dallin, ed., pp. 39-52; and Cooper, "The Scientific and Technological Revolution in Soviet Theory," in Fleron, ed., *Technology and Communist Culture*.

6. The most important sources are: G. E. Glezerman, ed., *Razvitoe sotsialisticheskoe obshchestvo: sushchnost', kriterii zrelosti, kritika revizionistskikh kontseptssi*, 2nd revised edition (Moscow: Mysl', 1975); V. I. Kas'ianenko, *Razvitoi sotsializm: istoriografiia i metodologiia problemy* (Moscow: Mysl', 1976); V. Sikorskii, *KPSS na etape razvitogo sotsializma* (Minsk: Byelorussian State University, 1975); B. N. Topornin, ed., *Gosudarstvo i demokratiia v period postroenniia razvitogo sotsializma* (Moscow: Nauka, 1974); V. I. Lesnyi and N. V. Chernogolovkin, *Politicheskaia*

mations lie just over the horizon, little is said of the timing of future changes. Rather the nature and evolution of developed socialism are discussed in terms of three factors: (1) those features which separate it from the earlier phase of the construction of socialism and full communism, (2) the inherent and unique characteristics of the present stage, and (3) the pattern of growth evident within a developed socialist society.

Before confronting the particulars of a developed socialist society, the concept must be placed within an appropriate political framework. Like the scientific and technological revolution, developed socialism serves political as well as ideological ends. The phrase was first coined by Lenin as a vague description of a mature socialist system.[7] Brezhnev referred in passing to "a developed socialist society" in several addresses from 1967 onward, and the concept appeared with greater force in his opening comments to the 24th Party Congress in 1971, but at the time there was no indication that it was intended as a major theoretical contribution. However, in the years that followed the 24th Congress, developed socialism was rapidly transformed into a major centerpiece of contemporary theory, spreading from its Soviet origins to East European theorists, who took up the concept to characterize the tasks of development within their countries.[8]

It is not accidental, as the saying goes, that the concept of developed socialism would fall upon receptive ears, for it provides convenient and plausible responses to theoretical and practical needs. In theoretical terms, it provides a middle ground between more primitive socialist formations and full communism; stripped of the optimistic timetable of the Khrushchev years, developed socialism emerges as a safe definition of a contemporary state struggling with the impact of intensive modernization. Moreover, it offers a timely counterpoint to the concepts of "post-industrial" or "technetronic" society, which Soviet theorists reject out of hand. In

---

organizatsiia razvitogo sotsialisticheskogo obshchestva: struktura i funktsii (Moscow: Moscow State University Press, 1976); P. N. Fedoseev et al., *Marksistsko-leninskoe uchenie o sotsializme i sovremennosti* (Moscow: Politizdat, 1975); D. A. Kerimov, *Sovetskaia demokratiia v period razvitogo sotsializma* (Moscow: Mysl', 1975); and E. M. Chekharin, *Sovetskaia politicheskaia sistema v usloviiakh razvitogo sotsializma* (Moscow: Mysl', 1975) [*The Soviet political system under developed Socialism* (Moscow: Progress, 1977)]. Surprisingly, only a few monographs have been published in the West, including: Robbin F. Laird, "Developed Socialist Society and the Dialectics of Development and Legitimation in the Soviet Union," *Soviet Union*, 4:1 (1977), pp. 130-149 and Alfred B. Evans, Jr., "Developed Socialism in Soviet Ideology," *Soviet Studies*, 29:3 (July, 1977), pp. 409-428.

7. See V. I. Kas'ianenko, *KPSS: organizator stroitel'stva razvitogo sotsializma* (Moscow: Politizdat, 1974), p. 11.

8. Evans, "Developed Socialism in Soviet Ideology," pp. 412-413.

practical terms, developed socialism is by definition a social and political system that has made it by the standards of the modern world; despite the recognition of the need for further transformation of the economic and social order, Soviet leaders evidence a clear sense of pride in having built what they see as a modern industrial state. And above all, it is a theoretical innovation distinctive to the Brezhnev years. As a significant and unique historical phase, it is undoubtedly to go down in history as Brezhnev's program, to be given theoretical voice in the concept of developed socialism and institutional body in the new constitution.

While there is no disagreement about the fact that the USSR presently constitutes a developed socialist society and will continue to develop within this framework for the next several decades, there are considerable differences of opinion among Soviet scholars concerning the precise features of such a system.[9] Some see it as a "developing concept" whose exact meaning is dictated by the complex interplay of economic, social, and political features and the specific national milieu, while others argue about its periodization and the nature of the transition process. Reviewing the literature in the field, V. I. Kas'ianenko finds that developed socialism entails (1) qualitative and quantitative changes in material production, including the material and technical base of industry and the transformation of "production relationships" in the larger social context, (2) advances in the "political organization and spiritual life of society," among which are numbered the transformation of the CPSU into a "party of all the people," the creation of the all-people's state, and the improvement of party leadership over the processes of social development, and (3) substantive alterations in the international situation, including the peaceful competition of the capitalist and socialist systems and the growing power of the socialist bloc.[10] He warns, however, against confusing developed socialism, which stands alone as a separate plateau, with more primitive or more advanced forms. On the one hand, it should not be regarded merely as a transition period closely linked to the earlier, more primitive period of the construction of socialism, for this fails to stress the "maturity" of developed socialism and suggests an aura of impermanence and potential instability. But on the other hand, one must not attribute to developed socialism all those features of a fully developed communist society so that it becomes "almost indistinguishable" from the final stage of development. To do so would be to accelerate the pace of transformation and to suggest that economic, social, and political forms possible only under a fully developed communist system

---

9. Kas'ianenko, *KPSS*, pp. 12-13 and *Razvitoi*, pp. 56-60.
10. Kas'ianenko, *KPSS*, p. 13.

would come quickly into being during the developed socialist phase.[11]

Whatever their differences, all commentators agree on the basic proposition that as a separate historical phase, developed socialism is to be a long period marked by the gradual transformation of social, economic, and political relationships. Reporting to the Supreme Soviet on the new constitution, Brezhnev struck a tone of deliberate caution concerning both the nature of the present stage and the pace of further growth:

> ... the stage of the perfection of socialism on its own basis, the stage of mature, developed socialist society, is a necessary element of the social transformation and constitutes a relatively long period of development on the path from capitalism to communism. Moreover, knowledge and utilization of all the possibilities of developed socialism is at the same time a transition to the construction of communism. The future does not lie beyond the limits of the present. The future is rooted in the present, and, by accomplishing the tasks of today—of the socialist present—we are gradually entering tomorrow—the communist future.[12]

This cautious tone is also reflected in the writings of Soviet theorists who concern themselves with the slow-paced nature of the transition process and the limited, embryonic emergence of future social and political forms. Three arguments are repeatedly stressed in the literature. First, it is possible to enter into the beginning stages of developed socialism without any appreciable alteration of the institutional structure. While the technical and economic forces which animate further change undergo continuing evolution during this period, the institutional structures—and this clearly means both the party and the state—change only gradually, acquiring added significance and increased functions.[13] Second, developed socialism is envisioned as following its own inherent laws of growth and change. As socialism "developing on its own basis," it is an economic, social, and political stage in its own right, conveying legitimacy to the political and social structures developing within it by virtue of its existence as a mature industrial system.[14]

11. Ibid., p. 14.
12. *Pravda*, October 5, 1977, pp. 2-3.
13. Chekharin, *Sovetskaia politicheskaia sistema* ... , p. 219.
14. Kas'ianenko, *KPSS*, pp. 14-15, and Glezerman, *Razvitoe sotsialisticheskoe obshchestvo*, p. 19.

The nascent development of future social and political forms characteristic of full communism is the third feature commonly stressed.[15] Two purposes seem evident: (1) to articulate a "safe" and gradual process of growth toward higher socialist and eventually communist forms, and (2) to provide a rationale for an enhanced role for party and state mechanisms, as redefined within the framework of developed socialism. Much of the practical emphasis of the literature falls on the increasingly important role of the party and state both as objects undergoing transformation during the evolution of developed socialism and as subjects whose enhanced goal-directed public role becomes the critical factor in consciously and "scientifically" directing the further transformation of society.

ECONOMIC, SOCIAL, AND POLITICAL CHANGE UNDER DEVELOPED SOCIALISM

Technology and the Economy. While Soviet planners have been noticeably reticent about specific projections over the next fifteen to twenty years—the long-promised fifteen year plan for economic growth and scientific and technological development has yet to be released—it is possible to discuss in general terms the medium- and long-term trends which are seen as shaping the next several decades. They may be grouped under the general categories of (1) a shift from extensive to intensive development, (2) the increasing role of the scientific and technological revolution, and (3) the gradual construction of the material base of communism.

The shift from extensive to intensive forms of economic development signifies both an alteration of the mix of capital, labor, and technological inputs required for further development and a restoration of the over-all growth rate. Viewing a sagging growth rate over the last decade, Soviet leaders have turned to new developmental strategies emphasizing increased labor productivity and technological modernization. No longer responsive to earlier growth strategies which stressed massive capital and labor inputs and disproportional development of leading sectors, the economy is seen as dependent on an increasingly well orchestrated application of scientific and technological modernization, increased labor productivity, improved management, and balanced sectoral growth. The process of intensification is viewed as a long-term feature whose impact will be felt throughout the entire period of developed socialism and continue well into the communist phase.[16]

15. Chekharin, p. 219.
16. Kas'ianenko, *Razvitoi*, pp. 107-108; Glezerman, pp. 67-68; Sikorskii, *KPSS na etape razvitogo sotsializma*, p. 123; I. I. Kuz'minov et al., ed., *Ekonomicheskie problemy razvitogo sotsializma i ego pererastaniia v kommunizm* (Moscow: Mysl', 1977), pp. 82-96.

Some of the most striking economic transformations are envisioned in terms of structural changes over the next several decades. Most important among these is the emergence of high-technology industries as the key growth sectors. While heavy industry will remain an important element, the highest growth rates will be seen in the fields of electronics, instrument making, chemicals, power engineering, and other high-technology branches. These sectors will emerge as the technological vanguard for the rest of the economy, generating considerable spin-off for less rapidly modernizing branches. Although little public mention is made of the defense and space industries, it is certain that they will also continue as major sources of spin-off for civilian industries.[17]

The second major structural transformation will occur as the so-called "non-productive" sphere gains in importance. Loosely defined as including scientific research, the service industries, certain utilities, education, culture, the arts, and all other activities not directly involved in the production of material wealth, it is slated to grow even more rapidly than the high-technology sectors of industry. The highest growth rates are predicted for the area of scientific research, which is increasingly being regarded as a productive enterprise. The growth of services will also account for much of the increased economic weight of this sector, although Soviet planners have been understandably careful to note the distinction between the service industries and consumer goods industries per se. The latter are also slated to grow in relative proportion to heavy industry until an appropriate balance is attained. Particular importance is also attached to the growth of post-secondary education and to other activities contributing to continuing adult education that serve to upgrade the qualifications of the work force or to improve the general cultural level.[18]

Closely associated with the increasing importance of science and education is the growth of a knowledge industry or an information industry. Included are both the increasing significance of science as a direct productive force and the growing importance of information storage, processing, and retrieval capabilities. It is in this area that the impact of the scientific and technological revolution is most strongly

17. Kosolapov, *Chelovechestvo na rubezhe XXI veka*, p. 21; L. S. Bliakhman and O. I. Shkaratan, *Chelovek v mire truda (sovetskie rabochie i intelligentsiia v epoche nauchno-tekhnicheskoi revoliutsii)* (Moscow: Politizdat, 1973) [*Man at work: the scientific and technological revolution, the Soviet working class, and intelligentsia* (Moscow: Progress, 1977), p. 35; 85]; Glezerman, pp. 68-85; and Kas'ianenko, *KPSS*, pp. 115; 170-173.

18. Bliakhman and Shkaratan; Kas'ianenko, *KPSS*, p. 186; Kosolapov, p. 126; Glezerman, pp. 23-26; Chekharin, p. 292; and L. M. Gatovskii et al, *Material'no-tekhnicheskaia baza kommunizma*, vol. 2 (Moscow: Mysl', 1977), pp. 287-373.

realized, and it is upon this sector's increasing maturity and ability to translate scientific and technological achievements into production advances, and information flows into timely and informed administrative decisions, that the intensification of the economy will ultimately depend. Soviet commentators leave little doubt that the creation of the "science-technology-production" link is one of the highest priorities animating current attempts to create viable research and production associations as well as one of the most serious problems facing economic planners. The further development of automated production systems, data gathering and control networks, and improved management systems is also seen as dependent on rapid advances in this sector. In short, while among the productive industries the lead is to be taken by high-technology industries, it is clear that the real leading force is now recognized as lying within what has heretofore been labeled the "non-productive" sphere.[19]

The scientific and technological revolution is also seen as producing wide-ranging changes in the nature of work. Soviet descriptions of the factory of the future portray highly educated worker-technicians tending fully automated production complexes. The nature of work itself is to become increasingly intellectualized, leading to a gradual blurring of the distinction between mental and physical labor, although work will not "degenerate" into meaningless "recreational activity."[20] Looking into the future, one commentator foresees that

> A worker as we know him will disappear, to be replaced by a worker-engineer. It has been estimated that the number of white-collar workers is growing ten times faster than the number of manual workers. The doubling of production results in quadrupling the number of engineers, technicians, and managers. Labor in the 21st century will be as much a creative activity as it will be a managerial activity. Everyone will be trained in economic management techniques, since a good knowledge of economics will be as indispensable to everyone then as the multiplication table is for us today.[21]

Soviet commentators are quick to point out, however, that the advent of the worker-engineer-administrator will be long in coming. The basic distinction between intellectual and physical labor will

---

19. Bliakhman and Shkaratan, pp. 112-115; 254; and Kosolapov, pp. 153-154; 200-202.

20. Bliakhman and Shkaratan, pp. 62-63; 201-204; Glezerman, p. 141; and E. I. Kaputsin, *Trud v usloviiakh razvitogo sotsializma* (Moscow: Ekonomika, 1977).

21. Kosolapov, p. 165.

continue throughout the period of developed socialism; the convergence of the two forms of activity will occur only gradually and on a highly selective industry-by-industry basis. In the beginning stages of developed socialism, the dividing line remains sharply articulated for all but the most technologically advanced industries. During this phase, progress is marked not so much by an increase in "the proportion of the country's total work force running automated process equipment . . . but rather [by] the complete and final elimination of arduous manual labor," a distinctly less ambitious criterion. Reservations are also offered concerning the shift from highly specialized workers to more generally trained worker-engineers. While generalized training in engineering, cybernetics, and management is set forth as the pattern characteristic of a more mature developed socialist society and of full communism, current trends in the USSR are acknowledged to be just the reverse, a pattern that will continue throughout the early stages of developed socialism because of the relatively late impact of the scientific and technological revolution.[22]

The scientific and technological revolution is also seen as having extensive impact on the rationalization of management. While any lengthy commentary on recent organizational reforms is beyond the scope of this essay, it must be noted that Soviet authorities have attached great importance to improved management at all levels, in part out of concern for enhanced efficiency within a bureaucracy where efficiency has been notably absent and in part to overcome time-honored departmental barriers to centralized direction. This new emphasis on management corresponds in theoretical terms to the increasing importance of the "subjective factor." As distinguished from the immutable, "objective" laws of historical development, the subjective factor refers to those areas of human endeavor subject to conscious manipulation by man. In simple terms, the growing importance of the subjective realm entails an enhanced role for the conscious planning of economic and social development.[23]

Over the next several decades, then, Soviet commentators foresee definite changes in the nature of management and planning as conscious, goal-directed activities. Arguing that managerial organizations of the future will look and behave much like present day research and development centers, they note the growing importance of general managerial skills which transcend particular sectors of the economy. Future emphasis in managerial work will fall upon the organization and control of enterprise and sectoral information networks and data banks, the selection and deployment of personnel,

22. Bliakhman and Shkaratan, pp. 201-202.
23. Chekharin, p. 227; and Kas'ianenko, *KPSS*, p. 175.

and the integration of complex and multi-sectoral activities. Particular attention is given to the latter, since the most difficult problems facing a developed socialist economy are seen increasingly in terms of coordinating activities in different sectors and/or regions.[24]

It is the third important economic trend during the period of developed socialism—the creation of the material base for a future communist society—that Soviet theorists approach with the greatest caution. In legal terms, the property relationships of a communist society will be built gradually during this period as collective property is converted to state or all-people's property. Of far greater importance are the projected changes in consumption levels and patterns of distribution. Despite the growing emphasis placed on the consumer and service sectors as the transformation of developed socialism goes forward, the proper formula for distribution remains essentially "to each according to his work." However, income differentials will continue to narrow over the next several decades, and a further leveling impact will be felt from the expanded role of the social consumption fund. But it is not until the attainment of full communism that distribution according to need may be implemented, and then with the share to each individual dictated by "scientifically determined consumption levels."[25]

Social Structure. The period of developed socialism will witness the gradual transformation of social and class relationships formed during socialist construction into the foundations of a communist society. While Soviet theorists emphasize the social unity of the "Soviet people" as an important component of developed socialism, they are quick to admit that significant distinctions will remain throughout this period. At present Soviet society contains the two "fraternal classes" of workers and collective farmers and the separate stratum of the intelligentsia. Relations between these elements are held to be "non-antagonistic" because of the absence of politically significant conflicting interests. Rather, the existing divisions are described in terms of the diminishing class differences between those whose labor is associated either with state or all-people's property (the workers and the intelligentsia), with cooperative or collective property (collective farmers and other cooperative enterprises), or in

24. Sikorskii, pp. 130-133; Kas'ianenko, *KPSS*, pp. 175-177; Glezerman, p. 153; and Bliakhman and Shkaratan, pp. 261-280. For Soviet management theory, see the annual series edited by V. G. Afanas'ev, *Nauchnoe upravlenie obshchestvom* (Moscow: Mysl', 1967-   ); P. I. Bagrii, ed., *Ekonomicheskie problemy razvitogo sotsialisticheskogo obshchestva* (Kiev: Naukova Dumka, 1977), pp. 150-241; and V. G. Afanas'ev, *The Scientific and Technological Revolution—Its Impact on Management and Education* (Moscow: Progress, 1975).

25. Kas'ianenko, *KPSS*, pp. 170-173; and Bliakhman and Shkaratan, pp. 139-141.

terms of continuing social distinctions based on functional and professional role, urban or rural residence, and mental or physical labor. It must be remembered that Soviet theorists speak of forthcoming changes both in the class structure and in the social structure of a developed socialist society. The former are interpreted narrowly within traditional theory and are expected to disappear gradually as the transformation of developed socialism goes forward, while the latter are more broadly interpreted to include other distinctions such as functional or professional role, type of residence, level of consumption, and so on. They are expected to grow more complex during the developed socialist period, simplifying into a more homogeneous social structure only after the attainment of full communism.[26]

During the developed socialist period, four important distinctions will continue to exist, although their intensity will diminish over time, albeit at very different rates.

(1) Distinctions based upon the use of collective property or of all-people's and state property: these, the only remaining class divisions, will fade as collective and cooperative property are gradually converted to higher forms, although Soviet theorists are noticeably reticent about a precise timetable—saying only that this distinction will be the first to be eradicated.

(2) Distinctions between urban and rural residents: historically this division has been closely associated with the distinction between collective farmers and industrial workers. However, as agricultural labor is gradually transformed into a form of work virtually indistinguishable from industrial labor, the significance will shift to the impact of urban and rural life styles. Even though agricultural work will then resemble factory labor, farm laborers will still live within a rural environment and presumably possess fewer of the amenities of life or opportunities for cultural enrichment than their urbanized counterparts in industry. A second process of change is also under way in the continuing growth of existing urban areas and the creation of new population centers in rural regions, which are expected to alter the life style and social consciousness of their residents, although differences will obviously remain well beyond the developed socialist phase.

(3) Distinctions between mental and physical labor: two contradictory transformations are envisioned during the period of developed socialism. Physical labor itself will become gradually more intellectualized, although Soviet theorists are careful not to absolutize this transformation to suggest the complete abolition of physical tasks. Rather, they offer a distinction between "physical labor," which entails arduous exertion with minimal intellectual

26. Bliakhman and Shkaratan, pp. 148-149.

involvement, and "manual labor," which suggests a combination of high intellectual content and skilled craftsmanship. The present beginning stage of developed socialism will simply witness a gradual shift in the balance from the former to the latter, with the abolition of heavy physical labor occurring long before the complete synthesis of mental and skilled manual labor. Intellectual labor will become increasingly specialized during the transition period, initially growing away from any convergence downward with the gradual upgrading of manual labor. However, with the transition to the beginning phase of full communism, the level of specialization among intellectual workers will fade gradually in all but a few cases, while the upward growth of manual labor toward higher forms will continue. Soviet theorists make it clear that the remaining distinctions between mental and manual labor will be the last to disappear.

(4) Distinctions among nationalities: while Soviet theorists foresee the gradual erosion of the importance of nationalities in economic, social, and political terms, these distinctions will survive in the form of secondary cultural differences long into the period of full communism. However, greater importance is attached to the impact of other social changes occurring as consequence of the spread of technology and industry, the conversion of agriculture to factory-type labor, and the creation of other reference groups in terms of professional and associational interests.[27]

Soviet theorists repeatedly point out that during the period of developed socialism, the social structure of society will grow increasingly more complex in the short run, especially to the degree to which the intellectual and occupational differentiation of society caused by the impact of the scientific and technological revolution races ahead of the emergence of highly skilled generalists within both the intelligentsia and the working class. During this period, the most significant social distinctions will be those associated with the nature of work, professions, occupational identification, type of community, and comparative standard of living. While these differences are held to be devoid of any political significance—they are not, after all, classes in the traditional sense—they do give rise, especially in a transition period, to differing social "interests" and "contradictions." They are especially important within the intelligentsia and the professional strata of society, where the process of differentiation occurs most rapidly.[28]

Soviet theorists devote special attention to social changes within

27. G. I. Pivtsaikin, *Obshchestvennye otnosheniia razvitogo sotsializma* (Minsk: Nauka i tekhnika, 1973); see also: Glezerman, pp. 132-151; Kas'ianenko, *KPSS*, pp. 181-194; and Bliakhman and Shkaratan, pp. 147-236.

28. Bliakhman and Shkaratan, p. 149.

The Soviet Image of the Future   219

the intelligentsia during the evolution of developed socialism. Defined as a stratum rather than a class, it nonetheless can possess a "class character" within the non-antagonistic framework articulated by Soviet scholars. While it will eventually merge with other elements, during the developed socialist period its numbers and distinctive economic and social roles are expected to grow rapidly for several reasons. First, the increasing importance of science and technology dictates that the intelligentsia will be the most rapidly growing stratum for the next several decades. The increasing importance of the subjective factor in further development is another reason for its enhanced role; greater attention to comprehensive and integrated planning necessarily implies added importance for research, planning, and managerial tasks falling, at least in the transition period, into the hands of the intelligentsia. Third, the intellectualization of labor itself contributes to the growing weight of this stratum, especially as the number of engineers and highly trained technicians working directly in production increases. Finally, structural shifts within the economy lend further impetus to the growth of this element. The expansion of high-technology industries and of those sectors that provide highly skilled services such as medicine or education inevitably demands ever growing numbers of highly trained personnel.[29]

Considerable attention is also given to the growing significance of specialized professional or occupational groupings. While they are obviously devoid of class identification in the strictest sense, they may nonetheless constitute important and highly self-aware "social groups" possessing "interests." The importance of such professionalization is expected to increase sharply throughout the entire developed socialist period, giving way only gradually to the emergence of less specialized worker-technicians with the maturation of communist production relationships. The professionalization of management is also projected as an important trend during this period. While Soviet theorists foresee the ultimate merger of production and management skills in the hands and minds of worker-technician-managers and the elimination of the separate managerial stratum, an important role is still maintained for those elements of the intelligentsia who will provide the technical and scientific guidance needed by industry. Theory holds that while basic technological training and general management skills will be easily mastered by the worker-generalist of the future, the most important positions as

29. D. M. Gvishiani et al., eds., *The Scientific Intelligentsia in the USSR* (Moscow: Progress, 1976); Kas'ianenko, *KPSS*, p. 192; Bliakhman and Shkaratan, pp. 257-297; and *Partiia i intelligentsiia v usloviiakh razvitogo sotsializma* (Moscow: Mysl', 1977).

technical specialists (but not managers per se) will be reserved for a highly educated and specialized scientific and engineering elite.[30]

The Party. During the period of developed socialism, the party's role and internal composition are to be marked by three gradual developments: (1) its role will increase throughout the entire period in response to the need for comprehensive guidance of economic and social development and the growing importance of its work with public organizations, (2) the style and content of party leadership will be modernized and rationalized in response to the needs of the scientific and technological revolution, and (3) the transformation of the party into a "party of all the people," which began concurrently with the advent of developed socialism, will intensify, setting the stage for its survival in redefined form long after the state has withered away.

Soviet theorists are explicit in their predictions that the role of the party will increase markedly during the period of developed socialism. While the traditional rationalizations for its leading role are cited ritually, primary emphasis has shifted to its role in guiding the scientific and technological revolution and in mastering the intricacies of an increasingly sophisticated economy and society. Theory holds that the complexity of the tasks facing Soviet leaders increases with the further maturation of developed socialism, requiring an augmentation of party leadership in all spheres. Other factors are also cited as contributing to this increasing role, including: (1) the growing importance of the subjective factor in the further evolution of social and political relationships, (2) the increasing need for ideological guidance, although Soviet theorists leave no doubt that the mechanisms of state discipline and economic levers will remain of paramount importance, (3) the expanded role of public and mass organizations, in which the party is expected to play an increasing role, (4) the heightened consciousness and social involvement of the masses, which require a commensurate increase in political consciousness and activity among party cadres, and (5) the growing importance of international factors, particularly inter-party relations among socialist nations.

Taken as a whole, the list offers few surprises. What is significant is that great care is taken to disassociate the process of generalizing the party's role and its greater involvement with mass organizations from any transfer of power, functions, or legitimacy to these organizations or to the public as a whole. While ultimately the party too will wither away, it is expected to persist well into the period of

---

30. Glezerman pp. 142-148; Kerimov, *Sovetskaia demokratiia v period razvitogo sotsializma*, pp. 155-181; and Bliakhman and Shkaratan, pp. 149-151.

full communism, although its "forms of work and internal structure" will undergo even further transformation. Soviet theorists are even reticent about speculating on the final withering process in the far-distant future, preferring instead to argue that the party will eventually turn into a "universal organization coinciding with the organs of self-administration" only when the political consciousness of all members of the society is raised to that of party members.[31]

The transformation of the party into a "party of all the people" is regarded as one of the most significant internal developments during the period of developed socialism, and while party theorists promise an acceleration of this trend, two reservations are usually offered. The first is that while the party now embodies the interests of all segments of the society, it retains its "class essence" as a party of the working class throughout the developed socialist stage. Soviet theorists stress the now seemingly stable majority of workers and peasants among rank-and-file party members and the involvement of other non-blue collar elements of the party in material production as touchstones of continuing proletarian legitimacy. The second limitation is that the party of all the people is to remain a relatively small proportion of the total population; in spite of the growth in total membership in recent years, it will continue to eschew mass recruitment.[32]

It is on the question of party leadership that the concept of developed socialism has had the greatest practical impact. Stressing the consistently increasing demands to be made on the CPSU as developed socialism evolves, Brezhnev and other party leaders have called for a thorough modernization and rationalization of the party's leadership style. Running throughout the exhortations for improved leadership are the themes of the improvement of the party's internal operations through the mastery of modern organizational techniques, and the growing importance of the party as the only force capable of providing the forceful leadership necessary for translating the achievements of the scientific and technological revolution into economic and social advances. Far from witnessing a conservative restoration of a self-possessed old guard content to muddle along the road to some imprecisely articulated future, internal developments

31. Sikorskii, pp. 39-47; 72-78; 118-119; Glezerman, pp. 268-277; Chekharin, pp. 251-268; *Partiia v period razvitogo sotsialisticheskogo obshchestva* (Moscow: Politizdat, 1977), pp. 8-20; V. S. Shevtsov, *KPSS i gosudarstvo v razvitom sotsialisticheskom obshchestve* (Moscow: Politizdat, 1974), pp. 53-60; and Lesnyi and Chernogolovkin, *Politicheskaia organizatsiia razvitogo sotsialisticheskogo obshchestva*, pp. 36-54.

32. *Partiia v period razvitogo sotsialisticheskogo obshchestva*, pp. 12-16; 32-33; Sikorskii, pp. 31-42; and P. E. Burak, *Partiinoe stroitel'stvo v usloviiakh razvitogo sotsializma* (L'vov: Vishcha shkola, 1976).

and party policies from the early 1970s onward suggest a mindful, if understandably politically cautious, recrudescence of an activist and reformist leadership. To be sure, the General Secretary's style is considerably less frenetic than that of his predecessor, and his initiatives have been marked by a careful regard for cadre interests and bureaucratic politics. Perhaps Bezhnev's greatest skill has been his ability to advocate a series of wide-ranging pragmatic reforms in industry and agriculture while reassuring the party elite and institutional interests that their fate is not in the hands of a hare-brained schemer.

It is at this critical point—the concept of what party leadership is to be within the next several decades—that the paradoxical nature of developed socialism has its most important implications. As a conservative or, perhaps more generously, as a cautious projection of a slowly evolving institutional order, developed socialism offers a stable institutional and political milieu within which limited and careful modernization may be safely attempted. In effect, it is a tacit promise that the rules of political battle and the institutional setting within which it occurs are unlikely to be altered capriciously, at least while Brezhnev or like-minded successors are in command. In such a setting, conflict over policies and reforms can be limited to just that—conflicts whose eventual outcome will have less than sweeping political and institutional consequences for the participants. In this vein, developed socialism as a theoretical framework is a mechanism to contain and manage certain kinds of conflict while simultaneously providing a breathing space for limited reforms.[33]

The other side of the paradox is more difficult to pin down. As an image of the future, developed socialism also carries within it powerful technical, social, and economic imperatives perhaps no less demanding than Khrushchev's optimistic call for the full-scale construction of communism, even though no timetable has been laid down. If anything, the call for immediate purposive action is even more pressing. While the ultimate goal of full communism is now inestimably in the future, the tasks of the here-and-now are more clearly articulated. The party must act now if the potential of science and technology is to be realized; it must plan now to deal with the increasingly complex problems of a developed socialist society; and it must do all of these things within an institutional framework at best wary and at worst hostile to sweeping reforms.

33. *Partiia v period razvitogo sotsialisticheskogo obshchestva*, pp. 27-38; Sikorskii, pp. 142-191; *Voprosy vnutri-partiinoi zhizni i rukovodiashchei deiatel'nosti KPSS na sovremennom etape* (Moscow: Mysl', 1974); and *Kommunisticheskaia partiia v politicheskoi sisteme sotsialisticheskogo obshchestva* (Moscow: Mysl', 1974), pp. 53-104.

The State and Public Organizations. Soviet theorists place primary emphasis on the theme of the perfection of the state mechanism during the period of developed socialism. Having initially ignored Khrushchev's notion of the all-people's state, they have now cautiously resurrected it as an integral part of developed socialism. Predictably, emphasis has shifted from its transitional features—that is, the rapidly growing role of public organizations and the withering away of the state, which Khrushchev alleged had already begun—to the elaboration of an all-people's state whose significance increases throughout the developed socialist period. Soviet theorists leave no doubt that the state will be alive and increasingly robust far into the future, even though nascent features of the coming social order will slowly emerge within its institutional framework.[34]

The growing role of the state under developed socialism is justified primarily by its increasing activity in the creation of the material and technological base of communism. Still seen as a "main element" in building communism, it is to undergo "further perfection" during the period of developed socialism in two ways. First, it is to play an increasingly active and sophisticated role in the planning and direction of economic and social development. The scientific and technological revolution is seen as placing increasing demands on state institutions and, taken within this context, the call for the "perfection of the state mechanism" is linked in instrumental terms with recent managerial and planning reforms. The logic at work dictates that a further improvement of the state apparatus necessarily entails a broadening and deepening of its ability to direct further economic and social change. Thus a qualitative improvement in the performance of state tasks results in a quantitative expansion and deepening of its impact. Echoing Lenin's "better fewer, but better" injunction, Soviet theorists ritually observe that this does not necessarily mean an expansion of the size of the state apparatus—although this is not precluded—but rather a progressive upgrading of the performance of state functions.[35]

The second development is referred to as "the strengthening of Soviet democracy," which is best interpreted as the gradual devolution of politically non-sensitive tasks to lower administrative levels, especially to the local soviets and, to a lesser degree, public organizations, and the increasing involvement of citizen-activists in the affairs of these bodies. What is significantly different from the Khrushchev years is the pace of this transfer, particularly concerning the growing role of public organizations and the involvement of citizens in

34. Lesnyi and Chernogolovkin; Kerimov; and Chekharin.
35. Kas'ianenko, *Razvitoi*, pp. 165-166; L. I. Zagainov, "Povyshenie ekonomicheskoi roli gosudarstva pri razvitom sotsializme," *Sovetskoe gosudarstvo i pravo*,[1] (1976), pp. 17-24; and Glezerman, p. 154.

pseudo-administrative functions. Not surprisingly, the role of public organizations has been scaled down and the emphasis shifted to the development of the soviets. But even with these reservations, this highly selective administrative deconcentration serves both practical and theoretical needs. It both provides the rationale for cautious experimentation in shifting some decision-making to lower administrative or territorial levels and demonstrates in relatively safe terms that the dialectical evolution of developed socialism continues its slow progress. As transitional institutions, the soviets are seen as sharing the characteristics of state administrative organs, public organizations, and public self-administration, with the center of gravity shifting from the first gradually through the second and eventually to the third as developed socialism matures.[36]

Public organizations are also expected to play an increasingly important role, although Khrushchev's confidence in their rapid emergence as major participants beside the state and party is hardly shared by contemporary leaders. Current literature stresses instead both the slow pace of any further transfers and the "supplementary" role these organizations play in relationship to the counterpart state agency. The evolution of public organizations under developed socialism must depend upon the further perfection of the state agencies themselves and their success in increasing the educational level, public involvement, and moral development of the masses, tasks which are to be shared, at least in the transition period, by both party and state.[37]

36. Sikorskii, pp. 132-142; 192-227; Kerimov, pp. 9-23; and Glezerman, pp. 160-161.
37. Lesnyi and Chernogolovkin, pp. 93-104; Sikorskii, pp. 202-207; Chekharin, pp. 220-229; and *Dobrovol'nye obshchestva pri sotsializme* (Moscow: Nauka, 1976).

Robert Conquest

The Soviet Order

In our time the division between the despotic and the civic political cultures (and political psychologies) is the dominant factor in world affairs. It manifests itself, above all, in the confrontation between the Soviet order and that of the West. Advances in communications and in weaponry have brought these opposing cultures into a most immediate, constant, and dangerous contiguity—but not understanding. The difference between the consensual political order such as has existed in the West for centuries and even millenia, as against the old despotic orders of post-Mongol Russia (and similar states) on the one hand and the messianic revolutionary despotisms on the other, forms a psychological and conceptual barrier difficult to break down.

The Soviet order is *sui generis*—and above all not to be apprehended under categories suitable to quite different political cultures such as our own. But it has its historical roots and its general principles: in part the entire Russian background, and in part the specific Communist political and ideological present. Its ruling elite are the products of centuries of history, of personal and collective experiences of indoctrination, and of the ability to survive those experiences and accept that indoctrination.

It is clear that the dominant Russian political tradition, after a pre-Mongol period of a much more Western style, was a specific result of the Mongol overlordship as such and its particular characteristics. The Mongol state had as its conscious aim world empire. At the same time its theory of a worldwide order based on justice and equality explicitly sought that aim by making all its subjects live a life of permanent service to the state, as can be seen in the great Mongol law code *Yasa*.

The Great Russians, after recovering independence, lived in an almost permanent state of mobilization against continual menace from the steppe. The threat continued for hundreds of years. Moscow was sacked by the Crimean Tartars as late as 1571. As a result, Russia always had to keep what was, by the standards of the time, a huge army on the frontier till winter made the routes of invasion impassable to raiders. The effort was a killing one. Pavel Miliukov wrote, "Compelling national need resulted in the creation of an omnipotent State on the most meager material foundation; this very meagerness constrained it to exert all the energies of its population—and in order to have full control over these energies it had to be omnipotent."

Effective defense entailed expansion, but rigorous centralization was enforced over huge territories. Although it might take a year for a government order to reach its recipient, decisions even on very petty matters, were made in Moscow. On the other hand, the great distances made it far more difficult for the scattered subjects to bring influence to bear on the capital or to coordinate complaints into popular movements.

As Trotsky also put it, not only Russian "feudalism" but Russian history itself is marked by its "meagerness"—the absence of real cities, the fact that in its attempt to compete with "richer Europe" the Russian state "swallowed up a far greater relative part of the people's wealth than in the West, and thereby not only condemned the people to a two-fold poverty, but also weakened the foundations of the possessing classes," whose growth was "forced and regimented." Though the autocracy of the period between the Mongols and the Emancipation was extreme by most standards, it was not (if only for want of the technical possibility) as complete as the post-revolutionary settlement. Nevertheless, it contained some major elements which have persisted, or have revived, under the Soviets.

As a Soviet official recently told the *New Statesman* correspondent:

> Our country has no civil tradition. The taste for association, for organizing communal life together, for getting to know each other and taking decisions together, never really

existed in Russia. Between the czar and the moujik there was nothing; equally, between one moujik and another there was nothing except for essential personal relationships. We were and we remain a huge body, colossal even, but shapeless and deprived of articulation, of that political fabric on which the modern states of Europe were built.[1]

This Russian state tradition was not the only social and intellectual tradition in Russia. Pre-Mongol Russia, Kievan Russia, with the traditions of Slavic tribalism and Norse law, had developed along lines comparable to European feudalism. The great merchant republics of northwest Russia were fine examples of the urban civicism then beginning to emerge in many parts of Europe. But the new model type state at Moscow crushed them, as it had crushed the remnants of Kievan feudalism.

The independent element in Russian thought and organization continued to manifest itself: in religious life, particularly in the monasteries, which long maintained a sturdy independence of the state; in the popular initiatives at the beginning of the 17th century; in what might have been a proto-parliament, the Zemsky Sobor; after the religious reforms of the mid 17th century, in the persecuted but bitterly resistant Old Belief, which was never assimilated to the state. On and beyond the borders of the central state, serfdom came late or never. Freer spirits swarmed to the border region to form the Cossack areas of the Ukraine and Siberia. In the Ukraine, the Republic on the Waterfalls had an organization of a strictly consensual type, and was only crushed late in Catherine the Great's time—leaving perhaps a more independent spirit there than in central Russia.

The Russian state tradition, on the other hand, was based on the intensive serfdom of the main regions and the increasingly rigid grip of the autocracy and its bureaucracy which began to come into full fruition during the time of Peter the Great. It was in reaction to this tradition that the Russian revolutionary tradition emerged. Though the Enlightenment and the great legal and political reforms from 1860 to 1905 had created a basis for a different evolution, nevertheless the state tradition of autocracy persisted powerfully and was reflected in a competing autocracy of revolution from 1825.

Lermontov, writing in 1830, already speaks of the fall of the monarchy leading to terror, plague, and famine from which a ruthless tyrant—"The Man of Power"—will emerge. As early as the 1850s liberal-minded Russians were noting the despotic tendencies of the revolutionary intelligentsia. Herzen made the prophetic remark,

1. K. S. Karol, *New Statesman*, January 1, 1971.

"I believe that there is some justification for the fear of Communism which the Russian government begins to feel: Communism is the Russian autocracy turned upside down!" The truly creative minds of Russia had a less sanguine and more profound view of the revolutionary future than is to be found among many Westerners of a more sophisticated time.

The Communist regime soon went back to the principles of autocracy and bureaucracy, to the bases of serfdom and despotism in the Russian state tradition. But, and here is a point which Solzhenitsyn has made very powerfully, the Communist regime brought in a new element of totalitarianism—an absolutism that really was absolute—and demanded the submission of all those elements in Russian life that even Nicholas I had not found it possible to crush. At the same time, it reduced all public morality to that which enabled the ruler's will to prevail, again going far beyond the absolution of any of the tsars.

The setting up of the totalitarian one-party state by Lenin in 1917 marked the end of the progress toward a civic order which had begun in Russia in the 1860s. But within the Communist movement itself, and among surviving intelligentsia, a tradition of critical thought—an inevitable concomitant of the dispute between revolutionaries and the regimes they had overthrown—still survived. The destruction of this tendency was Stalin's main achievement in the 1930s. When the Communist party had become no more than an uncritical mechanism of despotism, it became appropriate to use all the psychological and other resources of the general despotic tradition.

In this view, the Stalinist purges were necessary for the preservation of the regime. The most profound problem was to establish in the Soviet Union the pre-critical society of ancient times, in which the ideas and wishes of the rulers were to be accepted as infallible by modern society. But the party had come to power, in part, with the encouragement of the extreme critical attitude in regard to the previous order; those trained in such an attitude were unable to switch it off on demand. Revolution itself is inevitably bound up with inciting minds to criticism of the previously existing system; but the establishment of a despotic-messianic regime inevitably involves destroying the habit of criticism on which it had originally to rely. Stalin's inner party terror may be taken as the natural means of destroying the persistent, but now obsolete, critical attitudes among the revolutionary elite itself.

Because the Stalin purges destroyed that segment of the party tainted by a residual Europeanization, present Soviet leadership is derived from those social strata which were never influenced by the liberalization of the Enlightenment. As several thoughtful observers have noted, they come either from households of peasants, or from an urban working class just out of the villages. The present generation of rulers is, moreover, the first that is entirely the political product of the Soviet order. Khrushchev and Molotov, whatever their convictions, still retained the memory and, to some slight but unavoidable extent, the influence of pre-Soviet—even non-Soviet—ideas. Moreover, the thin slice of the political spectrum which came to power in 1917 was, in the 1930s, sliced ten times thinner. A very special type (from the point of political, but not only political, psychology) emerged. Since 1917, the whole political talent of the country except the adherents of a single doctrine were excluded; in the years that followed all but one nuance within this narrow section of the political spectrum were reduced to oblivion. In the actual years of the Terror, a new principle was applied: even those who fully agreed with the official line were disposed of if they did not exhibit absolute servility and absolute loyalty unqualified by qualms of conscience.

The members of the present Politburo, both old and young, owe their careers to the Terror. This applies not only to men like Kosygin and Brezhnev, who were among the few surviving *apparatchiks* to fight their way up through the political slaughter pens of the party machines of Leningrad and the Ukraine. It is also true of younger men like Mazurov, who was working in the political department of the heavily purged railways of Byelorussia in 1938. It should be remembered, moreover, that all who did not adequately denounce were themselves formally decreed to be among the guilty.[2] As Dr. Alexander Weissberg, the physicist, noted (of Ukrainian industry but the point applies more generally): "A few months later their successors were arrested too. It was only the third or fourth batch who managed to keep their seats. They had not even the normal advantages of youth in their favour, for the choosing had been a very negative one. They were men who had denounced others on innumerable occasions. They had bowed the knee whenever they had come up against higher authority. They were morally and intellectually crippled."

Every time that conditions allow a Soviet writer to delineate the *apparatchik* we get the same picture—from Vladimir Dudintsev's "Drozdov" in *Not By Bread Alone* in the mid-fifties, and the characters in *For The Good of The Cause*, to the recent *Ivankiad*. Perhaps even more telling is the veteran and respected writer Konstantin Paustovsky's direct account of personal experience:

2. As was officially stated. See, for example, Y. P. Petrov, *Party Construction in the Soviet Army and Fleet 1918-1961* (Moscow: 1964), p. 301.

> The new caste of Drozdovs is still with us, . . . there are still thousands and thousands of them. . . . Recently I took a trip around Europe on the steamer *Pobeda*. In the second and third classes there were workers, engineers, artists, musicians, writers; in the first class were the Drozdovs. I need not tell you that they had and could have absolutely no contact with the second and third classes. They revealed hostility to everything except their position, they astounded us by their ignorance. They and we had completely different ideas about what constituted the prestige and honor of our country. One of the Drozdovs, standing before "The Last Judgment," asked: "Is that the judgment of Mussolini?" Another, looking at the Acropolis, said: "How could the proletariat allow the Acropolis to be built?" A third, overhearing a comment on the amazing color of the Mediterranean, asked severely: "And is our water back home worse?" These predators, proprietors, cynics, and obscurantists, openly, without fear or embarrassment, carried on anti-Semitic conversations worthy of true Nazis. They were jobbers, quite, quite indifferent to anything else. . . .

The Italian left-wing Socialist leader Pietro Nenni, who had always been a good friend of the communists, wrote confidentially to Suslov after Khrushchev's 1956 "Secret Speech" that any destruction of the Stalinist myth must also call in question

> the judicial and political structure of the state, the very idea and practice of one-party government, and the conduct of economic and social affairs—in short, the entire system. . . . What is more, despotism and abuse will rear their heads again tomorrow as they did yesterday, if the denunciation of the 'shameful facts' of the Stalin era is not followed by a full and complete restoration of democracy and liberty.

When Khrushchev fell eight years later, Nenni published this letter, adding the comment that the new coup proved the point that "the good will and good faith of human beings, even those endowed with exceptional personalities, are powerless against the vices of the system." As Garaudy has put it,

> Not only did the criticism of Stalin, from the start, remain within these limits, but the weight of the structures and of the apparatus forged over a quarter of a century of bureaucratic centralism very quickly eroded the human choice: criticism was not pushed to the point where it would

have permitted a radical change . . . in reality, the present Soviet leaders hastened to turn back the page, and less than ten years after the XXth Congress, the criticism of Stalinism was completely interred. The leaders who constitute the essential framework of the Party and the State were formed by Stalinism and given position in Stalin's time on the basis of the criteria of the epoch: acceptance of official dogmas, the carrying out without discussion, at every level, of directives coming from above, and centralised, bureaucratic and authoritarian functioning in all institutions.

Western misunderstandings about the USSR are seldom misunderstandings about the form or even the general principles of the system. They stem overwhelmingly from something different: the natural tendency to project onto others our own motivations or something like them. It follows that the most important things we have to learn about the USSR are whatever illustrate with clarity the ways in which the minds of the leadership work. These may often be, on the face of it, superficial or even frivolous. Yet all the thousand theses written in Britain and the U.S. about changes in cotton prices in Uzbekistan from 1932 to 1936 tell nothing compared, for example, with attitudes toward the truth.

There are all sorts of minor examples. When a new edition of the most used Russian dictionary *(Ozhegov)* came out in Khrushchev's time, it had a single detectable change from the previous one: *khrushch*, a type of beetle, had previously been described as "deleterious to agriculture." This phrase was now omitted. On the other hand at the time of Khrushchev's fall in 1964, a Soviet opera company was in Milan playing *Boris Godunov*. A new programme appeared, in which a minor character of that opera, Khrushchev, was transformed into merely "a boyar." It is in such apparently minor phenomena, in the removal of pages from encyclopedias, in the faking of photographs, in the extraordinary lists of banned subjects laid down by Glavlit, that the mind of the regime displays itself most clearly. These are not aberrations but fair illustrations of the Soviet mind, of the attitudes of the Soviet political culture.

All this faking casts a particularly vivid light on the alien intricacies of the Soviet view of what is right and proper. But more essential is the matter of refusing to admit the commission of crimes on an enormous scale. An entirely false account of the Katyn massacre is still maintained. Historic restitution is still denied to the victims of Kolyma. As long as such things are suppressed, the present leadership remains not only the inheritor but also the accomplice of Stalinism.

Dmitry Ustinov, Minister of Defense (and formerly Stalin's

Minister of Armaments), addressed an audience of six thousand, the Soviet elite. He made two favorable references to Stalin, each time being interrupted by prolonged applause. The applause was, moreover, reported in *Pravda* the next day. There could hardly have been a franker demonstration of the views and allegiances of those who rule the Soviet Union. Moreover, as the Soviet philosopher G. S. Pomerants remarked a few years ago, praise for Stalin when he was alive was not open and acknowledged praise for a system of lies and terror, since these were then denied and concealed. Now, however, much of the truth has long been available in the USSR itself, so that (in Pomerants' words): "to restore respect for Stalin, knowing what he did, is to establish something new, to establish respect for denunciations, torture, executions. Even Stalin did not try to do that. He preferred to play the hypocrite. To restore respect for Stalin is to set up a moral monstrosity by our banner. . . . "

The Soviet order is characterized above all by the world view of its ruling group. Nor is this a matter of mere intellectual conviction, the acceptance of one ideology. Their attitudes go much deeper than that. They are unable to see the world in any other way. They were trained in and are a product of the lower levels of a dogmatic millenarian sect, which had destroyed the remnant of critical thought existing within it.

The main characteristics of their attitude, simply put, are first that it is a way of seeing the world which is in the strictest sense dogmatic—that is, it accepts the idea that a final philosophy, political philosophy and theory of society have been achieved; and that the nature of the perfect human order which will prevail throughout the future is known and can be achieved by theoretically prescribed methods. That is, it is a system of thought that, being true as against the falsehood of all others, implies a closed society.

Second, this way of thinking implies that the political leadership and political considerations generally are on a higher and more comprehensive plane than all other elements in society and are empowered to make the final decision in all fields. (It was this point that Leszek Kolakowski satirized in his definition of a "non-socialist state" as one where the writers said the same things as the politicians but always later.)

Third, it is based on a view of history—and of the world in general—which sees stuggles and clashes as the only essential mode of political or any other action. And long practice in putting this principle into operation has made it an attitude so deeply ingrained as to be almost automatic.

Fourth, the dogma's universal applicability throughout the world is equally deepset. All other political orders, even Communist ones which deviate in any significant way from that of the USSR (e.g.,

Dubček's Czechoslovakia or Mao's China), are in principle illegitimate and should be destroyed when possible, just as abberrant political or other views within the USSR are equally subject, in principle, to total suppression.

Brezhnev need not be envisaged as kneeling down and reciting the *Theses on Feuerbach* every night. He has enough ideology to get along, and the rest is soaked into his bones. This is not to say that conscious ideology does not play its part. We have accounts of long and serious sermons from Suslov, Ponomarev, and others to representatives of foreign Communist parties, even to the degree of insisting on a Marxist formulation that may be politically disadvantageous to the party concerned. For example, the confidential Soviet advice to the Syrian Communist party, published in the Beirut *Ar-Rayah* on 26 June, 1972, and commented on at length by Mohammed Heikal in the Cairo *Al-Ahram* on 18 August, 1972, can now certainly be accepted as genuine. It was a long, considered set-piece, in the preparation of which Soviet ideologists and political experts had made separate studies. It laid down Marxist criteria highly offensive to much of the Arab world, in particular, asserting that there is no such thing as an Arab nation—naturally the denial of the existence of the Arab nation is politically harmful, but to assert its existence in the program (of the Syrian Communist party) is not permissible because Marxism-Leninism denies it. The Russians went on to urge that the establishment of socialism piecemeal in various Arab countries, not Arab unity, was the "principal target."

Apart from the mere power-mania of the apparatus, the sole rationale of the disastrous collective farm system of agriculture is ideological. Collectivization was, from the start, carried out in a thoroughly irrational manner, irrationality being a characteristic to which we shall return later. There was no serious economic thinking: a crude administrative notion was effected simply by force. The success too was merely ideological, in the almost total destruction of private ownership. When a Politburo member a few years ago suggested a sensible relaxation as the only way to the much-sought improvement in agricultural production, he (Voronov) was removed. Similarly, the general economic reforms which came up in the mid-sixties have not been implemented, or only in such a form as to deprive them of their benefits, and this for "ideological" reasons.

The USSR has advanced further than any other order into a condition in which the shape and the actions of society are determined by the political and other ideas in the minds of their rulers. A highly articulate and explicit statement of this essential communist attitude was given by a member of an earlier generation, Gregory Pyatakov, just fifty years ago. Meeting a former Menshevik friend, N. V. Volsky-Valentinov, in Paris, he burst into an excited harangue:

According to Lenin, the Communist Party is based on the principle of coercion which doesn't recognize any limitations or inhibitions. And the central idea of this principle of boundless coercion is not coercion by itself but the absence of any limitation whatsoever—moral, political and even physical, as far as that goes. Such a Party is capable of achieving miracles and doing things which no other collective of men could achieve. ... A real Communist ... that is, becomes himself in a way a miracle man.

As Solzhenitsyn puts it,

... it was more than flesh and blood could bear to be hopelessly caught up in impossible grotesque, crippling schedules. You were trapped and held in a deadly grip. The system crushed you, driving you harder and faster all the time, demanding more and more, setting inhuman timelimits. This was why buildings and bridges collapsed, why crops rotted in the fields or never came up at all. But until it dawned on someone that people were only human, there was no way out of this vicious circle for those involved, except by falling ill ....[3]

The revolutionary attitude, with its corollary that nothing is more important than making specified changes in society, implies above all the primacy of politics. Since intense political conviction does not necessarily go with expertise in other fields, this usually means that radical-sounding theories are likely to be voted for by the Central Committee or other revolutionary ruling body, rather than less emotionally impressive (though better supported) ideas.

The system, far from tending to rationality, places a premium on quick and spectacular results however obtained. A. N. Larionov, First Secretary of the important Ryazan Province—a full Member of the Central Committee for many years—sought esteem in Khrushchev's time by promising to double his province's meat production in a year. He succeeded in this, with the support of all his subordinates, by slaughtering all the milk cows and breeding stock and illegally buying cattle on a large scale in other provinces (with funds illegally diverted from machinery buying) and so on. After a brief triumph and promises of an even better next year, Larionov, now a Hero of Socialist Labour and holder of the Order of Lenin, had to commit suicide in 1960 when it came out that he had ruined the area. His many imitators in other provinces disappeared.

3. Alexander Solzhenitsyn, *The First Circle* (New York: Harper and Row, 1968), p. 124.

Nor was this merely a Khrushchevite aberration. Six years later, under full Brezhnevism, we find similar occurrences. One of dozens of examples was a great efficiency drive in agriculture in the Kokchetov province.[4] This took the form of an enforced specialization according to which sheep, cattle and so forth were concentrated in the areas thought best for them. As a result, villages where sheep farming had been practised for centuries were left with no sheep, and dairy farms were suddenly filled with hordes of them. Pigs, however, were the greatest sufferers. They were banned on all except a few specialized farms, the rest being slaughtered immediately. As a result meat, milk and wool production in the province fell drastically. The peasantry, for the first time, had to import food. The local meat factories refused to buy pigs except from the special farms which had not got round to producing any, so the pigs left in private hands had to be marketed in provinces hundreds of miles away.

The quality of thought of the Soviet elite, apart from the dogmas of Marxism, seems to be primitive. A whole series of pseudo-sciences has been found compatible with Marxism, ever since Marx himself became addicted to phrenology. Lenin warned Gorki against the crackpot ideas of Bolshevik doctors, and medicine and biology were to be areas of great lunacy in Soviet times—the Schwartzman miracle cure of the twenties, and Kazakov's "lysates" in the thirties, Boshyan's microbe-synthesis in the forties, Lepishinskaya's spontaneous generation of cells in the fifties, the Kachugin "method" in the sixties—and above all the Lysenko blight—all owed their success to support from high political personalities. And so with the puerile Socialist realism aesthetic theory, the linguistics of Marr, and so on. The principle of accommodating science to a particular metaphysic, rather than leaving it to act autonomously, seems bound to produce distortion. The notion that Marxism is a basic, universal science leads to the condition in which many people professing it feel that they are already fully educated and, in effect, capable of judging any subsidiary studies without adequate humility or forethought.

Although the system is often described as totalitarian, or totalist, we all know that these terms are not adequate in practice. The system cannot work as its designers hoped, because it is based on a fallacious notion of politics and human psychology.

Moreover, if it be regarded as an Orwellian state in principle, it is an Orwellian state without the full courage of its convictions. Perhaps the most obvious way in which powerful ideas contradicting the whole concept of the Leninist order are permitted to penetrate the consciousness of the population is in the reprinting of Russian

4. *Kazakhstanskaya Pravda,* February 15, 1970.

classical literature—all of which, with negligible exceptions, in effect teaches non-Leninist attitudes. There are other spheres in which a lack of true totalism has awkward results: for instance, in Soviet treatment of the nationality problem. Rosa Luxemburg, it will be remembered, was totally opposed to any grants of national autonomy in the proletarian state. The Leninists, on the other hand, chose the method of encouraging it up to a point, while suppressing aspects of it which seemed disintegrative, as if national feeling, that wildcat of whose worldwide rages we are all aware, could just be "fixed" like some old tabby.

Then again, the Soviet rulers—and ironically enough this became particularly true in the Stalin period—wished to appear as respectable liberals, with elections and pseudo-parliaments. This had two disadvantages. First it was obvious nonsense and could only be believed by an effort of doublethink which could not but have a deleterious effect on the party intellect. Second, in certain cases it met contradictions—as with the sovereignty of Poland, Hungary, or Romania where, contrary to serious intentions, shadow institutions took on substance after all.

Further, the conviction that Marxism is a science, while providing suitable justification for the beliefs of Soviet Marxists, also introduced into their world less easily managed aspects of the scientific attitude. And whenever they were in fact proving themselves right by metaphysical assertion, they had to do it in a form which appeared scientific, thus setting up yet another strain in the party mind.

The Soviet system also had the conceptual weakness that it was and is supposedly a vehicle for rule by the industrial working class. To believe this, as the rulers in some sense evidently do, must require the equivalent of an ideological lobotomy. The extent to which the USSR is class-ridden has been pointed out elsewhere. And it is of course notorious that workers' risings of the type far exceeding anything seen in the "capitalist" West have been endemic since the early 60s.

What has happened in the past ten or fifteen years in towns from Chimkent to Dnepropetrovsk has not been sufficiently understood in the West. The equivalent in Britain would be food-riots in Middlesborough put down with dozens shot dead by police and army; strikes, developing into demonstrations, in Aberdeen—with hundreds of casualties; nationalist demonstrations in Merthyr, scores shot, hundreds arrested . . . and so on and so on, in dozens of examples. The mutiny on the Soviet warship *Storozhovoy* in November 1975 was reported in the West, but without much comment. Imagine if such a mutiny and attempt to take a vessel into a foreign port had taken place in the British or American Navies. What an outcry would have been heard about a collapse of morale! And rightly—nothing really comparable has taken place since the mutiny on the battleship Potemkin in 1905, which presaged the downfall of the then Russian state.

The social order of the USSR has, in fact, little resemblance to the official conception of it. Above all, it is both politically and economically class-ridden. The Communist *pays légal*, that is those citizens who are in practice entitled to discuss matters of state policy, is confined to a few thousand. Members of the Bureaux of Provincial Committees, together with equivalent party workers from the Army and elsewhere, number something between five and six thousand. There are in addition about 8,000 party workers attached to those Bureaux as professional activists, and they may have some minimal influence. The full membership of the Provincial Committees is about 20,000, and if we double that to include the equivalents in Army and similar organizations, we may stretch it to 40,000-odd people in some very slight way involved in political discussion at the extreme periphery. The whole *nomenklatura* is believed to number about 50,000. More realistically, discussion proper takes place among the members of the Politburo and the Secretariat, with the members of the Central Committee exerting influence on a lesser scale. Even members of this elite have, in some respects, lesser political rights than ordinary members of the adult population in the West. For example, they have no right to suggest that the economic and political system itself is faulty.

From another point of view, a careful estimate of the Soviet elite considered in terms of real income is given by Mervyn Matthews.[5] He found that approximately a quarter of a million people make 450 rubles a month or more and have access to secondary benefits. This caste enjoys privileges hard to justify on any grounds, particularly communist ones: the "thirteenth month" salary; the gold ruble extra pay for use in foreign currency shops; the special "distributor" shops for rare luxuries at low prices; the privileged blocks of flats; the special restaurants; the special holiday facilities; the high-grade hospitals and clinics. That this doublethink is a sensitive matter is clear. Mervyn Matthews points out that "Another touchstone is the secrecy which shrouds the doings of the most favoured Soviet citizens. It is noteworthy that (a) words like 'elite' and 'rich' are banned as a description of any Soviet social group (b) no information whatever on higher salaries is printed for open distribution (c) no official figures have so far been given for the national distribution of income, probably because this would reveal an unsocialistic degree

---

5. Mervyn Matthews, *Privilege in the Soviet Union: A Study of Elite Life Styles under Communism* (London: George Allen & Unwin, 1978).

of inequality (d) scarcely anything is printed on elite lifestyles or the benefits which an elite might enjoy (e) there is nothing nearly as comprehensive as a 'Who's Who' in the Soviet Union. Given the amount of discussion of pay differentials and lifestyles at lower levels, the obvious explanation lies in a complete censor's prohibition of the topic," as indeed recent evidence on Soviet censorship shows to be the case. These facts require doublethink in terms of proletarian rule.

Marx's dictum that "the proletariat have no country" was based on the idea that the industrial working class in his day had no stake in Western society and did not in any real sense form part of it. Nowadays such a principle should be differently applied. In the West the whole population is part of the political culture. It is in the USSR that polity and society are not coterminous. The polity, the *pays legal*, consists of (stretching it to its utmost) a few tens of thousands of party and other officials, and the great bulk of society is excluded from it. This constitutes a "contradiction," as the Marxists say, a conceptual weakness in the party mind, which has to repress the notion, as well as a potential physical weakness.

The leaders are capable of behaving with amenity in international affairs, of being on their best behavior, on certain occasions. At their meeting with the Czechoslovak communist leadership at Cierna-nad-Tisou, in the summer of 1968, though the discussions were sometimes fairly heated, they remained "comradely." When a few weeks later the Czechoslovak leaders were arrested, subjected to physical violence, and paraded as prisoners before a jeering Soviet Politburo, they were quite unprepared for the change of tone. As one of the Czechs put it, while it was no surprise that the Russians were narrow-minded dogmatists, what came as a shock was to find that they were also "vulgar thugs." The low level of intrigue noted after that occasion, when they had to release the Dubček leadership and return it to Prague, was equally striking—as when they promised but failed to release until the others refused to go without him their greatest bugbear, Kriegel, "that damned Galician Jew," as Brezhnev put it.

The Soviet economy has been ably dealt with elsewhere. I wish only to make the point that, strictly speaking, it is not an economy at all in the sense that its operations are in principle governed not by economic laws but by decisions taken preponderantly on a political-ideological basis. It is an economy only in the sense that distribution of goods in a barracks or a prison can be so considered. This raises the point that barracks and prisons are notoriously susceptible to developing a real economy, with supply sergeants and trusties much involved. This is, of course, the case in the USSR too, and we may regard extralegality as the lubricant without which the Soviet economy could not work at all. Still, it is only a partial and insufficient lubricant; and the Soviet economy can only be kept going by the application of, in the long run, excessive force. This is to say that an economy organized on Soviet principles is inconceivable without administrative pressures. Thus, again, the mere structure of the system, determined by ideological creed, involves a rigorous command system.

Curiously enough, the economic dogma which lies so heavily on the USSR is not about socialism at all but about capitalism—that capitalism is characterized by commodity relationships. It has been the avoidance of commodity even more than any positive insistence on specific socialist method which has invariably driven the USSR away from market solutions. A decision by the highest political authority is, in all spheres, the final one: if this is not enforced with the rigour of total logic it nevertheless provides the central economic thrust of the regime.

All attempts from the mid-sixties on to introduce a market component into the Soviet economy have failed because the authorities have always insisted on keeping central controls operative, even as to pricing. In the article I have mentioned by K. S. Karol,[6] he quotes a Soviet economist: "My mistake," he said, "was to believe too long that our leaders supported reforms to tackle the country's economic reality. I thought they understood, from their experience, that repressive measures would never achieve results and that they were therefore ready to employ purely economic tools. Now I see there was nothing to it."

Zygmunt Bauman notes

> the tendency of some Western observers to assume an affinity between managers of state or public-owned enterprises in a socialist society and owner-managers in a capitalist socio-economic system, and to conclude from this assumed affinity that the former entertain the same inherent, rationally-based sympathy towards political democracy as the latter. Both the assumption and the conclusion are false. In capitalist societies, as long as the state power remains relatively unobtrusive and does not challenge the central value-cluster on which the socio-economic equilibrium of the system is founded, the owner-managers neither owe their basic rights to the group holding political power at the moment, nor can they hold it responsible for any predicament they may be in.
> The situation of the managers in a state-ownership

6. *New Statesman,* January 1, 1971.

system is diametrically opposite. In contrast to that of capitalist owner-managers whose security is anchored outside the political sphere, their position is inherently political in nature, being founded soley and exclusively on a political equilibrium. What power they have is politically granted, politically guaranteed, and politically oriented.[7]

In Stalin's time and even more in Khrushchev's time, the leadership was organizing the economy with a view to "overtaking the West." It seems probable that the leadership then really believed that this was an aim they could achieve. Nowadays, the feeling one gets in all leading Russian circles and even the top leadership itself is that they no longer have much, or any, faith in such an outcome. The general decline reaches the political level as different sectors compete more and more sharply for materials and resources. To the normal tensions at the top over power and higher policy, this strong extra instability is added. Of course the Politburo wants, in a sense, a more prosperous and productive Russia. As Francis Bacon remarked, "It is common with princes (saith Tacitus) to will contradictories . . . for it is the solecism of power to think to command the end, and yet not to endure the mean."

The political difficulty of creating a flexible and modern economy is clear. Georg Lukacs has written that economic reform is not possible without a general increase in democracy, in particular in freedom of speech. Academician Sakharov makes the same point; and he based on the state of the Soviet economy a broad set of demands for what amounts to the elimination, on the Czechoslovak 1968 model, of the current police state. But for the Soviet leaders the opposite considerations clearly apply. If faced with the fact that economic reform is not possible without political reform, they will do without economic reform. The concessions made will be small and inadequate, economically speaking, though sufficient to prevent real disaster—as with Stalin's grant of small private plots to the peasantry, which was, and is, not enough to make Soviet agriculture even moderately efficient, but is enough (usually) to secure a basic ration from the farms.

One consideration which makes it virtually certain that under the present regime consumer goods will not tend to the Western level is that the USSR is now a military power capable of matching the United States simply and solely because it diverts into heavy industry and defense production a high enough proportion of its resources. If we compare it with the area of equivalent population in Western

7. Zygmunt Bauman, "Twenty Years After: The Crisis of Soviet-Type Systems," *Problems of Communism* (November/December, 1971), pp. 45-53.

Europe (not for the moment considering the U.S.) it is clear that Britain, France, Germany, Italy, and so on, more than an economic match for the USSR, would be a military match for it but for the special structure of the Soviet economy.

The superiority of the Western culture in science and technology is inherent in this situation. It is not merely a matter of the freer movement of ideas and the comparative absence of inhibition against expressing new ones—though these play their part. It is also a result of different attitudes toward the whole notion of research.

To the open culture, the idea that the advance of knowledge can be planned has the same absurdity as the idea that new social orders can be constructed. In the Soviet scheme, science is beset with difficulties arising from the twin errors that the party is in possession of a supreme philosophy empowering it to have a final say in every sphere of knowledge and that planning is applicable in research as in all other fields. As a result of all this, the general estimate among Soviet scientists is that the real costs of a given program in the USSR are as much as four or five times greater than those incurred in the West for the same results.

Another result, found throughout the economy as well, is a tendency to resist the reorganization of smoothly running conventional research, since this naturally means a temporary disorganization and slowing down, the submitting of applications for new materials which are hard to find, and above all venturing into untried fields where initial production plans may prove wrong and, thus, damaging to all concerned. At the 24th Congress of the CPSU, a further nuisance for scientists emerged as party organizations within the research institutes were empowered to exercise control over the administration.

None of this is to say that the Soviet economy is wholly unsuccessful. On the contrary, it has kept up what is, in the abstract, a significant rate of advance. But this has been the result of inordinate effort and strain—and, above all, it has left the country far below all the other industrial nations in per capita GNP, real incomes, and a whole series of indicators, while its comparative backwardness is in effect admitted by its technological imports. It does not operate in an abstract isolation but in a world of other powers with a different economic system, and this is continually and obsessively in the consciousness of those who rule the USSR, both as a fact intolerable to their most cherished dogmas and an insult to their power and competence.

What can we say of the Soviet present and above all of the Soviet future? First of all, it is plain that the system still in existence is that created by Stalin. No changes of substance have taken place. The Khrushchev interlude, when for a time it looked as though some sort of ameliorative evolution was possible, may have been, as Solzhenitsyn puts it, a "miracle;" but even Khrushchev failed to institutionalize the reforms (such as they were) that he had inaugurated.

The point was clear even then to many Russians. When Dr. Gene Sosin said to a Russian during the Khrushchev interlude that things were better, the reply was "Yes, but what about yesterday—and tomorrow?" Anna Akhmatova warned friends that in a system of this sort, without legal guarantees, a good Caesar might be simply followed by a bad one. Nero was overthrown and execrated, but twelve years later Domitian was on the throne. Chateaubriand, in his *Études historiques* points out that a whole series of good emperors from Nerva to the time when "with Marcus Aurelius, philosophy itself was placed on the throne" led to nothing, since no constitutional guarantees existed.

As we know, Khrushchev was succeeded by leaders who reversed his departures from traditionalism. They have not, it is true, restored the full rigors of Stalinism. But they still exhibit an extravagant suspicion and hatred of any non-official thinking. They have done their best (as we have seen) to minimize criticism of, or even information about, the Stalin period.

And we do not need to be reminded of the various literary trials, nor of the labor camps on a vastly smaller scale than in Stalin's time (yet still with the murderous rations of the 1930s, far lower than those of the Japanese killer camps for prisoners of war on the river Kwai). Above all, report after report of interrogations and investigations show the KGB men in charge arguing from the old narrow and totalist mentality, clearly ready for harder action than is, at present, customary.

The present Soviet leadership may feel that all it wants to do is to enjoy power quietly and not take further risks. The question that arises is what will be the attitude of the younger generation which must eventually—long though the wait may seem to be—come to the top. There is nothing specifically Soviet in the fact that even if politicians are capable of learning from their own experience, generations without that experience go ahead to repeat the errors of their predecessors. Nadezhda Mandelshtam says "I do not believe the older generation now at the helm wants to see a new orgy of terror and killing. Knowing so well what this means, they are cautious." But, as she puts it, the new "criminal stock" of more recent times which has not so far managed to climb to the top "... are young people with no memory of the terrible years who would be capable of anything." Andrei Sakharov and Roy Medvedev both agree about the dogmatism of the younger generation—the 45 year olds. They do not say that a new Stalinist terror is inevitable, and there are, of course, other

The Soviet Order 243

perspectives. Nevertheless, we cannot dismiss too lightly the thought that not only are the institutions of Stalinism still in existence, but the young who are recruited into the machine through (for example) the local secretariats of the Komsomol in universities or elsewhere, are precisely those most totally and narrowly devoted to a system in principle at war with all other thought and feeling among its own subjects and those of all other states. Moreover, as Mandelshtam says in the second volume of her memoirs, the terror machine is still in being: "Even when it is only idling, as today, it continues to function in essentially the same manner as before. At any moment, after lying dormant for a time it could start up again at full speed."

If there is to be a crisis of the Communist regime under the present leaders or their probable successors, I would expect it to come not as the result of any specific policies, but rather through unforeseen catastrophes with which their methods, and indeed their personalities, are not fitted to cope. They will soon have to face, in some form or other, a major dislocation which their present small-scale economies and conservation measures do not go very far to avert. The Soviet economy is in principle over-extended and this must bedevil the relations between the Soviet ideologists, military men, and administrators in various fashions, even to the point of shaking the entire structure of the state. But it is likely that there will be an even greater crisis of ideas than of economics. We are faced by an economy and a society whose inextinguishable tendencies run counter to the political integument which at present hems them in, thus creating conditions of a classical Marxist pre-revolutionary situation. The current regime has learned from Khrushchev that random reforms within the system have not done any good. But the immobilism to which they have retreated equally provides no solution, and it appears inevitable that pressures will continue to build up.

One does not see the current leadership taking adequate measures against this. Nor does one see any sign of potential successors who might. Although there have been occasions in the past when obsolete political systems have been transformed without serious trouble, these instances have been comparatively uncommon. Moreover, such an evolution has usually been possible only when plenty of time was given for the principles of change to soak into every corner of the social mind. In the USSR today, one would not expect a great deal of time to be still available.

The blockage to the free spread of ideas, especially into the minds of the ruling party, is unprecedentedly strong, though we should perhaps not underestimate the degree of erosion. But the greatest difficulty of all is simply that the machinery Stalin built is organizationally effective and ideologically disciplined to the extent that it can probably keep the political integument in being long past the stage at which other political forms would have failed. And this implies that the pressures, when they reach a critical point, will be very high indeed. In the meantime, we should be prepared for surprises over the next decade and should not fall into the temptation of believing the status quo to be as stable as it may appear to the superficial glance.

As Solzhenitsyn notes in his "Letter to the Patriarch," the past fifty years have been wasted, and more than wasted, in Russia. "Half a century of the past has already been lost, and I am not talking about trying to save the present. But how are we to save the future of our country?" If a start could be made in simply eliminating the extremes of totalitarianism, in initiating and implanting areas of legality, that would indeed be a real beginning. Academician Sakharov is often seen as one who sees more hope of an immediate democratization. But he both speaks of the "many fine democratic steps beginning with the reforms of Alexander the Second," and admits that the present vicious circle "cannot be overcome in a short time."

From the point of view of the West, it is true that, as Engels commented of an earlier time, "As soon as Russia has an internal development, and with that, internal party struggles, the attainment of a constitutional form under which these party struggles may be fought without violent convulsions . . . the traditional Russian policy of conquest is a thing of the past." That is not yet. In the meantime, various evolutions and revolutions are possible. But for the immediate future, Russia is stuck with a group of rulers who are faced by a society tending in every respect away from their concepts but who are in possession of an immensely powerful instrument for blocking social and political change. In foreign affairs we face an inept Soviet oligarchy with huge military resources, answerable to none and possessed of a surly hostility to all other forms of political life.

The points made here are clearly of the utmost importance to all foreign policy decisions made in the West. There is a school of thought, or at least of speech, which continually asserts that the Soviet order has changed in an absolutely essential fashion, that it is no longer the vehicle of an irreconcilable Leninist dogma. If this were true, it would be of great importance. To accept it as true if it is not true, on the other hand, would mean that we were basing our foreign policy on a major fallacy. One would think, therefore, that those who believe that such a change has taken place would offer evidence of some sort that this has indeed occurred.

Such evidence might include showing that the state and party institutions which are the vehicle of the Leninist dictatorship have changed; but no change whatever has taken place. Then, it might be shown that there was a tendency to pluralism in the thought of the

Soviet rulers, and hence to tolerance of other ideas. No sign of such a change has appeared, either in the conduct of the Soviet rulers towards unorthodox ideas within the Soviet Union or in their attitudes to political and other views they regard as heretical or wrong in the outside world. Finally, a tendency to reconciliation with other orders might be expected to manifest itself in the acceptance of a lower level of armament than that now in being, and the avoidance of a "forward" foreign policy in various parts of the world. This is not a very precise description of reality.

Those who advance the optimistic view seem to be lacking in general historical perspective. It has long been commonplace among historians—that is, those knowledgeable not merely about a particular subject but about history in general—that political cultures and political psychologies have great intrinsic momentum and are not easily deflected. Changes may occur, but they do not occur rapidly. It would be hard to find, throughout human history, an example of a group of oligarchs converted within a few years to democracy, or a group of adherents to a closed and totalist view of the world who suddenly changed into followers of John Stuart Mill.

The evolution of the Soviet state into something approaching true civic culture is not a short term prospect. If the West pursues the correct policies, however, it should be the single direction which lies open. And we should recall, above all, that such an evolution is essential in the long run if world peace is to be maintained and a cooperative world order to be created.

I here say nothing of the consequences of large scale Soviet military or foreign policy successes. These are indeed possible, if the West pursues inappropriate policies. And triumph abroad is the traditional recourse of a tyranny inefficient at home. Nor has "backwardness" prevented many a militarily competent barbarian nation from overwhelming superior civilizations.

Andrei Amalrik

The Soviet Union— Approaching 1984

If there exists a certain determined sequence of events, a certain fixed connection between cause and effect, then we can consider it possible to predict the future. Common sense generally proceeds from the assumption that what has been, will be, and that it is possible more or less to extrapolate existing tendencies. Despite all the catastrophes of our century, this view is firmly rooted, apparently in response to a profound need for stability as well as to the belief that whatever might change, man continues to remain the same "Old Adam."

Apparently, in 99 out of 100 cases, this view is correct. But in the one exceptional case a break occurs, a leap; those who renounce more attainable goals for the sake of less attainable goals, begin to play a role, and it is precisely here that long-range development is determined for many years. This break always catches us unawares; nevertheless it turns out not to be unexpected. Thus, the Russian revolution evoked the two opposing feelings: this was inevitable—but how could it happen?

In predicting the future, we are dealing with a practically unlimited number of combinations. The construction of so-called scenarios, i.e., five or fifty possible variants of development, seems to me no more than an intellectual game: you cannot bet on all the horses and win, especially in races where a horse which has not been entered in your program could win. At the present time, the least scientific approach remains the most reliable and is, in fact, intuitive, although much effort is expended on its rationalization. It is not surprising, therefore, that personal experience strongly influences the result of analysis.

For example, it would be an exaggeration to say that in American Sovietology there exist two schools: that of the Polish Jews and that of the German Jews. But it is undoubtedly true that the Sovietologists of Polish extraction appraise the Soviet system and the possibility of reaching an understanding with it much more skeptically, and even pessimistically, than their colleagues of German extraction. Likewise, it is possible to see a difference between the analyses of dissident emigrants and of those emigrants whose careers before emigration were pursued within the framework of the Soviet system. The former emphasize the importance of moral-psychological factors, while the latter stress considerations of economic determinism. The advice of the former to the West is to maintain a moral position and political resolve; the advice of the latter is to seek rapprochement with the pragmatists in the USSR and to render economic aid. Clearly, generalizing from one's own experience is inevitable.

With some oversimplification we may distinguish three general approaches to the study of the Soviet system:

1. As primarily a modern industrial state;
2. As primarily a state built on Marxist ideology;
3. As primarily a political structure of the Russian people and other nationalities of the former Russian empire.

So far as there have been significant, although not decisive, changes in the Soviet system in the last quarter of a century—changes mostly in the direction of a softening of the system—three theories of the future of the Soviet system have been proposed within the framework of these three general approaches.[1]

1. The theory of convergence postulates that the very conditions of modern industrial society will gradually reshape the Soviet system in a more liberal spirit. And so far as there is a tendency in the West toward partial socialization and a greater role of the government in the economy, this will gradually lead the two systems to a closer resemblance. From this point of view, which is incidentally quite Marxist, Marxism served in the period of industrial backwardness of

---

1. I refer to theories expressed and debated in *samizdat*, but roughly the same theories were developed in Western Sovietology with more professional scientific method but with less prophetic thrust.

Russia-USSR as a stimulus for accelerated development. As the goal of industrialization is attained, the Marxist ideology and the system of totalitarian control associated with it fall away.[2]

2. The theory of stabilization postulates that the totalitarian political system based on Marxist ideology, by means of the violent revolution and post-revolutionary purges, finally has assured its complete control of society, so that it no longer has to employ such brutal methods. The "momentum of fear," so to speak, carries on; the regime has become stabilized and can go on unchanged for centuries.

3. The theory of stagnation postulates that the inner revolutionary forces of the regime are exhausted or wearing out and that softening is not the result of conscious liberalization from above or below but of the decrepitude of the system. But, because of the special qualities of Russian history, the system rotting from above does not permit alternatives to be advanced from below, so the most probable outcome will not be a peaceful transformation but a breakdown, which may be hastened by a military conflict.[3]

It is clear that all of these approaches have some basis, for the USSR is in reality an industrial state based both on Marxist ideology and Russian tradition. It is hardly possible to analyze correctly the Soviet present, much less to foresee its future, within the framework of a single approach—although it is no easy task to find the correct balance among them.

The accelerated industrialization of the country preceded the victory of Marxism and to some extent prepared the way for it; yet, after the Revolution, the ideology itself took the lead in industrialization and imposed on it characteristics unknown to Western society. Russia, as a country, a people, and a culture, existed before the acceptance of Marxist ideology and before industrialization, both of which made a strong impression on the Russian psychology but hardly changed it. Evidently Marxism and industrialization are stages a country passes through in order to come to something different.

---

2. This point of view is clearly apparent in the book by A. D. Sakharov, *Thoughts on Progress, Peaceful Coexistence, and Intellectual Freedom* (Petersham: Foreign Affairs, 1968). In general, the view that the USSR will accept Western liberal ideas more easily as it attains economic prosperity seems to me very problematic. Not only liberalism but also fascism is a Western idea, and we find no direct correlation between well-being and freedom. The U.S. is not free because it is prosperous but, to the contrary, it became rich thanks to freedom. If one considers two totalitarian states, Italy and Germany, the poorer, fascist Italy, was relatively freer than richer, nazi Germany. Totalitarian China is not poorer than democratic India.

3. This point of view is presented in my book, *Will the USSR Survive until 1984?* (New York: Harper and Row, 1970).

Therefore, it seems sensible to me to examine the present and future from the point of view of the general regularities of Russian history.

First, there is the Eurasian character of the country. It is not only geographically but, so to speak, mentally located in Europe and Asia. The conflict between "Asian" and "European" elements, between Westernizers and Slavophils,[4] between the nationalistic and critical strains runs through all Russian history.

Secondly, the "Asiatic" element, with its inclination toward isolation, fixity, and collectivism, appears more constant than the "European," with its inclination toward contact, development, and individualism. Therefore Russian history has been characterized by long periods of political stagnation, broken by periods of convulsive movement, revolutions and reforms, leading to a re-examination of all customary values. Then everything congeals again for a long time, so that Russian history goes forward as though by jerks—and the greater the immobility a regime achieves, the more fearful the following convulsion.

Thirdly, the internal tasks of Russia are always subordinated to the external. Therefore the natural form of its existence is expansion, and the external enemy is the necessary justification for the subordination of the personality to the state. Expansionism is expressed in the ideologies adopted by Russia—the universal rule of the "Third Rome" or the universal rule of the "Third International." So long as external political expansion, not necessarily military, proceeds successfully, the regime does not have to worry about the internal situation; as soon as expansion halts or retreats, critical elements come to the fore, and there begins a period of reform and revolution.

Movement by jerks is explained by the fact that an authoritarian or even totalitarian regime is not in a position to guide and control all the processes going on in the country;[5] thus the gap between the directed and undirected sectors widens. There doubtless exists some mechanism of feedback from these uncontrolled changes, but in totalitarian states, in contrast to democratic states, it is extremely feeble—in the USSR there are no free elections, no political parties, no independent press, no serious polls of public opinion. Thus the gap grows until the authorities lose contact with reality or are forced hastily to institute far-reaching reforms.

At present there exist at least six such gaps known to investigators of the Soviet system; is there a threat that they will grow into an abyss?

4. One might better say "Tatarophils."
5. For example, the Soviet regime could organize collective farms but cannot get satisfactory harvests, could fix workers in their jobs but cannot raise the productivity of labor, and could monopolize the means of communication but cannot control the condition of minds.

THE GAP BETWEEN THE CHANGING STRUCTURE OF THE SOCIETY AND THE UNCHANGED STRUCTURE OF POWER

The structure of power was finally consolidated in the late 1920s and early 1930s, when the majority of the population was composed of semi-literate or illiterate peasants and the middle classes had been practically wiped out. At present, the overwhelming majority of the population has an education, a new middle class has arisen, and it does not want to be treated like a silent mass. This conflict can take on dramatic forms of open dissent, but to a considerable extent it is manifested as passive resistance that imperceptibly undermines the bases of the system.

The stratification of the allegedly classless Soviet society is not inherently simple. If we consider the economic conditions, social status, and occupational position of the "Soviet man," we see that wealth means nothing and social prestige is rather illusory, unless it is related to a person's position in the structure of power.

Therefore, it is rational to take the chief axis of Soviet society, the party-government system, and examine how Soviet people are placed along this axis. If someone should become influential within the limits of his professional specialty—for example, a scholar or writer—then, as a rule, on attaining a certain level, he is recruited into the party; only thus can he rise higher. But even non-party people serve the party-state and so take their place in the hierarchy.

It is possible, following Aristotle's division, to divide Soviet society along this axis into three layers, higher, middle, and lower. The drawing of exact boundaries requires serious study; in any case, it is clear that the limits of the middle class are very unstable.

The upper class includes those who occupy positions of command and are most fully identified with the system.[6] The new class was first drawn from the prerevolutionary middle class. To a degree they were idealists and, despite their mutation after the seizure of power, they retained some idealism for a time, against the evident general tendencies away from egalitarianism and internationalism and toward elitism and nationalism. The final victory of Stalin was the victory of these tendencies; at the same time, the elite was almost totally replaced by new recruits from the lower class. Those pro-

6. The division into classes clearly has, to a considerable degree, a psychological basis: a person feels himself part of one or another social group, equates his interests with its interests and behaves accordingly. In party *apparatchiks* this identification goes very far. I remember how one of the assistants of the Magadan obkom said, "We shot Voznesensky, and it appears he was an outstanding economist." But "we shot" Voznesensky at a time when this obkom worker was crawling under the table and was not in the slightest responsible for the execution.

moted brought with them the manners of their class and could find common ground with the masses on the basis of shared anti-intellectualism, anti-Semitism, xenophobia, and aversion for critical ideas. But the fact that they "rose from the people" stimulated them to separate themselves from their past as rapidly as they could, while their humble social origins freed them from the complex of "guilt toward the people," so characteristic of those who rose from the old middle class.

The ethics of the ruling class is rooted in two prerevolutionary institutions, the Bolshevik party and the tsarist bureaucracy. The organization of professional revolutionaries was elitist by philosophy as a party of the elect. The same can be said of members of the bureaucracy, who regarded themselves as servants of the ruler or the state, standing apart from and even in opposition to the population. It is not surprising that the party, taking over the position of the bureaucracy, began to set itself ever more firmly apart. At the same time, its leadership, appealing to the proletariat and the masses could not simply throw overboard egalitarian ideals.

The isolation of the ruling class and its detachment from reality increases constantly. In the first place, the ruling class replenishes itself only by co-optation, not allowing into its ranks those who sustain values formed in other layers of society. In the second place, there is responsibility only from bottom to top, and the ruling class is its own judge.[7] In the third place, the desire to preserve privileges, to place "authority" on a pedestal unattainable for simple mortals, and also considerations of personal security, raise a need for maximum distance and isolation from other layers of society. Finally, physical aging plays a role: despite the general tendency toward a decrease in the average age of the Soviet population, the average age of leading functionaries is rising.

The middle class may, justifiably, be called a class of specialists—academics, engineers, middle-rank administrators, members of the free professions.[8] In contrast to the higher class and because of pressure from the latter, it has been unable to solidify itself and is hardly aware of itself as a class. The awareness of the middle class of its interests is impeded not only by the psychological manipulations and control of the upper class but also by its constant replenishment from the lower class, recruits from which bring with them the lower class mentality. It may be stated that the whole underground

7. For this reason a judgment from outside, in the form of a foreign policy failure or military defeat is so important.

8. Strangely, part of the party *apparatchiks* and part of the dissidents belong to the same class. If we consider dissidents and former *apparatchiks* who have emigrated to the West, we observe that both the reason for emigration and the goals they maintained in Russia are in part similar.

"struggle of ideas" goes on within the middle class, while its members gradually come to identify themselves with their own class and ever less with the party-government system. The middle class has been the basis of democratic society everywhere, and no doubt strengthening it is the only chance for the liberalization of Soviet society.

One has the impression that, at present, the replenishment of the ruling class, especially its top section, will not come from the lower but rather from the middle and upper classes. This tendency promises that the next generation of power holders will feel itself more "in place," will be more professionally confident, less anti-intellectual, and more tolerant, more guilt-conscious and less arrogant. To be sure, this is all relative.

Thus there are two ways in which the regime might overcome the present quasi-stable, transitional situation: either by reforming the system of power to conform to the requirements of the educated part of society; or by reforming the society itself, in effect liquidating the new middle class by the methods used to liquidate the old.

THE GAP BETWEEN THE MULTINATIONAL CHARACTER OF SOCIETY AND THE CENTRALIZED CHARACTER OF THE STATE

In the USSR there are more than a hundred nationalities which have more than a million members; and the heterogeneity of the peoples, some of whom previously had their own governments, conflicts acutely with the unitary Soviet system. The union and autonomous republics, although they somewhat soften national antagonisms, are primarily decorative; and the efforts of the central powers to replace minority customs and languages by common Soviet, that is, Russian equivalents become ever stronger.

However, two powerful processes counter unification. In the first place, the national self-awareness of non-Russian peoples increases because of the national minority intelligentsias, especially of the second generation. This process is not rectilinear; on the contrary, in many developed nationalities the first generation of the intelligentsia strove to Russify itself as much as possible, casting off its national culture as "backward." Only their children begin to turn back to the national culture and counterpose it to the Russian. Local nationalism is also in some cases moderated by the fact that the standard of living of the Russians and their social status are lower than those of the local peoples, and the awareness of superiority provides some outlet for nationalistic sentiments.

In the second place, the national balance is changing in favor of the non-Russian peoples. Already the Russians constitute less than 50 percent of the population, non-Slavs more than 30 percent. The Russians only reproduce themselves, while the Islamic peoples have high birth-rates. By 1984, if this tendency is sustained, the Russians will be decidedly in the minority.

As in social conflicts, the basic masses do not express nationalistic feelings openly; but they passively present palpable resistance to what they call "Russification."

There are evidently here, also, two solutions for the regime: either a move toward decentralization, returning to the federal structure its real meaning; or intensification of centralization and Russification, gradually proceeding to the abolition of the union republics and the establishment of a formally unitary state.

THE GAP BETWEEN THE NEED FOR A VIGOROUS IDEOLOGY AND THE GROWING IDEOLOGICAL VACUUM

The growth of minority nationalism and the intensification of Russification, two mutually stimulating processes, are partly explained by the crisis of the ideology that binds the Soviet people together. A moral basis (politically, an ideology), is necessary for every political system, above all as the legitimation for a totalitarianism. Yet one perceives ever more clearly the transformation of Marxism (which has not fulfilled a single one of its promises) from a living ideology, as it was in Russia in the first half of the 20th century, into an obligatory but dead ritual. The youth, the best barometer of ideology, is obviously the most de-ideologized.

This ideological vacuum needs to be filled, and there is perceptible in Soviet society a covert but intensive search for a new ideology—by partisans of the regime to find means to uphold it, by opponents to change it.

Both supporters and opponents of the regime turn ever more frequently to Russian nationalism as an ideology called upon to save or destroy the regime. It is characteristic that in pre-revolutionary years the ideology of autocracy was more and more replaced by the ideology of autocratic nationalism, or nationalistic autocracy. There even appeared the term, "genuine Russian people," in contrast to the simply Russian.

Russian nationalism however, is an ambivalent phenomenon which includes incompatible traits. In the first place, there is imperial nationalism with a goal of a united and indivisible Russia, the boundaries of which should expand ever more until it becomes a world state—with the Russians naturally on top. However, the very term "Russian" thus begins imperceptibly to lose ethnic meaning and take on a political sense; loyalty to the nation is replaced by loyalty to the multinational state, just as the steppe-dweller was true to his Khan, not to his ""fatherland."

In the second place, there is ethnic nationalism, which does not want to go outside the borders but to shut itself up within them, to concentrate on the preservation of the language, national culture, and ultimately of the "race," not to bring into itself new peoples but to reject them as aliens. So far as these two nationalisms are not clearly separated but coexist in one, ethnic nationalism suffers from great indefiniteness.

Evidently, in the realm of ideology also one may perceive two solutions for the regime: either the revision of Marxism in the direction of Eurocommunist models, free discussion in order to work out alternative ideologies—and ultimately ideological pluralism; or, without formally breaking with Marxism, a shift to "National-Bolshevism," a Russian national ideology, a sort of Russian fascism, with great explosive potential in a multinational state.[9]

THE GAP BETWEEN THE ECONOMIC NEEDS OF SOCIETY AND THE ORGANIZATION OF THE ECONOMY

The mobilization of all the capacities of society for forced industrialization doubtless brought results in the shape of the rapid expansion of the economy and subsequently the gradual improvement of the standard of living. However, this improvement of the standard of living has come to a halt at a level much below that of the Western countries, and the growth of production has slowed. Moreover, signs of economic crisis are apparent in the inefficiency of agriculture, the decrease of the rate of return on capital investments, the disproportional development of different branches of industry, the oncoming fuel shortage, and the ever growing apathy of the workers.

The heart of the problem is the crisis of management. The state seeks to direct a modern economy with the methods of the 1930s. In the past twenty years, there have been attempted a number of reforms based more on common sense than on economic theory, but not one of them has been fully implemented. Even giving the managers more freedom does not of itself solve the problem, since this leads to conflicts between managers and workers, again requiring the intervention of the Party apparatus.

9. It is not impossible that between 1939 and 1941 Stalin gave thought to Russian national socialism, but the war with Germany excluded this.

The demands of the consumers, the demands of the military, unemployment,[10] sectoral labor shortages, the ineptness of central planning for the huge country, the shortage of needed goods and the overproduction of unneeded ones—all these problems are not being solved.

Roughly speaking, here again one can suggest two solutions: either liberalization of the system and coordination of the planned and market economies, with moves toward workers' self-management in the enterprises; or the militarization of the economy, the fixing of workers to their jobs, and the introduction of rationing.

THE GAP BETWEEN INTERNAL INSTABILITY AND FOREIGN POLICY AIMS

The foreign policy of the USSR, however it may be governed by practical considerations in any specific instance, pursues the messianic purpose of extending its influence over the entire world.[11] This can bring enormous foreign policy successes, but only at the price of internal exhaustion—several times external tasks have led to catastrophes within Russia.

The might and influence of the USSR in the world cannot be disputed, yet it is hardly in a position to solve several potentially dangerous foreign policy problems. Although the threat of a direct conflict with China has disappeared for the time being, the death of Mao Tse-tung has again rather increased the danger, inasmuch as the new, more pragmatic leadership immediately undertook rapidly to modernize military industry and the army. In Eastern Europe, although the USSR can long hold the region by force, its political and economic influence is shrinking. Eurocommunism may on the one hand be an instrument for the dissolution of Western Europe; but, on the other hand, it is an ideological weapon of Eastern European countries against the USSR, which lacks the flexibility to use Eurocommunism for its own purposes.

Decolonization has created great areas of political vacuum, in part with an anti-Western bias, opening up enormous possibilities for an aggressive and ideologized Soviet Union. It is true that the Soviet

---

10. If unemployment were recognized in the USSR and measured in the same way as in the U.S., it would be lower than in the latter country. Western economists studying the Soviet Union base their conclusions on Soviet data which, even if one assumes they are not distorted, by their lacunae in very important areas make an accurate picture impossible. By publishing some indicators and concealing others, the Soviet authorities can manipulate Western scholars.

11. In the 15th century, Russia was heir of two universal empires, the Byzantine and the Mongol, and in the 20th it took up the ideology of world revolution.

Union is being gradually squeezed out of regions where it was at first dominant; but this process is slow and doubtful, while the Soviets discover ever new arenas of action and act ever more confidently, as shown by Soviet-Cuban expansion in Africa. Yet interventionism constitutes an additional burden on the economy, on the one hand, while on the other there is danger of possible involvement of Soviet forces. To avoid this, Soviet leaders desire détente with the West. Ideologically drawn to the poor, they incline economically to the rich, calculating that stability in Europe and economic assistance from the West free their hands in the Third World. The West, without desiring it, has always been a factor for the strengthening of the Soviet system. It has been so not only as an ideological enemy, justifying Soviet repression and aggression, but as a constant stimulus for the technological progress of the USSR, which has always had to overtake and surpass the West.

Although the West was prepared to "pay" the Soviet Union with the understanding that it would not change the situation in its favor anywhere in the world, it was not prepared to finance Soviet expansion. However scornfully one may regard the absence of political will in the West, one cannot suppose that it will swallow one "Angola" after another. Moreover, the fawning of Western politicians before the USSR cannot disguise the fact that rapprochement is impossible without a certain amount of mixing of peoples and their increased personal contacts; but this is contrary to Soviet isolationism. The danger of the ideological erosion of its society restrains the USSR from reaping the political and economic advantages which rapprochement with the West would give.

Here again one can see two solutions: either efforts to come to an understanding with the West, under which the USSR would refrain from pressure on the weak spots in the world, joint containment of China, and opening of borders for free entry and exit; or intensification of pressures abroad, military interventions in Africa, Asia, and Latin America, possibly a military assault in Europe.

THE GAP BETWEEN POLITICAL REALITY AND THE FORCE OF POLITICAL INERTIA

The USSR, like any other country, is ruled by tradition: people "above" and "below" have become accustomed to a definite system of relationships. Only, as already remarked, changes accumulate in the psychology of the people and elsewhere. In view of the brutal tightness of the system, with its numerous underpinnings, the mechanism of change is its weakest point.

This is illustrated best of all by the absence of any legal means of succession to the highest power. In the first place, the position of General Secretary is decisive in practice but not legally; in the second place, there are no fixed bounds to his authority; in the third place, his tenure in this position is not limited, there is no legal means of re-election, and there is no way of his designating a successor.

Therefore every change of Secretary means a crisis of authority and factional struggle. It is quite evident that we are now approaching such a crisis. Even if Brezhnev's place is assumed painlessly by one of his Politburo colleagues, the successor will be able to remain only a short time because of his advanced age. At the same time, the senior group of the Politburo represents the last Soviet leaders with a glimmer of charisma, achieved through the Marxist ideological struggles of the 1920s and 1930s and principally in the war in the 1940s. By 1984, power will have fallen to people who lack ideology and moral justification. The question is whether the administrative tradition by itself will suffice to sustain power without basic changes. The force of political momentum will be braked by political reality.

Speaking of the mechanism of change, it is interesting to consider the question whether Soviet society has become more totalitarian or less so during the last quarter century. This obviously depends on the definition of totalitarianism. It may be noted, however, that under Stalin there existed a certain balance and competition between party, security organs, army, and state apparatus, with Stalin holding the strings in his own hands, while power is now concentrated at all levels in the hands of the party apparatus.[12]

Thus, after the death of Stalin, totalitarianism might have been overcome if separate elements of power had come into greater independence and competition, making it possible for the developing opposition to find a place for itself. Now, however, totalitarianism can evidently be overcome only by a narrowing of the role of the party or a transformation of its character.

It is possible that the army, the state apparatus, or the security

---

12. This may be illustrated by a diagram suggested by Dr. Teresa Rakowska-Harmstone at the time of my presentation:

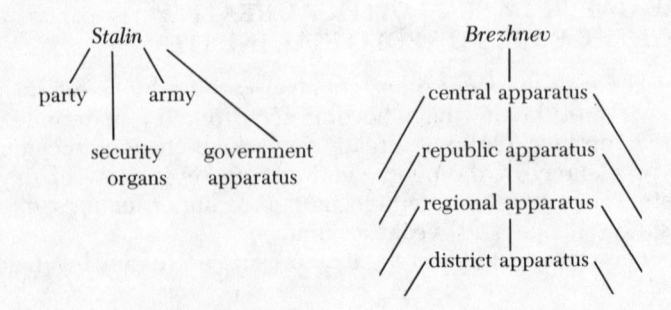

```
           Stalin                              Brezhnev
          / |  \                                  |
     party | army \                       ,central apparatus,
           |       \                     /    |              \
       security  government             / republic apparatus  \
       organs    apparatus              /     |                \
                                       / regional apparatus     \
                                      /      |                   \
                                     / district apparatus         \
```

organs may again endeavor to play an independent role. The army has never acted autonomously in Russian history except for several palace coups and the unsuccessful White movement in the 1918-1920 civil war; and the Soviet officer corps is politically hardly more consolidated than the middle class. However, in a moment of crisis the army, unable to act openly, might exert pressure from within.

It is likely, if the post-Brezhnev oligarchy begins to fall apart, lacking a general moral and ideological platform, that the two most probable solutions are: either movement toward a legal government, restoration of the real functions of the soviets, the dissolution of power and the fixing of its limits, terms of holding office and, consequently, institutions for checking power; or personal dictatorship, possibly military dictatorship.

This may be summarized in the diagram on p. 261.

The Soviet system is doubtless strong enough to cope with separate crises. However, several may coincide; for example, the death of Brezhnev or of his successor, two harvest failures in sequence, a refusal of the U.S. to sell grain to the Soviet Union, an uprising in Poland, or border conflicts with China. If in a time of crisis there are no clear political ideas at the summit and no reform plan or self-confidence sufficient to carry out a reform, given the paralysis of the middle class, the country may find itself in a desperate situation.

The lower classes—those whom Lenin called the "masses" and Americans speak of as "the man in the street"—at present generally accept the system passively, partly with inner indifference, partly with masked opposition, partly in illusory identification with the regime. The designations "we" and "they" can be used in quite different ways. "We" may be the workers, "they" the authorities; or "we" the workers, and "they" the intelligentsia. At the same time it is wrong to think that the "man in the street" is interested only in improving his material welfare. He wants to be taken into account, to be esteemed, to have his personality recognized with his inalienable rights—and here is his point of contact with the Human Rights Movement.

Since the "man in the street" in the U.S. is exceptionally esteemed as a voter and buyer, American sociologists are disposed to overestimate his role in the USSR. What does the average person think about this or that is a question I have often heard. What he thinks has no importance in the USSR during times of stability. It doesn't matter whether he supports the totalitarian regime or not. Of course, authoritarian or totalitarian regimes may welcome popular support, but it is secondary for them, because by their very nature they rest on nothing so shaky as the goodwill of the public, but on the solid bases of police, party, and army. They find a spontaneous demonstration of popular support frightening; its lack of organization represents a challenge.

However, if the passivity of the lower classes and their lack of political orientation correspond to the current interests of the ruling class, they may become very dangerous for society in a moment of crisis at the top, as the disoriented masses begin to clutch hastily at any destructive, demagogic idea.

Thus Russia faces catastrophes that can be avoided only by far-reaching reforms. To push the country to reforms, there must be a small crisis. I do not believe that there will be long to wait.

Bases	Problems	Solutions	Results
Russian state	internal political	personal dictatorship / legal government	national Bolshevism / humanized socialism
	external political	military expansion / agreement with the West	national Bolshevism / humanized socialism
Marxist state	ideological	national Bolshevism / trend to pluralism	national Bolshevism / humanized socialism
	national	unification / federalism	national Bolshevism / humanized socialism
Industrial state	social	liquidation of middle class / democratization	national Bolshevism / humanized socialism
	economic	militarization / liberalization	national Bolshevism / humanized socialism

Robert Wesson

Conclusion

For the first twenty years of its existence, the Soviet Union represented to the United States primarily the ideological challenge of a different way of life and a promise of justice and abundance based on premises repugnant to American values of political liberty, national sovereignty, free enterprise, and individualism. The bureaucratic Soviet state no longer does so; its idealistic attraction, as emphasized by Leo Labedz, is virtually dead. On the contrary, it presents a formidable challenge of power. It has established and hardened dominion over Eastern Europe, and it has spread its influence to Cuba, several countries of Africa, Afghanistan, and Vietnam. It has built up military forces which many persons believe at least equal to those of the United States; and it continues to enlarge its physical might, as detailed by William and Harriet Scott. It has shown the ability to push into areas of weakness, such as Ethiopia, and pessimists have spoken fearfully of the possible "Finlandization" of Western Europe. From the American point of view, the Soviet Union poses the only important threat to the world balance, the only real danger of nuclear incineration, and the overriding reason for a defense budget of $126 billion.

With no other state is it consequently so important to settle differences, and there have been many efforts toward détente and understanding. Yet such efforts have been repeatedly truncated by new clashes between American and Soviet policies and interests. During the Khrushchev era, every two or three years there were new crises; over Berlin, the Congo, Cuba, and so on. Under the Brezhnev leadership, likewise, there have been alternate warmings and chillings. The invasion of Czechoslovakia in 1968 was followed by a turn toward détente, climaxing with the visits of respective leaders to Moscow and Washington in 1972-73, followed by new frictions, clashes over the Near East, Soviet interventions in Africa, human rights issues, and difficulty in reaching agreement regarding nuclear armaments despite manifest utility for both sides. Despite the reluctance of many to acknowledge the regrettable reality, conflict between the U.S. and the Soviet Union seems to be unavoidable, the product of differences in the two societies.

Consequently, one of the greatest questions for American foreign policy and for the world order is whether, or to what extent, we should expect the Soviet Union to continue to be a powerful opponent to the ways and values of the Western industrialized societies, particularly the United States. The question has been posed again and again, of course, from the days when Western observers were confident that Lenin could not retain the power he ruthlessly seized, down to the convergence theory popular a few years ago, which stated that differences would melt away in shared modernization and industrialization. The Soviet system has proved remarkably stubborn and adaptable, confounding not only prophecies of destruction but prognostications of deep change.

It is hence bold to entertain the thought that there may now be severer strains in prospect, possibly entailing instability of the long stable system. We are tempted, however, to do so, viewing the visible trends of recent years. Weaknesses are coming into perspective, such as the danger of a difficult succession crisis, the slowdown of economic growth, the irreversible disarray of the world Communist movement, the self-awareness and perhaps growing capacities of the non-Russian minorities, the surfacing of an apparently irrepressible movement of intellectual dissent, in addition to sundry social ills long familiar in the West but assumed to be insignificant in the realm of Communism, such as crime and corruption. Perhaps most important of all is the least tangible, the exhaustion of the ideological and moral impulse that long made an inherently cumbersome system fairly workable.

In other words, after the Soviet Union has surmounted grievous trials—the revolutionary upheaval, the years of civil struggle, collectivization and Stalin's frantic industrialization program, the grotesque purges, and the world war in which close to half its industrial capacity was at one time lost to the enemy—there has been a loss of impetus. Now there arises a problem of a novel character for the Soviet state. When there are no more violent struggles and no more social and economic transformations, can the Soviet state continue in approximately the same condition and maintain approximately the same distinctiveness in the modern world? There is certain to be change beneath the surface in an age of change; can the Soviet state resist erosive forces as it has repelled violent assaults?

This is the broad question which was addressed by the contributors of this volume, whether the Soviet Union may be expected, barring unforeseeable (but not therefore unlikely) events, to carry on in a manner recognizably like the present, at least to the extent that the present-day Soviet Union is recognizably like that of forty years ago, with the same rule by a self-selected party justified in more or less the same terms. Or are the tensions and contradictions growing within the Soviet system strong enough to lead to an expectation of some sort of breakdown and systemic change away from the party-state structure, the maximally controlled economy, and Marxist-Leninist ideological legitimation?

Perhaps the strongest reason for anticipating change is the seemingly irreversible trend toward economic slowdown. Ever since Stalin's First Five Year Plan in 1928, economic growth has been a major forte of the Soviet system and a basis for its claims to superiority; it was claimed and widely believed that only the socialist planned economy could rationally direct investment for rapid and purposeful growth of production. For a time, the Soviet planning seemed to work very or at least fairly well and the Soviet share of world output rose steadily. Since about 1950 more attention has been given to light industry and agriculture, and per capita consumption has increased impressively along with a considerable increase of leisure.

The level achieved is not high, however, by standards of the West; and Soviet consumption levels remain behind nearly all of Eastern Europe. The Soviet economy has lagged in technological innovation, moreover, in the same way that official Soviet literature, music, and culture show little originality and brilliance. Since World War II, Soviet economic performance has been no better than that of Western Europe; and the trend, especially since about 1970, has been toward a weakening of performance indicators. Soviet growth has depended much more on enlarged inputs of labor and capital than on innovation and productivity; but the labor force, because of decreased birth rates, cannot be much expanded—a problem that also affects the military. Meanwhile, the productivity of capital investments has been steadily declining—although in other industrial countries the return on capital has increased with the rise of the technological level. The capital growth needed to produce a given amount of additional output is several times as high in the Soviet Union as in the U.S.

Consequently, the Soviet Union faces a need to increase investment at the expense of either the standard of living or the military. The former might have negative effects because of reduction of incentives as well as political costs, when incentives are increasingly needed to compensate for labor shortage and to motivate people in a consumption-minded age. The diversion of resources from the military to investment, on the other hand, is probably politically excluded.

There remains the alternative of improvement of productivity, and this may be considered the key question of the Soviet future. If means can be found to keep growth of productivity up to world levels, other problems may be solvable; if not, all difficulties are sure to be compounded. The outlook is poor. The Soviet Union is unique in the small part—under half—of its economic growth attributable to technological improvement, and the system continues to be resistant to innovation. The core of the problem is lack of autonomy and incentives for those who are called upon to innovate. The rewards are for certainty of production through old ways, while innovation inevitably means uncertainty. There is no satisfactory way for planners to motivate innovation; it cannot be planned—and in the planning system it is difficult to separate real from spurious innovation. No less important, perhaps even more so, there is no way in the planning scheme to penalize for failure to innovate—there can be nothing corresponding to fear of losses and possible failure in a competitive market.

One possible or partial remedy is increased foreign trade and the importation of technology and, if possible, capital from the West, to compensate for domestic deficiencies. But imports require exports; in the lagging Soviet economy, these must increasingly be raw materials, and foreign capital seems requisite to much increase of raw material output. Foreign trade has multiplied several times over since 1970, and the Soviet Union is being forced to some extent into an unwanted interdependence with the capitalist world. Yet the Soviet state cannot fully share in the world economy and the benefits of interaction and intercommunication without losing its character; and the costs of aloofness, in terms of ideas and stimulation, are large.

Another possible answer might be economic reform to encourage innovation and better use of resources by permitting freedom of prices and more latitude to on-the-spot managers. But experiments, as Joseph Berliner points out, are only a "tinkering;" they are always resisted and usually defeated, failing because of the conditions which make them necessary. Flexibility requires smaller enterprises, but the only major reform of the 1970s, the formation of "production associations" has created larger units of production. Workers and managers as well as party cadres are usually opposed to the uncertainties of a free market. Any important rationalization would reduce the role of the Soviet factory as a social insurance agency and turn redundancy and leisure on the job into painful unemployment—when security of employment is one of the most effective boasts of the Soviet economy. Andrei Amalrik holds that there is already substantial real unemployment, despite claims to the contrary and despite shortages of qualified workers in many areas. Moreover, any release of prices would certainly cause the present largely concealed inflation to leap up.

Alternatively, permitting private enterprise in services and small-scale production and trade, somewhat in the manner of Poland and Hungary, should permit an easy improvement of the standard of living. Berliner offers the Soviet leaders the probably sound advice that they should institute a new NEP, imitating Lenin's successful use of private enterprise in the 1920s, to pull Russia out of the economic slough. Such a turn seems excluded on political grounds; it is ideologically inadmissible, as Conquest stresses. It would mean a comedown for countless controllers, party bosses and, it seems, the workers in general, who resent those who become richer than they by "speculation." Any considerable opening to private enterprise would have political implications, moreover, promising a growth of non-party power. This would be especially critical in non-Russian areas, such as the Caucasus, where private trade is already much stronger than in Russia proper; a private sector would almost certainly be the basis for a nationalistic movement.

It may be that the Soviet Union can continue to increase production into the 1980s, as Schroeder believes; but the regime can no longer point convincingly to rapid improvement of the standard of living to justify its authority. There are continual problems of imbalances, shortages, and surpluses caused by the incapability of the planning mechanism to gear production to wants. Prices of necessities have to be subsidized (at a huge cost to the state budget) to compensate for creeping inflation. The illegal or partly legal extraofficial economy continues to grow, drawing resources away from the planners' goals. Social problems, crime, alcoholism, poor labor discipline, and corruption, plague the economy. In short, things do not go well, as one easily deduces from published statistics; it is suggestive that Soviet authorities have in the past few years drawn the shroud of secrecy tighter and ceased giving out various data formerly made available.

Economics present other problems for the Soviet hegemony in

Eastern Europe, where Jan Triska finds shortages of materials, energy, and manpower. The time when the Soviet state could profitably exploit its vassal states is long past. They continue to be major military and political assets, partly because of weapons production and cooperation with Soviet foreign policy in all spheres, especially the Third World; but, increasingly, they require diversion of resources which the Soviets can scarcely afford. In Eastern Europe, as in the Soviet Union, economic growth is slackening, social mobility is declining, and grumbling increasing. The countries need more technology and credits from the West, for which they lack means of payment. If imports have to be cut, consumption will suffer, and political consequences will surely follow. Hard-pressed to hold on and unable to consider withdrawal, the Soviet Union would seem driven toward a major reorientation and integration into the world economy, for which it is not prepared.

Economic slowdown reflects a decreased capacity to implement the political will. The state also finds itself under attack from a sector of the very intelligentsia that it has created. In the past year, "hammer blows struck by the KGB" have brought dissent to a low ebb; in the opinion of Professor Barghoorn, however, dissent cannot be eliminated, and it may well grow in scope and effect in the future. It arises mostly from the clash between the "ought," as promised by the party and hoped for by the highly aware and educated, and the "is" of lack of progress coupled with intellectual stifling and abuse of power. A substantial underground literature has been produced, mostly in protest against official violations of rights formally recognized by the Soviet system; and the movement has built up a moral capital and spirit unbroken by repressions. As in the tsarist past, a liberal sector of the highly educated classes forms a sort of counter-elite standing in principled opposition to and moral superiority over the official elite. There are many political currents among critics of the regime, but the existence of open dissent, the non-acceptance of party controls, is more important than the content of protest. However, to a degree surprising for those who stress the autocratic Russian tradition, the movement is democratic in spirit.

The dissident movement has thus far been non-violent in the face of the overwhelming power of the authorities. Yet there is a potential for violence because of frustrations; and if the authorities are able to remove the non-violent upper-class leadership, protesters of lower-class background are more likely to turn to violent expression. However, if the active dissidents were multiplied by ten, they would hardly represent a threat to the Soviet state. The few who sacrifice their careers and, often, freedom by speaking out are outnumbered a hundred or a thousand times by the disaffected. In many cases where authorities demand that a group, such as the workers in a laboratory or teachers in a school, expel one of their number for "anti-Soviet" activities, no one will speak up in favor of the accused, but perhaps a quarter will refuse to vote for punishment, despite multiple pressures and the absence of any but a moral reward for abstinence. Only 40 percent of the members of the Academy of Sciences could be prevailed upon to denounce Sakharov despite his many sins against the Soviet state.

In the same spirit, ordinary Soviet people are increasingly prone to grumble about the irritations of daily life; and if grumbling becomes a habit it might lead to general political alienation, as has occurred in Poland. The party probably feels some fear of mass unrest, in the view of George Breslauer; at least the political authorities can hardly feel free to cut back severely on consumption as necessary to provide adequate capital. As Robert Conquest points out, there have been some violent outbreaks, such as the big Novocherkassk riots against raised prices of meat and milk in 1962; and the threat is less from an average discontent than from crisis situations arising from the disequilibria of the system.

While a small band of intellectuals are moved to protest against the Soviet regime on grounds of political principle, much larger numbers assert themselves in one way or another against the domination of an alien central authority. Many observers have seen the multinationalism of the Soviet Union, in which the Russians comprise only half the population, as the Achilles heel of the system. Nationalists are ruthlessly suppressed, but recent years have seen a marked upsurge of ethnicity, which merges into nationalism, demands for autonomy and, ultimately, separatism. Soviet policy promotes assimilation or amalgamation, and small nationalities succumb, while persons detached from a national base tend to identify with the central power; but the solid national areas, Ukraine, Baltic, Caucasian, Central Asian, and so on, maintain their own identities. Clashes of interest are inevitable in the system whereby benefits are politically apportioned, and interests are increasingly aggregated on an ethnic base. There is no constitutional mechanism for conflict resolution, and national interests are poorly represented in Moscow; resentments consequently grow. The various factors which promote the growth of ethnicity elsewhere are all operative in the Soviet Union. The situation is in fact worse because under the Soviet prohibition of competing political organizations the ethnic political structures are the only aggregative groups.

There is no remedy, in the analysis of Teresa Rakowska-Harmstone. Modernization raises self-awareness and contributes to conflict rather than defusing it. The commitment to equalization has declined since 1970, and the gap between poorer and richer groups has widened again. This situation is complicated by the higher birthrates of some groups, especially Central Asian nationalities—a problem particularly for the Russian leadership of the armed forces. Concessions are difficult, partly because of the feelings of superiority, partly because of fears that concessions encourage further demands. Repression causes more bitterness and resistance, although force can probably keep the minorities quiet at a high cost. Federalism is excluded as a practical policy by the dominance of a single nationality. Antagonism to China exacerbates the situation because it mobilizes Russianism, which irritates non-Russians. Russian nationalism, which dominates the upper levels of the party, is grossly contradictory to Leninist ideals of trans-national social transformation.

It thus appears that, in various areas, the Soviet system is running down or facing difficulties more menacing than in the past, and it is difficult to point to major positive trends. Other negative tendencies include the aging of higher cadres, the increasing separation of elite and masses, and the growing cumbersomeness of an immobile apparatus. If all these problems are added together, one might draw a very dismal picture, not only because they add up but because their effects multiply. The wearing out of ideology makes less enforceable the controls of the planned economy, the adequate function of which requires a spirit of dedication on the part of at least a small fraction of directing personnel. The fading of the revolutionary spirit makes reforms more difficult when they are more needed, and it undermines the effectiveness of repression. The decline of solidarity erodes discipline in all areas. The weakening of the economy, falling behind expectations if not actually deteriorating, causes widespread disaffection and grousing, against which repression is impractical. The discontent of the non-Russian minorities is probably manageable as long as the economy prospers, but frictions are sure to proliferate if the pie to be divided ceases to grow. The thesis of rapid improvement under socialist planning has been a mainstay of party rule; without it, the special place of the party seems much less warranted. Economic slowdown, along with ideological decay, contributes to growing corruption; people feel entitled to supplement incomes and have few compunctions about using positions for material benefit. If Soviet society becomes somewhat demoralized at the lack of evident progress or positive inspiration, productivity may be expected to suffer further. There is no visible way out of the morass; the more change appears in order, the less feasible it seems to become. There is no remedy to arrest economic decay or the decline of quality of leadership. The forces of disruption seem gradually but steadily to mount, awaiting some sharp provocation or evidence of weakness of the leadership.

It is most predictable that Soviet institutions will be "seriously tested," as emphasized by Myron Rush, in the approaching succession crisis. The current General Secretary, born in December 1906, may remain on the scene for some years; but the unsteadiness of his health makes it likely that there is already some undercover contest for his power, and the longer his enfeebled hands remain at the helm the more conflict-ridden the succession is likely to be. There is no formal presumptive heir, and the most likely candidate is apparently Kirilenko, who is slightly older than Brezhnev and lacks experience in foreign and defense policy. Not only has Brezhnev not provided for a succession, he has removed the younger Politburo members who might seem capable of stepping into his shoes. At the time of the demises of Lenin, Stalin, and Khrushchev, each leader was surrounded by a group of subordinates ten to fifteen years younger who were able to carry on in his absence. However, the average age of the members of the Politburo was 68 years in 1978, and there is currently no high-level junior corps to take over the reins.

Moreover, a succession represents uncertainty and likelihood of change because there is no regularized way of selecting the General Secretary and no definition of his power. It is conceivable that the oligarchs might, for their own security, attempt to restrict the office to render it innocuous and consequently incapable, with unforeseeable results on the system. On the other hand, an influential group or agency might seek to force its own choice of General Secretary on the Politburo, especially if this were divided.

A Soviet succession has a secondary crisis when the leader undertakes to consolidate his personal power. Thus, after Lenin and after Stalin there was a prolonged contest between the General (or First) Secretary and his former equals. The struggle of Brezhnev to advance himself was subdued, but there will be an additional complication in a Brezhnev succession. Any younger man will feel the need to raise himself—not over his former equals but over a corps of senior figures accustomed to superiority over him.

Such uncertainties raise a likelihood of forces outside the Politburo playing a larger role. Especially if difficulties reflect on the competence of the oligarchs, outside groups or agencies might seek to impose their choice for General Secretary on a divided Politburo. The military or, secondarily the police, are the sectors best capable of intervening, although it is conceivable that the administrative apparatus might assert itself. A new leader, unless backed by force, will almost surely be in a weakened position. At the same time, he will probably be called upon to deal with a host of problems which have been avoided in the present reign and the confrontation with which will cause political strains and divisions.

Thus far the analysis seems fairly clear and factual. But when we try to project the further course, opinions diverge. Basic outcomes may be divided in three, and there are good arguments to support each: that the party-state will continue more or less as it has; that it will evolve toward a looser, less closed, less ideological, more liberal, decentralized system, that is, in the direction of Western pluralism; or that it will lurch rightwards, as though convulsively to protect itself by force, and militarize, recentralize and retighten, turning to what Amalrik calls "National Bolshevism."

Amalrik presents a strong argument that the "either-or" is compulsive, and that the system must almost certainly go in one direction or the other. Other analysts, however, hesitate to predict a breakdown of the Soviet system or any major alteration in the near future. This is understandable in view of the failure of many such predictions in the past and the demonstrated viability of the system over a human lifetime. It is also recognized that our information is incomplete and that the Soviet system may, in new circumstances, show strengths thus far unperceived. Many have a feeling that the party will adapt so far as it is driven to and pull through, perhaps ingloriously but competently enough to survive more or less indefinitely. If popular discontent rises, there may be a mixture of concessions, perhaps more of form than substance, with energetic repression, the apparatus for which definitely remains in being. It may be possible to paper over many contradictions. As long as the party maintains control of the *nomenklatura*, the power of nomination to all important positions and hence the gift of careers, it is difficult to challenge; and millions of persons have a vested interest in maintaining something like the present stratification. As the system grinds along, people adapt to it, psychologically as well as economically, and leaders and the populace have an interest in keeping structures as they are.

The military have thus far had good reason to be satisfied with the Soviet order. Not only do they receive a large share of the national product, but they can congratulate themselves that the Soviet Union is still rising although it may be near its peak, in the world "correlation of forces," in the Soviet phrase, as seen by much of the world and Soviet authorities in particular. The Soviet Union still has a long-term foreign policy orientation in which the military plays a leading part; as long as this continues, it seems improbable that the marshals will favor or permit any major change threatening to their positions.

The dissidents hardly have a program beyond the plea to the authorities to act more humanely and to apply their rules more equitably. They could well do so with little or no infringement of the party's monopoly of power. A good deal of free talk in Hungary, for example, hurts the position of the ruling party not at all—and possibly benefits it—as people vent their feelings harmlessly. There is no prospect at all that the party will surrender control of the economy and, as long as nearly everyone works for the state, opposition is likely to be thin. The political effects of economic troubles are, moreover, unclear. While shortages doubtless cause antagonisms, it may be that demands will be for more effective planning and sterner regulation rather than liberalization. In Poland, powerful protest movements in 1970 and 1976 forced policy changes but led to no renunciation of economic controls or decrease of the ability of the party to adopt whatever measures it deemed desirable.

Much the same might be said of the condition of the national minorities and, in a slightly different way, of the vassal states of Eastern Europe. While no solution is in prospect, neither is an uncontrollable explosion. There is no common front of minorities, and if Georgians, Estonians, and Uzbeks dislike the Russians, they also dislike each other. Their restiveness grows, but its effect may be to make party rule seem more necessary as the only means of keeping order. There is no basis for federalism, and independence is hardly practicable for small nations, such as Estonia and Tadzhikstan, that have been economically most welded into the larger Soviet sphere. Even if they are unhappy, it is hard for them to doubt the inevitability of Russian domination, at least in foreign and defense policy. If they should begin to evince doubts to the extent of mass defiance of Soviet authority, in all probability a bloodbath would bring back realism. The Hungarian example is instructive. The events of 1956 seem to have killed aspirations to independence for a long time and given the relatively easygoing party more acceptance than in most Communist countries.

In Eastern Europe, as within the Soviet Union, it is sufficient that Russian domination be regarded as immovable; and people know that the limits to liberalization are the limits of Russian toleration. In a sense, the region invites super-power domination; and if the Soviet Union did not act as suzerain there would presumably be an unstable power vacuum, as there was between the wars. Meanwhile, institutional and economic bonds are woven as tightly as possible, and generations grow up perhaps despising the Russians but unaware of any other order of the universe.

The question then becomes whether a system of party dictatorship, established in the Soviet Union for a largely peasant, backward country on the basis of a revolutionary-egalitarian ethos can maintain itself more or less indefinitely in an (unevenly) industrialized and urbanized country as a stratified system of privileges, although it seems to be economically, culturally, intellectually, and ultimately perhaps politically dysfunctional. The answer, in complete contradiction to the implications of Marxism, may well be yes. The Leninist party-state form has shown itself able to adapt to many things, and it may well adapt to stability and stasis also.

It has certainly shown a considerable ability to reshape its once revolutionary ideology, as Donald Kelley shows in his discussion of "Developed Socialism." This theory, a set of ideas vaguely corresponding to the discussions in the West of the "Post-Industrial Society" and its variants, in effect uses ideas of change to support stability, postulating an indefinite period of transition to the higher order of Marxist communism, mingling technological modernization with the fullness of party management. It offers a typical Soviet compromise, preservation of long-term dimly utopian goals and preoccupation with system maintenance, where talk of the "Scientific-Technical Revolution" replaces concern for social change. Its promise for the foreseeable future is more of the same. It is, of course, dialectical: specialization is to increase to prepare for the ending of specialization; the state is to be strengthened to make possible its promised withering away.

The ability of the Soviet leadership essentially to limit the future to more of the same chiefly requires that the party remain united and prepared to use force to maintain itself. If the party is solid and ruthless, the various troubles outlined would seem more annoyances than real danger to the party's continued possession, as it has possessed since November 7, 1917, of the governmental power over the Russian-dominated domain. To the extent of our knowledge, principled disagreement within the party has tended to decrease for many years, and there is no sign that any leaders would place adherence to a policy over the security of the party. The only imaginable division might come through inability to agree on a successor to the General Secretary; but anxiety to avoid a split might facilitate agreement. There is much less likelihood of the party's shrinking from the use of whatever force it felt necessary; inhibitions in ruthlessness are not to be expected in men brought up under Stalin, or under Brezhnev either.

There is thus some reason to see the political future of the Soviet Union much like the present for a good many years. Change is difficult and somewhat dangerous and, unless jolted, most people usually prefer to manage as best they can with familiar ways, making only minor adjustments to repair occasional intolerable deficiencies. Substantial reforms have been introduced in Russian history only over the resistance of the apparatus, and the apparatus seems now to be governing as never before. The masses would enjoy the economic and social security that the system gives those who accept it, and the elite would enjoy their comfortable superiority. A gradual erosion of the system would still be inevitable, of course, but it might require a long time, as under tsarist rule "society" gradually grew at the expense of the state.

On the other hand, if corruption, disorders, shortages, and the tyranny of the little bosses should drive the people to explosive despair, they would seem more likely to turn to a strong man to put things in place than to problematic democratic reforms. Likewise, if party leadership is weakened for whatever reason, it seems probable that the chief beneficiaries will be the armed services, the only force obviously capable of challenging the party and asserting a title to guide and cleanse, if not govern the state. The trend has in any case been in that direction. Stalin thoroughly subordinated the army to himself; under Khrushchev, the military cooperated with the party; under Brezhnev, it was increasingly brought into the upper ranks of the party and received a major role in domestic and foreign policy. After Brezhnev, its status can be expected to rise.

The role of the military has little to do with the international situation; it has enlarged under détente as in times of greater tension—a typical manifestation is the great expansion of military and paramilitary training for school children in the last decade. The standing which the Soviet military has already attained is attested by the fact that in a relatively quiet international situation it receives, according to most accepted estimates, 12 to 13 percent of the national product, more than double the percentage in America and much higher than in any non-Communist industrial country except Israel. Some, including the Scotts, feel that in terms of real value the Soviet percentage is more like 18 to 20 percent. A key question is whether or how the economy can support Soviet defense expenditures without cutting into civilian consumption or reducing investments, with greater long-term costs.

The role of the military corresponds to the decrease of *élan* in the party and to the replacement of Communist transformational ideology by an ethos of nationalism, Communism, and militarism rolled together. If challenges rise from restive minority nationalities, East European efforts to obtain greater autonomy, popular movements at home, or a threat from China in the East, the military will be called upon to protect the Soviet order as unifier, Russifier, stabilizer, and guardian. Although there seems to be no question of the military entirely displacing the party, which is needed as mobilizer and organizer of society, the military may be expected to move forward so far as the party shows incompetence. But it is to be noted that military dominance is characteristic of the politics not of the advanced industrial states but of the Third World.

If militarist-nationalist elements gain more authority in the fading of revolutionism, the keeping of order will have priority, and defensive xenophobic attitudes will take the place of the social-revolutionary vocation. The system needs to uphold the antithesis to an evil outside world; and if this can be done only in a semi-fascistic manner, it will probably be so done. Economic progress will be sacrificed to political needs, in this view, and Russia may become (if it is not already) the most conservative of major powers. The prime desiderata would be order at home and strength in the world.

There are reasons, however, to be skeptical of a re-Stalinization or "National Bolshevist" turn. A truculent despotism is not sustainable in modern states without a powerful vocation. A would-be dictator cannot simply conjure up a legitimation for force adequate to overrule and annihilate divisive forces. The apparatus of coercion is still there, perhaps larger and potentially more effective than in Stalin's day; but Stalin's rationale of protecting the revolution is gone.

Despotism, moreover, is anti-modern. If the present Soviet Union has difficulty securing technological innovation and keeping the lag behind the modern West from becoming excessive, a much tighter, more ideologized, anti-intellectual system would condemn itself rapidly to backwardness and weakness. One may assume that, although a fascistic turn might be a danger under some troubled circumstances, it could not be a long-term solution.

It is also arguable that a much harder-line state is unlikely (barring major violence on the world scene) because the Soviet state maintains about as tough a posture as it can without excessive costs. Relaxations, such as there have been have come about not because of leaders' love of liberty or distaste for excercising power or the compulsions of countervailing institutions, but from practical necessity and the need for better results. Khrushchev opened up a little because it was evident that Stalinism was strangling the country. Fear of losing control, it seems, has led the Brezhnev government back a little. But the Brezhnev regime has made concessions to foreign trade contrary to its inclinations for the sake of the economy; and much re-Stalinization would be fatal for dreams of modernization, respectability, and leading power in the world. It is for this reason that Mao's successors have rapidly discarded much of Maoism; redness and revolutionizing, even under the aegis of the great leader, were impoverishing China.

Movement toward more or less liberalization, a certain relaxation of the party reins, more attention to the standard of living, some increased latitude for cultural and intellectual expression, and so forth, would be influenced by desire for economic development, by the need for rationality of an industrial society with a declining commitment to proletarian social transformation, or any other mobilizing cause. An important question for this development is the attitude of the totally post-revolutionary generation that must one day take the reins. Conquest expects them to be quite as ruthless as their fathers, but they are hardly likely to be possessed by the same compulsions. As pointed out by Amalrik, the present generation of leaders came from the poor and uneducated classes predominantly, and are hence anti-Semitic and anti-intellectual. The new leaders will have been born to an easy existence and educated as middle to upper class; one may expect at least a certain softening of attitudes.

The upper and middle classes are, moreover, undoubtedly subject to some degree of Westernization, exposure to attitude and values, limited though it may be, of the more pluralistic societies. In tsarist days, the Russian upper classes wished to be modern in terms mostly of speaking French, having foreign governesses and French furniture, but also in embracing modern progressivism and values. It did not make them democrats, but it made them less effective supporters of autocracy. Soviet leaders like foreign clothing and cars and probably listen to foreign radio. To what extent they feel the need to measure themselves by more liberal and humane standards we do not know, but comparisons for the Soviets are increasingly external. The greater the relative success of the Western world and the more disappointing the results of the Soviet experiment, the more attractive the values of the former. These two directions are not mutually exclusive, of course; elements of both may be combined, or the Soviet state may fluctuate somewhat, as it has in the past, and change may be difficult to define. A new leadership might seek popularity by liberalization or harden policies to enlist military backing, only to swing in the contrary direction when it felt itself more secure. Moreover, much depends on events and climate on the world stage, from a possible military showdown with the Western world to such placidity as to make it difficult to maintain ideological tensions. The health and prosperity or decay and crisis of the West will have deep effects on the evolution of the Soviet Union. Like its tsarist predecessor, the Soviet state looks mostly westward and reflects, albeit in distorted fashion, events and ideas in the West, always striving to be Western in technological level and cultural achievements while maintaining an authoritarian political essence.

One's estimate of long-term Soviet or Russian prospects must to a large extent depend on one's view of human nature and modern civilization, and pessimism about the one tends to imply pessimism about the other. It seems certain, however, that difficulties accumulate for the essentially unmodern Russian-Soviet political and economic system. How they may eventually be resolved is one of the greatest questions of our times.

Contributors

ANDREI A. AMALRIK has received much of his education in Soviet prison camps. A Muscovite by birth, he was expelled in 1963 from Moscow University because of ideological errors in his dissertation on "Normans in Kievan Russia." He spent 1965-66 in exile in western Siberia, 1970-73 in prison and forced labor (Kolyma), and 1973-75 in Magadan. In 1975 he was exiled to the West, where he has been lecturer at Utrecht University, George Washington University, and Harvard University; currently he is Senior Research Fellow at the Hoover Institution. Three of his books have been published in the U.S., best-known being *Will the Soviet Union Survive until 1984?*

FREDERICK C. BARGHOORN, Amherst A.B. and Harvard Ph.D., was with the State Department for eight years, half of them spent in Moscow. In 1963 he acquired world-wide celebrity when President Kennedy secured his release from the KGB. Since 1947 he has been with the Department of Political Science at Yale, as professor since 1956. He has also held visiting appointments at Columbia and Chicago and has acted as consultant to several government agencies. He has published numerous articles and books on the Soviet Union, many of them dealing with propaganda and ideology. His research recently has concentrated on problems of "democratization" in the USSR.

JOSEPH S. BERLINER is Professor of Economics at Brandeis University. Recipient of three degrees from Harvard, he has been Associate Director of Harvard's Russian Research Center, has worked as a consultant, and taught at Syracuse University before going to Brandeis. He has been President of the American Association for the Advancement of Slavic Studies and of the Association of Comparative Economic Studies. He has published numerous articles. The most recent of his several books is *The Innovation Decision in Soviet Industry*.

GEORGE W. BRESLAUER received his Certificate in Russian Studies and Ph.D. from the University of Michigan. He is Associate Professor of Political Science at the University of California, Berkeley. He has published numerous articles on recent Soviet politics and several books, most recently *Five Images of the Soviet Future: A Critical Review and Synthesis*.

ROBERT CONQUEST has served in the British diplomatic service in Sofia, the United Nations, and the Foreign Office. He has held numerous high level fellowships, and he has published several volumes of poetry, science fiction, literary criticism, a co-authored novel, and countless articles. His numerous books on Soviet topics include *Power and Policy in the USSR*, *The Great Terror*, and *Kolyma*. At present he is a Senior Research Fellow at the Hoover Institution.

DONALD R. KELLEY received his Ph.D. from Indiana University, has taught at Monmouth College, and is Associate Professor at Mississippi State University. He has published numerous articles, coauthored *The Economic Superpowers and the Environment*, and authored *Soviet Politics in the Brezhnev Era*.

LEOPOLD LABEDZ, the longtime editor of *Survey*, was educated in Warsaw, and has studied at the universities of Paris, Bologna, and London. He did post-graduate work at the London School of Economics and was Senior Fellow at the Russian Institute of Columbia University. He was for several years visiting professor at Stanford University and is now a Fellow of the Centre of International Studies of the London School of Economics. He has lectured in many countries and published articles beyond number, mostly in British journals and newspapers. The most recent of his many books on Soviet affairs deals with the literary opposition, especially *Solzhenitsyn, A Documentary Record*.

KLAUS MEHNERT was born of German parents in Russia and spent his childhood there. He was educated in Germany, receiving his doctorate from the University of Berlin. He has spent many years in the Soviet Union, China, and the U.S., and has taught at universities from Berkeley to Shanghai to France. He has been editor of *Osteuropa* for 27 years, and has published many books on the Soviet Union, China, and the New Left.

TERESA RAKOWSKA-HARMSTONE is Professor at Carleton University, Ottawa. Born in Poland, she served briefly in the Polish Ministry of Foreign Affairs and the United Nations. A Harvard Ph.D., she has taught at Rutgers and McGill. Most of her many publications deal with the Soviet nationality problem, especially in Central Asia.

MYRON RUSH, Professor of Government at Cornell University since 1964, has served as Senior Fellow at the Research Institute on Communist Affairs (Columbia University) and Scholar in Residence in the National Foreign Assessment Center of CIA. He is author of *How Communist States Change Their Rulers* (1973), *The Rise of Khrushchev* (1958), *Strategic Power and Soviet Foreign Policy* (with Arnold Horelick, 1966), and other books and articles.

GERTRUDE E. SCHROEDER is Professor of Economics at the University of Virginia, with speciality in the Soviet economy and comparative economic systems. A Johns Hopkins Ph.D., she has worked with various government agencies and has been Assistant to the Economic Counsellor of the American Embassy in Moscow. Most of her thirty-odd articles have dealt with Soviet wages, economic management, and consumer problems.

COL. WILLIAM F. SCOTT has had two tours, each of two years, as senior United States Air Attaché in Moscow. A graduate of the United States Military Academy, he has a doctorate from Georgetown University. He is a regular lecturer at Georgetown University, an occasional lecturer at various universities and war colleges, and a consultant to several research organizations. He has published many articles on Soviet military forces; one of his recent books is *Soviet Sources of Military Doctrine and Strategy*.

Contributors

HARRIET FAST SCOTT was with Col. Scott during his tours as Air Attaché in Moscow, and she has made a specialty of Soviet strategic doctrine. An occasional lecturer at various war colleges and universities, she is also a consultant to a number of research organizations. She translated, edited, and commented on Marshal Sokolovsky's *Soviet Military Strategy* and has published extensively on Soviet military affairs.

DONALD W. TREADGOLD, Rhodes scholar and Oxford Ph.D., has been at the University of Washington since 1949 and is Chairman of the Department of History. He has been visiting professor at the Academy of Sciences' Institute of History in Moscow. He is recipient of many awards and distinctions; he was a director of the American Association for the Advancement of Slavic Studies 1968-75 and President 1977-78; for eight years he edited *Slavic Review*. He has published many articles and several books on the history of Russia and his secondary specialty, China.

JAN F. TRISKA holds the J.D. from Prague University Law School, LL.M. and JS.D. from Yale University Law School, and Ph.D. in political science from Harvard University. Since 1960 he has taught at Stanford University. He has held office in many learned societies and professional organizations, including the American Political Science Association and the American Association for the Advancement of Slavic Studies. He is a member of the editorial boards of a half dozen scholarly journals and has published some forty articles and chapters in books, as well as ten books of his own, dealing mostly with Soviet foreign policy and Eastern Europe.

ROBERT WESSON is Professor at the University of California, Santa Barbara, and Senior Research Fellow of the Hoover Institution. He studied at the Fletcher School of Law and Diplomacy and the Russian Institute of Columbia University, from which he received his doctorate. He has published two books on political-historical theory, *The Imperial Order* and *State Systems*, as well as several works on Soviet topics, most recently *Lenin's Legacy*.

Index

Africa, Chinese policy toward, 37
Africa, Soviet policy toward, 10, 16, 27, 257
Akhmatova, Anna, 242
Albania, 26, 29, 37
   break with Soviet Union, 47
Alcoholism, 118
Alexander II, 244
Alexeeva, Ludmila, 166, 169
Amalrik, Andrei, viii, 41, 267, 272, 276
America, 33
   See also United States
Amur River, 40
Andropov, Yu. V., 72
Anti-party group, 188
Anti-semitism, 9
April Theses, 5
Armenia, Armenians, 11, 137-38, 149
Azcárate, Juan, 29
Azerbaidzhan, 138, 149

Bacon, Francis, 240
Baltic Republics, 11, 149
BAM railroad, 82
Barghoorn, Frederick, viii, 97, 268
Batalov, Eduard, 22
Bauman, Zygmunt, 239
Bell, Daniel, 131, 133
Bergson, Abram, 94
Berliner, Joseph, viii, 266
Blackmarket: *See* Second economy
Bloch, Sidney, 172, 173
Bolshevik party, Bolsheviks, 3, 4, 5, 252
Bonner, Elena, 166
Border troops, 72
Boundary, Sino-Soviet, 40
Breslauer, George, viii, 269
Brest Litovsk, treaty of, 21
Brezhnev, Leonid I., vii, 9, 10, 13, 19, 24, 25, 34, 36, 84, 114, 125, 150, 179-82, 186, 193, 196-203, 209-11, 222, 233, 258, 259, 271, 274, 275
   and détente, 21
Brinton, Crane, 23
Britain, 7, 8, 29, 30

284 Index

Bromley, Yu. V., 133, 150
Brzezinski, Zbigniew, 22, 29, 43
Bukovski, Vladimir, 162, 163, 171
Bulganin, Nikolai, 199
Byelorussians, 137

Carrillo, Santiago, 29
Central Asia, manpower, 84
   population growth, 92
Central Committee, 178-80
Chalidze, Valery, 169
Chernenko, Konstantin U., 179
Chiang Kai-shek, 33
China, 7, 9, 10, 18, 25-27, 30, 178
   accusations against, 28
   fear of, 40-41
   modernization, 41
Chou En-lai, 26
Christian Committee for the Defense of the Rights of Believers, 169, 173
Christianity, 13
   See also Orthodox Church
Chronicle of Current Events, 158, 175
Churchill, Winston, 8
CIA, 42, 93
Civil War, Spanish, 7
Collectivization of agriculture, 5-6
Comintern, Communist International, 4-5, 7
   See also Third International
Communist party, Soviet, 24
   in developed socialism, 220
Connors, Walter, 58-59
Conquest, Robert, viii, 269, 276
Constitution of 1977, Soviet, 10, 150
Cordon sanitaire, 46
Council of Defense, 73
Cuba, 25
Cuban missile crisis, 9, 16
Czechoslovakia, 11, 150
   invasion of, 10, 47

Dahl, Robert A., 160
Damansky Island, clash at, 72
Daniel, Yuli, 10, 158
Declaration of Basic Principles, 21
De-Stalinization, 156, 161-63
Détente, 10, 21, 85

Deutsch, Karl, 142
Deutscher, Isaac, 5
Diet, Soviet, 112
"Doctors' Plot", 9
DOSAAF, 83
Dubček, Alexander, 238
Dudintsev, Vladimir, 229
Dzyuba, Ivan, 172

Eastern Europe, assistant to Soviet foreign policy, 59-60
   dissent in, 58
   economic growth, 58
   foreign workers in, 52
   importance for Soviet Union, 60
   indebtedness, 48
   military expenditures, 56-57
   national income growth, 49
   population growth, 51
   productivity, 52
   reforms in, 47
   trade with Soviet Union, 49-50
   trade with West, 47-49
Educational level, Soviet, 112
Educational reform, 91
Engels, Friedrich, 3, 244
Estonians, 136
Ethnography, Soviet, 132
Eurasianism, 250
Eurocommunism, eurocommunists, 18, 26, 109, 142
Expansionism, Soviet, 16, 17

Favier, Jean Louis, 15
Federal system, Soviet, 141
Feshbach, Murray, 90
First five year plan, 5
Ford, Gerald, 10
Foreign trade, Soviet, 62-63
France, 8
Franco, Francisco, 7
Friedrich, Carl J., 45

Galanskov, Yuri, 163
Gamsakhurdia, Zviad, 166, 167, 172

"Gang of Four", 31, 32
Garaudy, Roger, 230
General Secretary, 178, 179, 181-83, 189, 196, 198-201
Georgia, Georgians, 4, 138, 149, 158-59
Germany, 4, 25
Germany, Federal Republic of, 43
Germany, Nazi, in Eastern Europe, 46
Gibbon, Edward, 17
Gierek, Edward, 47
Ginzburg, Alexander, 28, 162, 163, 165, 166, 170, 171
Ginzburg, Evgenia, 162
Glazunov, Ilya, 165
Gluzman, Semen, 172
Goldman, Marshall, 55
Gomulka, Wladyslaw, 47
Gosplan, 81
Grain requirements, Soviet, 93
Gramsci, Antonio, 29
Great Fatherland War: *See* World War II
Great Wall of China, 40
Grechko, A. A., 69, 70
Grigorenko, Piotr, 162, 166, 172
Gromyko, Andrei, 181
Growth rate, Soviet economic, 89-91, 95, 99, 119, 265
Gurr, Ted Robert, 160, 161

Haeckel, Ernst, 39
Hassner, Pierre, 19
Heikal, Mohammed, 233
Helsinki Agreement, 55
Helsinki Watch Group, 164-66
Herzen, Alexander, 170, 227
Historical Review, 32
Hitler, Adolf, 7, 8
Hong Kong, 38
Hua Kuo-feng, 29, 32, 34
Hungary, 272
 1956 uprising, 10, 273
Huntington, Samuel, 19
Hunter, Holland, 55

Ideology, 4, 17, 19, 20, 21, 25, 132, 233, 254, 255

Ilyichev, Leonid, 34
India, 36
Indoctrination, 12
Inflation, Soviet, 117
Innovation, Soviet, 101-2
Intermarriage of Soviet nationalities, 138, 139n
Investment rate, Soviet, 94-95

Jackson-Vanik Amendment, 10
Japan, 25, 26, 36
Jews, Jewish movement, 137, 164, 167
Judaism, 13

Kadar, Janos, 62
Karol, K. S., 239
Kas'ianenko, V. I., 210
Kazakevitch, Channel of, 40
Kelley, Donald, viii, 107, 274
Kennan, George F., 19
KGB (Committee of State Security), 32, 65, 170, 172
Khabarovsk, 40
Khrushchev, Nikita S., 6, 9, 13, 24, 47, 67, 68, 71, 91, 93, 114, 124, 126, 156, 162, 180, 185, 188, 197-200, 206, 209, 229, 242
 and future state, 222-24
 and Pasternak, 162
 omission of name, 231
 "Secret Speech", 6
 seen by Chinese, 33
 succession, 184
Kievan Russia, 227
Kirilenko, Andrei P., 180, 183
Kissin, S. F., 23
Kissinger, Henry, 10, 21, 42
Klebanov, Valdimir, 169
Kolakowski, Leszek, 232
Kommunist, 26, 27, 29, 35, 36
Komsomol, 243
Korenizatsiia, 145
Kosolapov, V. V., 207
Kosygin, Alexei, 125, 180, 202, 203
Kovalev, Sergei, 169
Krasin, Victor, 172
Kriegel, Frantisek, 238
Kulakov, Fedor D., 183

Index

Labedz, Leopold, viii, 4, 263
Labor force, Soviet, 119
Larionov, A. N., 234
Latvians, 11, 136
Lenin, Vladimir I., vii, 3, 5, 13, 23, 79, 107, 109, 132, 209, 234, 235
Leninist nationality policy, 132-34
Lermontov, Mikhail Yu., 227
Levine, Isaac Don, 3
Little Entente, 46
Litvinov, Pavel, 163-64
Lowenthal, Richard, 19
Lukacs, Georg, 240
Luxemburg, Rosa, 236

Main Political Administration, 73
Malenkov, Georgii, 9, 124, 199, 200
Malinovsky, R. Ya., 67, 68
Malinovsky, Roman, 4
Mandelshtam, Nadezhda, 242-43
Manpower, Soviet, 87
Mao Tse-tung, 7, 8, 31-35, 39, 41, 42, 47
Maoism, 35, 36
    See also Mao Tse-tung
Marchenko, Anatoly, 167
Marshall Plan, 8
Marx, Karl, 3, 205, 235, 238
Marxism, 3, 13, 19, 23, 236, 249, 273
    See also Ideology, Marxism-Leninism
Marxism-Leninism, 12, 20, 24, 141, 142, 205
    See also Ideology
Matsuoka, Yosuke, 25
Matthews, Mervyn, 237
Mazurov, Kirill T., 229
Medvedev, Roy, 159, 160, 193, 242
Medvedev, Zhores, 19
Mehnert, Klaus, viii
Mercader, Raman, 3
Middle East, Soviet policies in, 10
Mideast war, 76
Mikoyan, Anastas, 147
Military doctrine, Soviet, 66-69
Military service, Soviet, 83
Military Strategy, 68
Military Thought, 67
Miliukov, Pavel, 226
Mill, John Stuart, 245

Ministry of Defense, 73
Molotov, Viacheslav, 229
Mongol state, 226
Monnerot, Jules, 23
Moslems, 138
    See also Central Asia
Mzhavanadze, Vasilii P., 147

Nagy, Ferenc, 47
National air defense, Soviet, 75, 77
NATO, 18, 34, 78
Nazi-Soviet pact, 7, 16
    See also Stalin-Hitler pact
Near East, Soviet policies in, 27, 30
    See also Middle East
Nenni, Pietro, 230
New Economic Policy (Lenin's), 105, 156
Nicholas I, 228
Nixon, Richard M., 10, 42
NKVD, 7
Nomenklatura, 185, 196, 237, 272
Novocherkassk riots, 269
Novy Mir, 162

Orlov, Yuri, 28, 165, 166, 171-73, 174
Orthodox Church, Orthodoxy, 7, 9, 13, 164, 173
Orwell, George, 161
Osipov, Vladimir, 159, 162, 165, 169

Pasternak, Boris, 162
Paustovsky, Konstantin, 229
Peking Review, 31, 33
Pelshe, Arvid, 181
Petroleum production, Soviet, 93
Podgorny, Nikolai V., 180
Podrabinek, Alexander, 167
Poland, protests in, 47, 58, 273
Polikanov, Sergei, 174
Politburo, 11, 178-83, 186, 189, 192
Polyanskiy, Dmitrii I., 180
Polybius, 14
Ponomarev, Boris, 233
Pravda, 24, 28, 36
Private plots, 6

Production associations, 103
Pyatakov, Gregory, 233

Quack science, 235

Rakowska-Harmstone, Teresa, viii, 269
Rapawy, Steven, 90
Red Army, 4, 69
Reddaway, Peter B., 172, 173
Romania, disturbances in, 57
Romanov, Grigorii V., 183
Roosevelt, Franklin, 8
Rudenko, Michael, 165
Rush, Myron, viii, 271
Russian Social Democratic Labor Party, 3
Russians, leading role, 136
  national consciousness, 12
Ryabikov, V. M., 81

SALT negotiations, 10, 75, 85-86
Sakharov, Andrei, 19, 159, 160, 164, 166, 172, 240, 242, 249n
Samizdat, 11, 13, 158, 159, 248n
Savings deposits, Soviet, 116
Schmidt, Helmut, 39
Schramm, Stuart, 39
Schroeder, Gertrude, viii, 5, 90, 96, 267
Scipio Africanus, 14
Scott, Harriet Fast, viii, 263
Scott, Col. William, viii, 263
Second economy, 117-18
Secretariat, 180, 186
Serbs, 151
Seton-Watson, Hugh, 151
Shafarevich, Igor R., 19
Shcharansky, Anatoli, 28, 165, 170, 171, 174
Shchekino experiment, 196, 202, 203
Shcherbitskiy, Vladimir V., 183
Shelepin, Aleksandr N., 180, 183, 187
Shelest, Piotr, 147, 180
Shostakovich, Dmitry, 172
Shragin, Boris, 160
Sino-Soviet conflict, 23, 31-33
  See also China

Sinyavski, Andrei, 10, 158
Sinyavski-Daniel trial, 163
Slavophils, 250
Smolensk archives, 10
Socialist commonwealth, 151
Sokolovskiy, V. D., 68
Solzhenitsyn, Alexander, 18, 160, 162, 165, 228, 234, 244
Sosin, Gene, 242
Soviet navy, 78-79
Stalin, Joseph, 5, 6, 7, 8, 9, 16, 23, 25, 157, 161, 180, 258, 264, 275, 276
  in World War II, 74
Stalin-Hitler pact, 21
  See also Nazi-Soviet pact
Standard of living, Soviet, 113-14, 117
State and Revolution, 23
Stavka (Supreme Command), 73-74
Storozhovoy mutiny, 236
Strategic rocket forces, 75
Suslov, Mikhail, 180, 233

Tatars, 136n
Teng Hsiao-ping, 32, 40
Third International, 17, 250
  See also Comintern
Third Rome, 17, 42, 250
Tito, Iosip, 8, 46, 47
Torgsin shops, 37
Treadgold, Daniel, viii
Triska, Jan, viii, 268
Trotsky, Leon D., 3, 4, 69, 226
Truman, Harry, 8
Trybuna Ludu, 27
Turkic peoples, birthrate, 11
Tvardovski, Alexander, 162
Twenty-Fifth Party Congress, 186
Tyl (rear services), 80

Ukraine, Ukrainians, 11, 137, 145, 149
United States, 7, 9, 18, 25-29
Ussuri River, 40
Ustinov, Dmitry, 181

Venclova, Thomas, 166
Versailles Treaty, 7

288 Index

Vietnam, Vietnam war, 10, 37, 85
Volga Germans, 136n
Volsky-Valentinov, N. Y., 233
Voprosy Dalnego Vostoka, 35
Voronov, Gennadi I., 180

War communism, 23
Warsaw Pact, 56-57
Warsaw uprising (1944), 8
Weissberg, Alexander, 229
Welfare state authoritarianism, 192-9
Westernizers, 250

Wolfe, Bertram D., 5
World War II, 13

Yakir, Peter, 162, 172
Yakunin, Gleb, 169
Yalta agreement, 16
Yevtushenko, Yevgenii, 41
Yugoslavia, 150, 151
  defection, 46

Zhdanov, Andrei, 8
Zinoviev, Grigoriy Ye., 13
Zlobin experiment, 203